THE
COMPLETE
IDIOT'S
GUIDE® TO

Street Magic

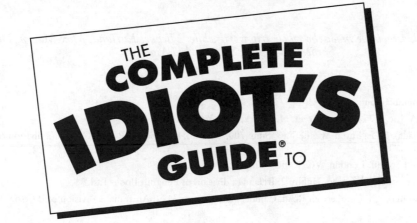

THE
COMPLETE
IDIOT'S
GUIDE® TO

Street Magic

by Tom Ogden

ALPHA

A member of Penguin Group (USA) Inc.

For four friends who have made the whole trip worthwhile: Michael Kurland, Max Maven, David Shine, and Dustin Stinett. And Mom.

ALPHA BOOKS

Published by the Penguin Group

Penguin Group (USA) Inc., 375 Hudson Street, New York, New York 10014, USA

Penguin Group (Canada), 90 Eglinton Avenue East, Suite 700, Toronto, Ontario M4P 2Y3, Canada (a division of Pearson Penguin Canada Inc.)

Penguin Books Ltd, 80 Strand, London WC2R 0RL, England

Penguin Ireland, 25 St. Stephen's Green, Dublin 2, Ireland (a division of Penguin Books Ltd.)

Penguin Group (Australia), 250 Camberwell Road, Camberwell, Victoria 3124, Australia (a division of Pearson Australia Group Pty. Ltd.)

Penguin Books India Pvt. Ltd., 11 Community Centre, Panchsheel Park, New Delhi—110 017, India

Penguin Group (NZ), 67 Apollo Drive, Rosedale, North Shore, Auckland 1311, New Zealand (a division of Pearson New Zealand Ltd.)

Penguin Books (South Africa) (Pty.) Ltd, 24 Sturdee Avenue, Rosebank, Johannesburg 2196, South Africa

Penguin Books Ltd., Registered Offices: 80 Strand, London WC2R 0RL, England

Copyright © 2007 by Tom Ogden

International Standard Book Number: 978-1-59257-675-3
Library of Congress Catalog Card Number: 2007926853

09 08 07   8 7 6 5 4 3 2

Interpretation of the printing code: The rightmost number of the first series of numbers is the year of the book's printing; the rightmost number of the second series of numbers is the number of the book's printing. For example, a printing code of 07-1 shows that the first printing occurred in 2007.

Printed in the United States of America

Note: This publication contains the opinions and ideas of its author. It is intended to provide helpful and informative material on the subject matter covered. It is sold with the understanding that the author and publisher are not engaged in rendering professional services in the book. If the reader requires personal assistance or advice, a competent professional should be consulted.

The author and publisher specifically disclaim any responsibility for any liability, loss, or risk, personal or otherwise, which is incurred as a consequence, directly or indirectly, of the use and application of any of the contents of this book.

Most Alpha books are available at special quantity discounts for bulk purchases for sales promotions, premiums, fundraising, or educational use. Special books, or book excerpts, can also be created to fit specific needs.

For details, write: Special Markets, Alpha Books, 375 Hudson Street, New York, NY 10014.

Publisher: *Marie Butler-Knight*
Editorial Director: *Mike Sanders*
Managing Editor: *Billy Fields*
Executive Editor: *Randy Ladenheim-Gil*
Development Editor: *Lynn Northrup*
Production Editor: *Megan Douglass*
Copy Editor: *Jan Zoya*

Cartoonist: *Shannon Wheeler*
Cover Designer: *Kurt Owens*
Book Designer: *Trina Wurst*
Indexer: *Julie Bess*
Layout: *Ayanna Lacey*
Proofreader: *John Etchison*

Contents at a Glance

Part 1:   **The Street Magician**   1

1   Take to the Streets   3
What is "street magic" anyway? Let's take a look at how it's changed over the centuries, from medieval mountebanks, to busking, to today's contemporary street performers.

2   Being Magic   17
There are a dozen reasons why people start performing magic. What's yours? And don't worry: You can *do magic! Find edgy but safe and affordable tricks to perform as you overcome any self-doubts.*

3   Creating Your Character   25
Style is everything. Here's how to create a unique and powerful image using dress, attitude, and choice of tricks. And what you say and how you say it is as important as the tricks themselves. Here's how to weave myth, legend, and magic to make a powerhouse performance.

4   The Magician Prepares   39
The Rules of the Game: keeping secrets, practice versus rehearsal, working with the audience, and other techniques for trickery.

Part 2:   **Defying Gravity**   53

5   Levitate This!   55
Things are supposed to stay put! But you're about to learn how to make all sorts of common, everyday objects float at your fingertips.

6   Up, Up, and Away   75
Look, up in the sky! It's a bird. It's a plane. No, it's you! Here are five practical one-person self-levitations, including the super-secret version made famous by street magicians on national television.

Part 3: **Unnatural Acts** **95**

7 Extreme Card Magic **97**
*Pick a card! These babies have been selected to rock with
maximum impact. Handle the deck like a cardsharp,
including ways to force a person to pick any card you want
them to.*

8 Light My Fire **127**
*Where there's smoke, there's magic. With their emphasis
on matches, fire, cigarettes, and ash, these tricks carry the
possibility—or even the promise—of danger.*

9 That's Gotta Hurt **149**
*How much is too much pain? And why are people so darned
entertained watching you inflict it upon yourself? This
chapter's for all you magical sadomasochists out there—
you know who you are!*

10 Pimp This Trick **177**
*Everything old is edgy now when you dress up these clas-
sic tricks with a bit of street smarts. Make the everyday
extraordinary by turning tricks with things around the
house.*

Part 4: **Things That Go Bump in the Night** **217**

11 The Undead **219**
*Any wizard of any worth should be able to contact the
Spirit World; and as a street sorcerer, you're no exception.
When you perform these tricks, you get to communicate
with the Other Side.*

12 Get Bent! **237**
*There are psychokinetic forces all around us, so these tricks
appeal to psychics and psychotics alike. It's sometimes hard
to tell them apart when you bend people's brains with these
warped bits of telekinetic wonder.*

13 The Powers That Be **273**
*While claiming to use hidden forces from the Unseen
World, you provoke unusual and startling events in the
natural world by sprouting seeds, restoring dead leaves to
life, controlling your pulse, and making magic with stones
from a ceremonial fire circle.*

Part 5: Technotrickery 303

14 Can You Hear Me Now? 305
Does anyone not *carry a cell phone 24/7? It's worth risking the roaming charges and even crossing service plans to dial up these freaky feats of cell-phone prestidigitation. Now you're talking!*

15 Music to My Ears 321
Find the magic in your music by performing technological tricks with iPods, earbuds, CDs, DVDs, and more.

Appendixes

A What's That, You Say? 343
B The Source 349
C Tell Me More! 355
Index 365

Contents

Part 1: The Street Magician   1

1 Take to the Streets   3

Are You Going to Scarborough Fair?..4

The Buskers...5

Jeff McBride and the Commando Act..6

The Levitators...7

The New Guys in Town 9

2 Being Magic   17

What Is Street Magic? 17

Can *I* Do Magic? 18

Why Magic? 19

It Costs *How* Much? 20

Practicing Safe Magic! 21

Overcoming Self-Doubt...22

3 Creating Your Character   25

Finding the Magic That's "You" 26

Get With the Routine...28

Character Counts 30

Word!..33

4 The Magician Prepares   39

The Big Three..39

Practice *Does* Make Perfect 41

The Devil Is in the Details 42

Theft 46

The Too-Perfect Theory 46

Crowd Control 47

What to Do When … 49

The Curse of TV Magic...49

Part 2: Defying Gravity   **53**

5 Levitate This!   **55**

The Floating Roll 55
Static Cling 61
The Levitating Lady 66
The Rising Ring 70

6 Up, Up, and Away   **75**

Fly By 76
Crawl Space 78
Undercover Ascension 80
Got Ya Covered 83
The Balducci Levitation 87

Part 3: Unnatural Acts   **95**

7 Extreme Card Magic   **97**

In the Beginning … 98
Pick It and Stick It 99
Is *This* Your Card? 104
May the Force Be with You 108
Revelations 113
Karate Kard 118
The Singed Card 122
The Slop Shuffle 123

8 Light My Fire   **127**

Heads or Tails 127
Under Cover 131
Ashes to Ashes 137
Snuff Happens 141
Don't Butt In 145

9 That's Gotta Hurt   **149**

Stretching a Point 150
Thumb Tack 152
Pin Head 155
Pin-etration 158
Pierced! 161

Blistered 165
Nose Candy 169
Eyescream 172

10 Pimp This Trick   177

The Jumping Rubber Band 177
The Great Escape 181
Go Fly a Kite 186
Trapdoor Trickery 192
Salt of the Earth 195
The Gypsy Switch 198
The Conjuring Caps 202
Up Yours 207
Up the Sleeve 209
The Vanishing Dagger 211

Part 4: Things That Go Bump in the Night   217

11 The Undead   219

The Ghost Whisperer 220
The Pentagram of Doom 223
Spinning in Your Grave 227
The Miracle of Life (and the Tragedy of Death) 230

12 Get Bent!   237

Bent Out of Shape 237
The Rubber Spoon 238
The Bending Spoon for Beginners 240
The Bending Spoon: The Real Deal 244
You Bent It! 248
The Breaking Point 251
Busted! 255
Oh, Fork! 256
Double Whammy 259
The Folding Coin 262
Paper Psychokinesis 265
PK Pen 268

13 The Powers That Be   **273**

The Seed of Life...274

Leaf Shredder 279

The Circle of Life 281

Tourniquet Trickery 288

In a Heartbeat..289

Look into My Eyes 291

Pro "Choice" 298

Part 5: Technotrickery   **303**

14 Can You Hear Me Now?   **305**

Meet Mr. Wizard...305

Fantastic Foto 310

Flowers Direct 315

15 Music to My Ears   **321**

Buds from Nowhere..321

Cut and Restored Buds 325

Nano to No Pod..328

The Vanishing iPod...331

The Mindreading iPod 335

In the Loop...338

Appendixes

A What's That, You Say?   **343**

B The Source   **349**

C Tell Me More!   **355**

Index   **365**

Introduction

Believe it or not, there is a real discussion right now in the magic world as to whether or not street magic, as it's currently seen on television and the web, is a legitimate genre of magic and whether it will even exist in another 100, or even 20, years.

Whether it's a phase, a fad, or a trend, one thing is certain: it is a phenomenon! And this book will help you take a giant step toward being a force to be reckoned with out on the streets.

What You Will (and Won't) Find in This Book

Most magic books, both beginner and advanced, group their tricks by the props with which you perform the magic—card tricks, coin tricks, and so on. Because street magic is so dependent on the themes and stories surrounding the tricks, as well your "character," I've grouped these tricks according to their general "themes," which will come in handy when it's time to create your own presentations to go along with the magic. In some instances, I offer various endings. So, too, I suggest different scripts (commonly called "patter" lines) for some of the tricks.

The question immediately arises, out of the literally thousands of magic tricks out there, many already explained in print, on DVD, or on the Internet, why and how did I decide which ones to include in this book? And why did I exclude others, even though you've seen them on TV?

My first concern was whether the trick was *appropriate* for a street magician to perform. A street magician is a very different creature than a birthday-party magician who makes balloon animals and maybe pulls a rabbit out of a hat. You want tricks that reflect your role as an urban shaman. Do you want to be seen pulling colored hankies out of an empty top hat? Get real. What would *you* want to be seen performing?

My second main concern was whether the tricks were *practical*. Which, of course, leads to the question of whether the trick is even *possible*. I don't want to burst anyone's bubble, but much of what you're seeing on TV and on the Internet today just can't be done in the real world. It was created for a camera lens to be seen on video, not in person. The tricks look great on TV or the web, but, for a variety of reasons, they can't be performed impromptu and actually fool people. There was no reason to include any of these tricks, because it would simply be exposing them, not teaching you how to perform them.

For some tricks, there were safety issues. Performing some of the stunts, such as swallowing a thread and pulling it out of your belly button, just have too many inherent risks involved. Any instructions that would have to start out with something like,

"First create a secret pouch under your skin, making a 1-inch slice with a razor blade …" didn't make it into the book.

Other tricks are hands-off because they are copyrighted and marketed in booklets or DVDs by their owners. Most of the tricks in this book have been around for hundreds of years. They can be included because they're in what's called the "public domain." The creators of a few of the newer tricks have been generous enough to allow me to include their pet tricks in this book.

Then there are tricks that require special props, and I made the decision that none of the tricks in this book should require you to find a magic shop (either a storefront location or on the web) or to spend more money to purchase a piece of apparatus. All of the stuff you need to do the tricks found here can be picked up at drugstores, grocery stores, office supply stores, or in the places where you're performing.

Finally, and perhaps most important, none of these tricks suck. Much of what calls itself street magic is actually just a gag or a stunt, which—if you performed it—would make you the equivalent of an urban prankster. Now, there *is* a time and a place for these types of bits of business, so I've sprinkled a few of the best ones among the hardcore tricks. They help break up the pace of your performance. But what you're primarily looking to achieve, and what I've tried to put in this book, are cool, high-impact, practical, commercial, doable tricks for the street magician.

How to Use This Book

The Complete Idiot's Guide to Street Magic is divided into five parts, each of which reveals a particular aspect of the art:

Part 1, "The Street Magician," gives a streamlined history of magic, concentrating on the mountebanks, buskers, and street performers. Other chapters discuss developing your character and style, showmanship, and magical ethics.

Part 2, "Defying Gravity," contains just what you'd expect: how to make yourself and other objects float in midair.

Part 3, "Unnatural Acts," offers dozens of unusual tricks that can be performed with otherwise ordinary objects, from a rubber band to a regulation pack of playing cards.

Part 4, "Things That Go Bump in the Night," features bizarre magic, with occult and supernatural themes, such as ghosts and spirits, mind-reading, telekinesis, and bending spoons.

Part 5, "Technotrickery," is wired for the modern street magician, teaching tricks that use iPods, digital cameras, and cell phones to create unexpected wonders.

You'll also find three helpful appendixes. Appendix A, "What's That, You Say?," lists the definitions for the jargon and special meanings for words used by magicians. Appendix B, "The Source," is a collection of the many books and DVDs consulted while writing this book. Appendix C, "Tell Me More!," is a treasure trove of information for those of you who want to continue in your quest for magical secrets. You'll find contact information for the country's leading magic shops, clubs, magazines, and schools, as well as some websites to help you in your Internet searches for street magic.

Box of Tricks

Throughout the book, I've added four types of "extras" in special boxes next to the instructions and text.

The Magic Word

This is where you pick up the slang, jargon, and unusual word usages of the magician.

Curses

Heed these dreaded warnings! They point out what *not* to do—potential problems or mistakes that, if not avoided, may result in your being injured or the trick not working.

Charms

Here you'll find handy tips to help you perform the tricks more easily or to give a better performance. Magicians sometimes refer to this type of insider information as the "real work."

Tricky Tidbits

Here you'll find miscellaneous information, anecdotes, and short tales that help illuminate the trick at hand. You may be able to use some of the stories, buzzwords, or phrases found in these Tidbits as the basis for the presentation of your tricks.

In addition to the titled sidebars, occasionally you'll run across short features that highlight the background of a trick or the biography of a particular important individual in the history of magic. I've presented these as boxed text.

Apology to the Lefties

Like most magical literature, these instructions are written with the right-handed reader in mind. These tricks are perfectly adaptable to perform using the opposite hands, of course. Unfortunately, I just didn't have the extra pages to give a separate set of instructions to every trick and sleight.

Acknowledgments

There are several people whose contributions I must acknowledge. I appreciate all the support and especially the patience of my executive editor, Randy Ladenheim-Gil, who was passionate about this book from the beginning. She conceived the need for the book and fought for its acquisition. Thanks for standing by me as I obsessed over every piece of the manuscript. I must also thank Lynn Northrup, also previously my development editor for both editions of *The Complete Idiot's Guide to Ghosts and Hauntings*, for actually requesting to work with me again on this book. Thank you, too, to my production editor, Megan Douglass, for coming on board. And, as always, thanks to my agent Jack Scovil of Scovil Chichak Galen Literary Agency, Inc.

In addition, I must thank Bob Farmer and Mac King for the contributions of their tricks "The Miracle of Life (and the Tragedy of Death)" and "Eyescream," respectively. I must also thank all of those people who provided various types of assistance and cooperation in helping me bring this book to the light of day: Stan Allen (editor of *MAGIC* magazine), Michael Ammar, Tobias Beckwith, Christopher Carey, Tim Ellis, Richard Kaufman (editor of *GENII* magazine), George Schindler, David Shine, Sue-Anne Webster, and Meir Yedid.

Thanks to the Technical Advisors

As with my *Complete Idiot's Guide to Magic Tricks*, Max Maven acted as the consultant for my trick selection and offered continuing advice. This included the sensitive issue of whether a trick was ethically permissible to be included, as well as identifying the creators of the effects whenever known. In some cases, he recommended specific routines and sleights to accomplish many of the tricks. Max has been an advisor to more than 70 television shows and numerous famous magicians. He is also a celebrated performer headlining in clubs and theaters across the United States and in more than two dozen countries. His published work includes more than 1,600 creations in the conjuring literature as well as *Max Maven's Book of Fortunetelling* (Prentice Hall) for the general public.

Throughout my writing, I also consulted regularly with Dustin Stinett, who acted as a research assistant and general sounding board. Dustin is a product reviewer and feature writer for *Genii* magazine as well as an aficionado and student of the craft with a passion for research. Whether it's about magic's past or contemporary history, Dustin loves putting his library of books and periodicals to work when delving into a question.

Thanks to the Photographers

More than 200 photographs appear in this book, most of them painstakingly shot over several long sessions with Jason Daniel of Titus Photography (titusphoto.com). A hobbyist magician as well, Jason had an innate understanding of just what the photo had to show and recognized the need for precise angles, which were often very difficult to capture.

Also contributing to this book were Claude Piscitelli and Jay Witlox of Luxemburg, who shot the terrific photos of magician David Goldrake. The performance photographs of Jeff McBride were supplied by Paul Draper (www.Realmagic.org), who is also a mentalist, magician, and popular speaker. He currently lives and performs full time in Vegas and appeared as an expert on The History Channel's *Houdini: Unlocking the Mystery*. The portrait shot of Criss Angel is courtesy of Hocus Pocus Focus, Inc.; the headshot of David Blaine is courtesy of MagicTimes.com; and the photo of Argentine magician Alba in Chapter 9 is by Brad Ball. And thanks to Cyril Takayama and Jeff McBride, who generously provided their own portrait shots for use in the book's first chapter.

Unless otherwise noted in the captions, all other photographs were either taken by or are from the collection of the author.

Thanks to the Models

I have to extend my thanks to the eight magicians who modeled for the many performance and locations shots in this book: Alba, Jonathan Castile, Edsel Chiu, Jason Daniel, Tom Isaacson, Steve Miller, Gaston Quieto, and Adam Wylie. Extra-special kudos must be given to two more magicians, Jeff McBride (mcbridemagic.com) and

David Goldrake (davidgoldrake.com), who went above and beyond the call of duty by taking it upon themselves to arrange for their own photographers and models and then providing the pictures for this book.

Street magic is only as good as its audiences. Thanks to all of the spectators who appear in the photos: Tori Bunting, Donna Carroll, Andre Franco, Holly Frantz, Deejay Lee, Robin Sol Lieberman, Abbi McBride, Renée McHenry, Erika Roberts, Dino Serna, Karen Setyan, David Shine, Meagan Smith, Lisa Wardell, and Jennifer Wilson.

Trademarks, Copyrights, Logos, and Endorsements

Finally, the legalese. All terms mentioned in this book that are known to be or are suspected of being trademarks or service marks have been appropriately capitalized. Alpha Books and Penguin Group (USA) Inc. cannot attest to the accuracy of this information. Use of a term in this book should not be regarded as affecting the validity of any trademark or service mark. Also, unless specifically recommended in the text, the mention or depiction of a performer, product, or website should not be construed as or implied to be an endorsement.

Part 1

The Street Magician

I know what you're thinking: "When do we get to some tricks? I want to learn tricks!" Don't worry, we'll be getting to the tricks soon—and lots of them. But first, let's get the basics out of the way. How has magic changed over the centuries to become what we see on TV and on the streets today?

Perhaps even more important than the tricks you'll be learning is the style in which you decide to perform them. It's your approach, your angle, your 'tude that makes your magic different than all the others out there—in fact, unique.

So in this part we'll examine how to set your style, pick your wardrobe, and cultivate your appearance. You'll decide what kind of tricks you should perform, what sort of things you'll be saying while you perform them, and how to deal with different types of audiences. Finally, we'll review some of the fundamental principles of magic, such as the importance of practice, keeping secrets, knowing whether to repeat a trick, and what to do when something goes wrong—the so-called "tricks of the trade."

It's time to take to the streets.

Take to the Streets

In This Chapter

- The first street magicians and buskers
- Sheshal and the first magical levitations
- The emergence of modern-day street magic: David Blaine, Criss Angel, and others
- Street magic goes international

Magic was used by priests, wizards, and alchemists since time immemorial to terrify and control their followers. Although the dates are debated, the first time magicians used magic for mere entertainment purposes seems be during the Middle Ages, when performers roamed the streets of Europe, doing a bit of juggling, singing a few songs, or performing a few magic tricks in exchange for a hot meal and a place to bed down for the night.

Before long, entertainers were performing casually staged shows in local fairs and on busy streets, finishing up a small show by passing around a hat to collect donations. Up through the twentieth century, this style of magic was generally known as "busking" or "street magic."

In 1997, the definition of "street magic" changed overnight when a young magician named David Blaine made it the subtitle for his first television special. From then on, "street magic" became synonymous with the style of impromptu, in-your-face magic that Blaine (and others who soon followed) became known for.

Are You Going to Scarborough Fair?

By the end of the 1600s, magic was finally becoming acknowledged for what it was: mere sleight-of-hand entertainment. *Mountebanks* freely traveled from village to hamlet. In the early eighteenth century, Samuel Pepys mentioned street magicians in his famous diaries, and William Hogarth depicted them in his artwork. As merchants began to assemble at large regional fairs such as the famous Southwark Fair in England, showpeople (including such magicians as Isaac Fawkes) added to the mix by setting up their own booths to entertain the crowds.

The Magic Word _____

Although the term **mountebank** specifically refers to a traveling pitchman who sells quack medicines (often by drawing in a crowd with tricks, jokes, and stories), the word has come to mean any flamboyant trickster. "Mountebank" comes from the Italian phrase *monta im banco*, which means "someone who stands up onto a bench."

Isaac Fawkes, in an eighteenth-century engraving attributed to Sutton Nichols, performing one of his most famous tricks, in which he produced eggs, money, and birds from an empty bag. The Egg Bag, a version of this classic trick, is still performed worldwide by magicians today.

Magic might have remained an outdoor street entertainment if it hadn't been for performers who wanted to establish it as a theatrical art form. By the mid-1800s, magic was being seen on the stages of legitimate theaters and being welcomed into the private homes of polite society. The twentieth century saw the era of the great illusionists who trouped their full evening stage productions worldwide, featuring all of the now-classic tricks, from sawing a girl in half to floating her in midair. Names such as Harry Houdini, Howard Thurston, Dante, Harry Blackstone, Doug Henning, and David Copperfield spanned the last century of magical entertainment.

At the same time, a separate genre called close-up magic came into its own, distinct from what was being performed on the stage. Also variously referred to as tabletop magic, pocket magic, and even micro magic, this type of sleight-of-hand isn't performed for large groups. Instead, it's visible to only a few spectators at a time and is performed almost exclusively with cards, coins, and other small handheld objects.

The Buskers

But even these performers were influenced by the magic coming from the streets. After all, street magic is, by necessity, "close up" because the props could only consist of what the performer was able to carry on his or her person while traveling the highways and byways.

Street *buskers* combined the classic close-up tricks with ones that were large enough to be seen by small groups. The main criteria for a trick to be included in a street magician's act were that it could entertain and hold an audience, not necessarily its mystery quotient.

The Magic Word

An English slang term, a **busker** is any type of street performer who gathers a small crowd, performs a short show, and then collects donations from the passersby.

Several performers now in more mainstream venues began their careers as street magicians. Television's Harry Anderson (*Night Court, Dave's World*) got his start as a magician on the streets of San Francisco. Las Vegas's Penn & Teller first performed as street performers (Teller as a magician, Penn Gillette as a juggler) working out of the greater Philadelphia area in the 1970s before joining forces.

You can still see this type of show at marketplaces (such as Covent Garden in London), at tourist attractions (such as Pier 39 in San Francisco), on oceanside boardwalks (such as Venice Beach in Southern California), and public areas such as in New York City subway stations and city parks—in fact, anyplace where a few people can be gathered to watch a show. Among the best-known contemporary buskers are Gazzo, Jim Cellini, David Graves, and Chris Capehart.

Perhaps the best-known American practitioner of the busking style of street magic is Jeff Sheridan. He began working his avant-garde magic on the streets and in the parks of New York City in the late 1960s, and he became one of the most recognizable street artists of that era. Much of his work was chronicled in Edward Claflin's 1977 book *Street Magic*. He is still recognized as one of the most influential street magicians of the latter twentieth century.

Jeff McBride and the Commando Act

Jeff McBride, who studied with Jeff Sheridan, coupled his magic and illusions with his lifelong studies of masks, martial arts, Asian theater, and movement to create a unique blend of magical theater that culminated in an off-Broadway show, *Mask, Myth & Magic*. Although still in demand as a performer, McBride is perhaps now most famous as the founder of "McBride's Magic and Mystery School" (www.magicalwisdom.com), an experiential retreat for magicians to reflect on the mystical aspects of their art. McBride also creates "enviro-magic," in which magical "happenings" surround visitors in unexpected venues. Jeff McBride's contribution to the current scene of street magic includes the release of the powerful material he developed over two decades as "The Commando Act," which he describes as "Real Magic for Real World Conditions"—practical yet astounding street magic that can be done at a moment's notice without hours of preparation in just about any conceivable performance situation.

Magician Jeff McBride.

(Photo by Richard Faverty of Beckett Studios. Photo courtesy of Jeff McBride.)

The Levitators

Magic from the streets continues to influence stage performers to this day. In fact, one of the most effective tricks of all time, the levitation of a woman, was first inspired by rumors of a street magician who performed the miracle in India.

India has always been known for its strange, odd, and curious entertainers, including snake charmers, sword swallowers, glass eaters, fire eaters, fire walkers, and, of course, magicians. In 1827, magicians in Europe first heard tales of an amazing Indian *fakir* by the name of Sheshal who was able to remain suspended about 4 feet in the air for up to 40 minutes at a time.

Sheshal performed in the streets of Madras. The magician stepped onto a stool behind a cloth and readied himself. When the blanket was removed, Sheshal was sitting cross-legged, suspended in the air without any support, except that his right wrist lightly rested on a piece of deerskin draped over a pole which, in turn, was attached to the stool. At the end of the performance, the curtain was raised again, and Sheshal emerged from behind the cloth.

The Magic Word

Fakirs are Hindu ascetics who live by begging and whose religious acts sometimes include the performance of incredible feats of physical endurance. The term is now used more generally to mean any Indian street performer whose "show" consists of strange or torturous stunts.

Street magician Sheshal in an engraving from Descriptive Letter Press *to the* Indian Microcosm, *Madras, 1828.*

In the case of Sheshal's performance, no one actually *levitated*. That is to say, no one rose into the air. Instead, he performed what magicians call a *suspension*, in which a person hangs in the air without falling despite nothing being underneath for support.

In the 1850s, the French magician Jean Eugene Robert-Houdin was one of the first stage illusionists to capitalize on the fame of the Indian suspension. In Robert-Houdin's version, his young son Eugene climbed onto a stool in full view of the audience. A pole was propped up under each of the boy's arms. The stool and one pole were removed, and the boy was lifted into a horizontal position, where he remained suspended on the single pole.

An engraving of "La Suspension Éthéréene," from Memoirs of Robert-Houdin, *1859, first U.S. edition.*

For the next 150 years, magician after magician developed more impressive and devious ways to create the illusion that someone actually floats. And, although almost none of them bear any direct resemblance to Sheshal's original, all modern levitations can trace their way back to that first suspension in the streets of nineteenth-century India.

And, indeed, it's a levitation—the one performed by modern-day street magician David Blaine—that, in large part, ushered in the current wave of interest in street magic. Although Blaine's first television special, *Street Magic*, featured more than a dozen other effective tricks, none generated the response that came from his one-man self-levitation. He appeared to float straight upward and hover several inches above the ground directly in front of the people watching him. Weeks after the TV special aired, the levitation was all that anyone who saw it seemed to want to talk about.

Much of the impact came from the fact that Blaine was outdoors, dressed in jeans and a shirt, just a few inches from where the people were standing. You could tell from the expressions on their faces that the spectators were stunned: they believed they were actually witnessing a miracle.

Tricky Tidbits

Although David Blaine's exact method may differ, he was no doubt inspired by an illusion known to magicians as the Balducci Levitation. You'll be learning how to perform the original version of this trick in Chapter 6.

The New Guys in Town

Today's crop of street magicians draws on magic's past—including its darker, occult side—to create something even more innovative and powerful.

At first, it was unclear whether this new "street magic" was a separate genre, because its practice seemed to be limited to just a few performers whose work has been seen primarily on television and not by average people on the streets. But as interest in their approach to magic grew and generated its own breed of adherents, today's "street magicians" are identified as having a unique style, independent of the medieval mountebanks, the buskers, or contemporary close-up strolling magicians.

So who are these new faces of magic? I thought you might be interested in taking a look at some of the top performers who have changed—and are continuing to transform and define—the world of magic today.

David Blaine: Street Magic

David Blaine (davidblaine.com) was born in Brooklyn, New York. In *Street Magic*, his first ABC television special in 1997, Blaine created a whole new paradigm for magic by combining roving, guerilla-style street magic with reality television. His crew used portable handheld cameras to capture not only Blaine's sleight-of-hand but also the audiences' responses. And it was the spectators' immediate and honest reactions that showed how strong this style of performance could be in the right hands. Because of the impulsive and sometimes brash nature in which Blaine approached his audiences, the magic seemed to be completely impromptu and spontaneous, even when (unknown to the spectators) extensive preparation or special props had been needed to bring about the miracles.

Street magician David Blaine.

(Photo courtesy of MagicTimes. com.)

Blaine's second television special, *Magic Man*, which aired in 1998, followed the pattern established by his first special, and it included a fascinating section that explored voodoo beliefs in Haiti. His third special, *Frozen in Time* (2000), showcased a live endurance stunt—as would all of his subsequent specials. Indeed, Blaine has become just as famous for his difficult, life-threatening stunts, in which he tests the physical limits of his body, as he has for his street magic. They've included …

- "Premature Burial" (April 1999), in which Blaine spent 7 days buried in a glass coffin at the bottom of a pit in Manhattan, remaining in full view of passersby.

- "Frozen in Time" (November 2000), in which Blaine stood encased in a block of ice in Times Square for just shy of 62 hours.

◆ "Vertigo" (May 2002), in which Blaine stood on top of a 90-foot pillar in Bryant Park in New York City, where he remained for more than 34 hours before jumping down onto a 12-foot-tall "landing mat" made of stacked cardboard. The stunt was featured as part of a TV special with the same name later that year.

◆ "Above the Below" (September-October 2003), in which Blaine was suspended in a 7 foot × 7 foot × 3 foot clear Plexiglas box over Potters Field Park on the bank of the River Thames in London for 44 days without food. This formed the basis for a 2003 TV special in the U.K.

◆ "Drowned Alive" (May 2006), in which Blaine was submerged for just over a week in a giant, water-filled globe located outside Lincoln Center in New York City. The stunt ended with Blaine escaping from handcuffs and chains while trying (and failing) to break the world's record for holding one's breath underwater. The attempt was broadcast live as part of a two-hour television special.

◆ "Revolution" (November 2006), in which Blaine spun for 2 days chained in a giant gyroscope raised 50 feet in the air in the Times Square area. The stunt climaxed with an escape, which ended with Blaine falling from the apparatus and through a stage located beneath him.

David Blaine has also published *Mysterious Stranger* (Villard, 2002), which is a combination autobiography and history book about magic. It also includes instructions for about a dozen tricks. Interestingly, the book also had an "interactive" aspect, because it included a treasure hunt with secret clues that was reportedly solved by a reader two years later. Blaine has also released a DVD, *Fearless*, which contains edited versions of his first three TV specials.

Criss Angel: Mindfreak

Born on Long Island, New York, Criss Angel (crissangel.com) is an illusionist, street performer, and musician best known for his *Criss Angel Mindfreak* television series on A&E. Often clad in black and leather and sporting a mane of jet-black hair, Angel has a buffed torso that he displays to full advantage during his physically punishing illusion work.

In 1998, "Criss Angel: World of Illusion" headlined the 12-day run of Madison Square Garden's annual Halloween spectacular. This led to his own show, *Criss Angel Mindfreak*, which ran for almost 600 performances at The World Underground Theater in Times Square, from November 2001 to January 2003.

The Mindfreak himself:
Criss Angel.

(Photo courtesy of Hocus Pocus
Focus, Inc.)

To help publicize the show, midway through its run in February 2002, Angel performed a live stunt in Times Square, in which he hung from eight fishhooks for more than 5½ hours. In August, he performed another major stunt, this time in a Manhattan city park, in which he remained chained underwater in a clear tank, visible to passersby for 24 hours before making his escape.

Needless to say, Criss Angel's performances, distinct "look," and edgy and gritty style didn't go unnoticed. In October 2002, ABC Family aired his first hour-long special, *Criss Angel Mindfreak*. The two-hour television special *Criss Angel Made in Japan* followed, appearing on TBS in Japan in October 4, 2003. In the same month, on Halloween night, Angel's special *Supernatural* aired on the Sci-Fi Channel back in the United States.

Criss Angel had more than proved his television legs by July 2005 when A&E debuted his series *Criss Angel Mindfreak*. Although the 16 episodes all included impromptu magic performed on the streets or in the Aladdin Hotel & Casino in Las Vegas, each one also featured a major death-defying stunt or illusion. These included being blown up by explosives, driving blindfolded, and being burned alive. Reminiscent of his 2002 stunt in Times Square, in one episode Angel had his back pierced by four large hooks and was then suspended beneath a helicopter and flown over the Nevada desert. And, of course, he performed several levitations, both of himself and others, in public areas out on the street.

The second season of *Mindfreak*, also based around the Aladdin and elsewhere in Las Vegas, consisted of 21 episodes. Feature tricks included Angel walking on water, making an elephant vanish, and sawing a spectator in half on a park bench. The third season, which began airing in June 2007, features 28 episodes mostly shot in and around the Luxor Resort and Casino and other MGM MIRAGE properties in Las Vegas. All of Angel's television shows also feature reality-style, behind-the-scenes segments showing the preparation and anguish over the danger connected with performing these major showpieces.

Most recently, Criss Angel has signed a 10-year contract with Cirque du Soleil at the Luxor beginning in summer 2008. Throughout all of this, Criss Angel has continued his music career. He has produced and performed his original music on four CDs for APITRAG records, as well as composing much of the music for his A&E series. (A fifth CD, *Criss Angel Mindfreak: The Official Soundtrack*, was released by Koch in 2006.) His first book, *Mindfreak: Secret Revelations*, was released in April 2007, and many of his television specials as well as the A&E series are available on DVD.

 Curses _____

Many of the demonstrations that are performed by street magicians on television are extremely dangerous and can only be performed successfully after hours of careful rehearsal. Remember, too: the tricks are only illusions. If you try them without knowing the secret—and sometimes even if you *do* know the secret—you can really hurt yourself. You should never attempt any trick or stunt that might cause you bodily harm or physical injury.

The Streets of London

The new wave of street magic isn't confined to the United States. So far, it's also taken the U.K. and Japan by storm. In England, two names have stood out in the field of street magic in the past few years: Derren Brown and Paul Zenon.

Born in England in 1971, Derren Brown (derrenbrown.co.uk) has combined his interests in magic, psychology, hypnosis, and human behavior to create an unusual form of psychic entertainment—not mind-reading exactly, but something that depends on a mixture of magical techniques, misdirection, and the power of suggestion.

In 2000, Brown appeared in a Channel 4 television special, *Mind Control*, which spawned two sequels and a six-part series. In October 2003, he played Russian Roulette live on a

Channel 4 television broadcast; and the following May he recreated a live séance, also for Channel 4. In April 2005, a new series, *Trick of the Mind*, began airing on E4 television, and subsequent editions have followed each year since.

In addition to his television work, Brown is a popular live artist, and his theater show *Something Wicked This Way Comes* won an Olivier Award for Best Entertainment. He's released highlights from his first series on DVD as *Derren Brown—Inside Your Mind*, and his first book for nonmagicians, *Tricks of the Mind* (Channel 4 Books), was released in October 2006.

Although Derren Brown has never billed himself as a magician—and certainly not a street magician—many of his television routines have been taped live, on the streets, interacting with unsuspecting people who were suddenly asked to take part in one of his psychological tests. The challenge aspect of the performance with its hit-or-miss possibility of failure, coupled with the unrehearsed spectators and their genuine reactions of amazement, makes much of his television work fall well within the new definition of street magic.

Paul Zenon (paulzenon.com), meanwhile, proudly proclaims himself to be "Britain's oldest juvenile delinquent," having pulled off his first scam (a fake raffle) at the tender age of 8. He was born in 1964, and as a teenager he worked summers at a magic and joke shop in Blackpool before busking his way around the Mediterranean.

He soon started working in clubs as a magician and comedian. By the 1990s, he had also segued into children's magic, which resulted in four television series on BBC1. Before long, he became a regular variety guest on British television and began touring his live show.

In the late 1990s, Zenon became known for his aggressive, yet comedic, form of street magic, much of it performed in pubs and on the sidewalks of London. His performance style tended toward his being a "charming cheat" rather than a "mysterious stranger." He had four "street magic" specials screened on ITV in England, as well as in about 20 countries worldwide: *Paul Zenon Turning Tricks, Paul Zenon's Tricky Christmas, Paul Zenon's Trick or Treat,* and *White Magic with Paul Zenon*.

He revealed the workings of many of his favorite routines in his 2005 book *Street Magic* (Carlton Books). His other books, also published by Carlton, are *100 Ways to Win a Tenner* (on bar bets and cons; 2003) and *Paul Zenon's Dirty Tricks* (on revenge-oriented gags and pranks; 2004.)

Cyril and Magic X

Cyril (cyrilmagic.com) was born Cyril Takayama in 1973 in Hollywood, California, and since moving to Japan he has become a major star of magic. Renowned for his impossible street illusions, he has parlayed his popularity into a series of magic television specials in Japan as well as one in Korea. He's probably magic's first "cyber celebrity," because the short clips of his street magic posted on YouTube have made him one of the most viewed and discussed magicians in the world.

Japanese magician Cyril.

(Photo courtesy of Cyril Takayama.)

In addition to his TV specials—11 as of January 2007!—he keeps up a hectic live tour schedule, primarily in Japan. Among Cyril's major awards in the field of magic is the top prize in Grand Illusion at the 1994 F.I.S.M. convention. (F.I.S.M., or International Federation of Magic Societies, is often referred to as "the Olympics of Magic.") Cyril has also won Siegfried & Roy's 2001 Golden Lion Award, and in April 2007, the Academy of Magical Arts (which operates out of the Magic Castle, the famous private club for magicians in Hollywood) awarded him its highest honor, "Magician of the Year."

Cyril is also a member of Magic X (myspace.com/magicxlive), a group of street magicians from Southern California who, in addition to their live shows, appeared in their own television special, *T.H.E.M. (Totally Hidden Extreme Magic)*, which first aired on NBC in 2004. *T.H.E.M.* was a hidden-camera reality show in which unsuspecting people were punked as they witnessed or were made the target of incredible magic stunts. Only afterward was it revealed to the spectators that a team of street magicians had pulled off the illusions.

(The magicians appearing in *T.H.E.M.* were Enrico de la Vega, Chris Gongora, Cyril Takayama, Danny Cole, Lisa de la Vegas, Justin Kredible, Thomas Meier, Michael Grasso, and Jason Neistadt. Many of them, like Cyril, were once members of the Junior Society of the Magic Castle.)

Other magicians who have produced television shows that featured street magic include Chris Korn and J.B. Benn (six episodes of *Mondo Magic* and well as TV specials shot in Singapore for release in Asia), Alain Nu (four episodes of *The Mysterious World of Alain Nu*), Marco Tempest (*The Virtual Magician*), and Keith Barry (*Keith Barry: Extraordinary*).

Well, that just about wraps up 3,000 years of magic history, from the ancient Magi to the street sorcerers of modern day. So now it's time for you to play your part: get ready to pick your tricks, dress them up in tales of the fantastic, and take to the streets. So who will be the next great street magician? Will it be you?

The Least You Need to Know

◆ Itinerant magicians have strolled the streets of Europe and the Middle East for at least two millennia.

◆ The suspension trick performed by Indian street magician Sheshal led to the creation of a new illusion: the levitation.

◆ David Blaine pioneered and established the contemporary concept of street magic through his many TV specials as well as with his public tests of physical endurance.

◆ Criss Angel has continued to popularize street magic through his A&E series *Mindfreak* and other television appearances.

◆ Street magic has gone international, with such performers as Derren Brown and Paul Zenon in Britain, Cyril in Japan, and Magic X in the United States.

Chapter 2

Being Magic

In This Chapter

◆ Street magic defined

◆ Who can do magic?

◆ Reasons to perform magic

◆ How much it's gonna cost

◆ Why ya gotta play safe with your magic

◆ What might be holding you back

Now that we've had a chance to take a look at the history of our Dark Art (as that lady across the street keeps calling it when I do card tricks), it's time for you to take your first tentative steps toward being a true street magician.

What Is Street Magic?

In ancient times, magic was full of mystery and the miraculous. Now, all too often, it's just for kiddies and all just "fun and games." As a sidewalk sorcerer, you can reverse that trend because the street is your stage. You're in the open air where there are no smoke or mirrors and nothing to hide behind.

Let's take a look at some of elements and attributes that make up street magic. Street magic is …

S sexy, spiritual, sacred, scary, startling, strange, supernatural, spine-chilling, sinister, shocking

T threatening, taboo, tense, touching

R real

E edgy, evil, eerie, enigmatic

E extreme, excessive

T terrifying

M mystifying, moving, meaningful, mystical, menacing

A aggressive, alarming, authentic, affecting, appealing, alien

G gutteral, genuine, guerilla-like, gross

I impromptu, impulsive, intimidating, intense, in-your-face

C cool, character-driven, charismatic, creepy, compelling, captivating

How many of these qualities can you incorporate into your work as a street magician?

Can / Do Magic?

I know this sounds sappy, but as a street magician, you have the power to achieve the impossible. Just think that over for a couple of seconds: you can do things that are absolutely impossible, that defy all of the laws of nature and reason as well as the laws of the physical universe. Most people can't conceive that such invisible, unseen realities or forces exist. So when you hear things like "I can't believe what just happened" and "I saw it with my own two eyes," you know you've done your job.

Secrets are easy to expose. But to *perform* the trick well requires much, much more. You *can* do it: but it will take time, patience, and perseverance. I'm telling you this up front so that you won't be disappointed. If you start showing your tricks too soon, you'll have friends or strangers telling you, "I see how it's done."

 Curses _____

I hate to burst your bubble, but despite what you may have read or heard elsewhere, there is no such thing as "easy-to-do" magic that you can "perform instantly" with "no practice required." These words are written on the side of the box or in a website advertisement to get you to buy the trick.

You can be better than any of those street magicians you see on YouTube. Trust me, you can and *will* be.

Why Magic?

People get into magic for all sorts of reasons. Almost everybody has seen a magician perform live or on television. But very few folks take the next step—to actually try to learn to perform magic. Here are some of the most common motivations people have for starting in magic:

- **To fool people.** It really is a kick to watch people's faces when you've completely floored them!

- **Power.** Much of street magic is about power. In fact, magic always has been. Shamans had control over the elements and over the Spirit World. Priests worked with Higher Powers. Magicians looked to the natural world to find out how, by using their special powers, they could affect the world around them.

- **To be special.** It's always great to be able to do something that no one else can, isn't it?

- **To be the center of attention.** If you're the type who likes to always have the spotlight shining on you, street magic is for you. You can have people wanting to watch you without having to beg, "Hey! Look at me!" all the time.

- **A burning desire to perform.** Different than having a need for attention, many people just want to be "on stage" in some branch of the performing arts. Some say it's the only time they truly feel "alive."

- **Secrecy.** You're the ones who always wear that silly grin that says, "I know something you don't know." You like being "in on things." If this were medieval times, you'd own several of those grimoire spell books.

- **The puzzle aspect.** You like to know what makes things tick. You're probably into Sudoku. In fact, you can do them in a minute flat. Depending upon your generation, you may have been one of those Rubik's Cube whiz kids.

- **To have and provide fun.** No, a street magician isn't a professional "life of the party" who wears a lampshade for a hat and does silly stunts just to provide a barrel of laughs. But even the most solemn or sinister street magic should have an innate element of fun. Don't ignore the fun factor in everything you do.

- **To make friends and meet new people.** Magic is the perfect icebreaker. Almost everyone loves to see short, direct, well-performed magic. Once you're already talking, it's only a small step to making a new friend.

- **To make "friends with benefits."** Yes, you can flirt with magic. But bear in mind that even though magic can make you seem charming and mysterious, if you push it too hard, you can just as easily come off as creepy, pompous, or geeky.

- **To make money.** In the old days, back, say, 20 years ago, street magic was the realm of the professional buskers, who "passed the hat" after each mini-show. Although you'll probably just want to accept your accolades and disappear back into the crowd after you've performed—the ultimate shock and awe—don't be surprised if from time to time someone slips you a tip to thank you for performing for them.

- **Entertainment.** Hopefully this last one is high on your list. Even though you may go into magic for a variety of other reasons, at its core, magic is all about entertaining other people.

It Costs *How* Much?

If you were David Copperfield, you might spend tens of thousands of dollars on your illusions (if, say, you wanted to make the Statue of Liberty disappear). But as a street magician, you have the option of spending next to nothing. The choice is yours.

After you've worked your way through the tricks in this book, you may also wish to invest in a few more books to expand your magical knowledge of all the possible tricks that are out there for the taking. (Skim through my suggested book list in Appendix B.) And as more and more street magicians appear on television, you may want to get that hot new trick that everybody's doing or talking about. (Sometimes it almost seems like everybody's in the same "Trick of the Month" Club. Maybe you can find the trick you need at one of the local magic shops or online magic dealers mentioned in Appendix C.) You may find that you want to pursue some of the more complicated street tricks that are only possible to do if you own special apparatus or buy the DVD in which the trick's creator performs and explains the effect.

You probably won't wind up putting all of these new tricks into your repertoire. Believe me, we magicians all have piles of played-with-once-but-never-put-in-the-act stuff in our magic closets at home. But with each new trick you buy, you'll be learning new methods and new possibilities that you might be able to adapt into a creation of your own, even if you never do the original trick itself.

> **Tricky Tidbits** _____
>
> The most important thing you can invest is your time. Commit to spending the time that you'll need to learn, practice, rehearse, and polish your tricks. Thomas Edison said, "Genius is 1 percent inspiration and 99 percent perspiration." I think the same goes for magic: 1 percent of magic is learning the secrets; everything else is working on your presentation and performance. After that, the effectiveness of your street magic won't depend on how much money or time you spent. It'll depend on the magical experience you can provide for others.

Practicing Safe Magic!

From the days of the Indian fakirs up through Houdini and beyond, magic has always been filled with death-defying stunts and demonstrations of physical endurance. Today, the tradition is carried on by David Blaine and Criss Angel, among others. Just take a look at what some of these guys have done and the way they've punished their bodies for your amusement and entertainment pleasure.

Chapter 9 of this book is called "That's Gotta Hurt," and in it you'll find tricks that, if they weren't magic, would really, really hurt. Some risks are worth taking. But no trick, no matter how amazing, no matter how much reaction you'd get, is worth hurting yourself or putting yourself or others in real danger. So when you're performing magic with any of the following, take extra care and precautions:

- **Fire.** It burns. 'nuff said?

- **Sharp objects.** Even scissors can kill. Remember how your mother warned you about running with scissors?

- **Cigarettes.** Caution: Cigarette smoking is addictive and _will_ be hazardous to your health as well as the health of those around you. And the ash falling off the tip isn't too attractive, either. So, if you _must_ do tricks with cigarettes, be careful how you light them, inhale them, hold them, and dispose of them.

- **Liquids.** They spill. And, yes, later they dry; but in the meantime, you've made the street magic experience rather unpleasant for your spectator. And depending upon what's tipped over, you might leave an unwanted stain behind as a permanent reminder of their encounter with you.

◆ **Loose objects that can drop on the floor, causing you or others to slip and fall.** I know it sounds silly now, but wait until someone breaks a leg and you're served with a lawsuit.

◆ **Any edible giveaways.** Be careful what you put in your mouth or the mouths of others. As my mother also used to say, "Who knows where it's been?"

Curses

You shouldn't need to carry a fire extinguisher when you do any of the tricks in this book, because the use of flame is minimal and contained. Still, use every reasonable safeguard to avoid being burned or hurting anyone else. Setting off an un-intentional blaze isn't what I mean when I say these tricks are hot. This goes for all the tricks that have anything to do with matches, lit cigarettes (if you're careless with them, you could set off a fire), ash, or the voodoo-style mind-reading and telekinesis tricks that use fire as part of the ritual ceremonies.

In the end, some tricks are just too dangerous to perform. In *The Discoverie of Witchcraft* (1584), Reginald Scot explains how "to thrust a dagger … into your guts … and … recover immediately.… [You] seem to kill yourself, or at the least make an unrecoverable wound." He then goes on to describe a magician who messed up trying to perform the illusion and actually did kill himself. Scot still explained how to perform the trick, but he suggested that anyone think long and hard before attempting it. His advice? "See you be circumspect."

Overcoming Self-Doubt

We all get stage fright from time to time. Even though we've practiced and rehearsed and maybe even performed magic for people in the past, we sometimes put up mental barriers that block us from being effective performers. Here are some of the excuses beginning street magicians often make that keep them from reaching their potential. And, yes, I'm going to tell you how to cancel out your concerns, one at a time:

◆ **"I'm too uncoordinated."** Magic is a learned skill. Everybody's better at some things than others. I can cut a deck of cards with one hand, but I can't hammer a nail straight. In the case of magic, "practice makes perfect" is more than a motto. It's a way of life.

- "My hands are too small." You don't need huge hands for magic. Some of the best sleight-of-hand magicians in history had short, stocky fingers. "If the glove don't fit, the magic gotta quit" isn't a valid excuse.

- "I'm not fast enough." Magic isn't about speed. It's about being smooth and looking natural. (I'll talk about "being natural" in Chapter 4.) Speed, in fact, often draws unnecessary attention to your hands. When they move too quickly, the spectators may not see exactly what you did, but they know when you did it. And it sure looked suspicious. No matter how fast you move—and regardless what the old cliché says—the hand can never be quicker than the eye, because eyes see things at the speed of light.

- "I'm too old to start a new hobby." Sorry, this excuse doesn't cut it. Despite the saying, "old dawgs" *can* learn new tricks. No matter what your age, you never stop learning in life. Street magic will be just another facet of your ongoing, life-long education.

- "I'm not smart enough." You don't need to be a brainiac to do magic. In fact, the secrets to most magic tricks are quite simple. Yes, you will have to be able to read and follow instructions, but you're doing okay so far, aren't you?

- "I'm not sneaky enough." It's true: sometimes you will have to be able to lie with a straight face. But you don't have to be the Arch Deceiver to get away with magic tricks. People don't know our secret methods, so it's much easier to fool them than you might think.

- "I'm afraid I'll make a mistake and look stupid!" Remember Murphy's Law: "If something can possibly go wrong, it will." Some gloom-and-doom people add, "And at the worst possible time." Unfortunately, it's a fact of life. Every magician—I repeat: *every* magician—has had tricks go wrong. But on those very rare occasions that it happens, it's not the end of the world. It's not a life-or-death situation; it's just a trick. If it'll make you feel any better for now, however, we'll be taking a more detailed look in Chapter 4 at some of the things you can do when disaster strikes.

- "I get scared." We all do from time to time. But practice and preparation can cut stage fright to a minimum. With each successful street encounter you have, your ego and self-confidence will grow.

- "I don't look like a street magician." There's no right or wrong "look" for a street magician. You just have to look appropriate for the type of magic you've chosen to perform. We'll tackle wardrobe, grooming, and attitude in the next chapter.

◆ "Magic is evil and the work of the Devil." And your point? Yes, once upon a time they burned us at the stake for doing card tricks. But not anymore. At least, let's keep our fingers crossed.

Okay, so you can perform magic; it shouldn't cost you a bundle and we've unleashed your "inner street magician." Let's move on to look at how to select tricks, script them, and develop a unique style for your street magician character.

The Least You Need to Know

◆ Anyone can perform magic. It's a learned, practiced motor skill. You don't have to carry some special DNA magic gene.

◆ People get into magic for a variety of reasons, from wanting to fool people and do something special to needing to be in the spotlight and having a burning desire to entertain.

◆ Street magic is as costly or inexpensive as you want it to be. Your major investment shouldn't be money but your time.

◆ Some people create mental barriers that prevent them from getting out there to perform. In time, all obstacles can be overcome.

Chapter 3

Creating Your Character

In This Chapter

◆ Finding tricks that are right for street magic

◆ Getting your routine down

◆ Developing a personal style

◆ Scripting your street magic

Jean Eugene Robert-Houdin, a nineteenth-century magician who's often referred to as "The Father of Modern Magic," once said, "A magician is an actor playing the part of a magician." And it's true. You don't really have magical powers. (Do you?) But by the time you get finished creating your street magician character, people will swear that you do.

An important first step is deciding how you want your audience to perceive you. Yes, there are different types of magicians. Your look and style will be determined by what kind of tricks you choose, your demeanor, how you dress, the type of props and accessories you carry, and the stories you tell.

Finding the Magic That's "You"

There are thousands of magic tricks to choose from as you're starting to build your magic repertoire. But not just any trick is right for a street magician. Can you imagine a street magician pulling a string of silk scarves out of his sleeve? No way! If you want to have street cred, you'll have to take all sorts of things into account as you're selecting the magic for your bag of tricks.

Make It Streetwise

No matter how much advance preparation a trick takes, it must seem impromptu, spontaneous, and off-the-cuff when you perform it. Not every trick lends itself to those restrictions, because you'd have to get the gimmicks ready just before you're ready to "go on" or you'd have to walk around carrying some sort of bulky load on you.

Also, take a look at the props or the objects you'll be working with. Do they make sense in the setting where you'll be performing? Playing cards seem to fit in anywhere. You can find spoons to bend right on the table at the bar or restaurant. But, getting back to those silk hankies: wouldn't they look a bit out of place if you were performing for people standing in line at the movies? To stay in character, your tricks and the props you use in your magic have to fit in.

That's Inappropriate!

You already understand this concept: there are some things you wouldn't dream of saying or doing in front of certain people. It would just be wrong. Likewise, you have to pick and perform the right tricks for each particular audience. No matter how amazing a trick might be, if you're doing it for the wrong people, you won't get the response it deserves.

That's why it's always good to know your audience. Knowledge is power. For example, if you know (or suspect) that the people you're working for share a particular phobia or taboo, you can either increase their comfort level by avoiding those topics, or, if you dare, you can increase the stakes by bringing them up. On the other hand, if you know that your spectators have a certain interest or fascination, you can use that to your advantage. When you talk about one of their pet subjects, they'll pay close attention and become more involved in what you have to say and do.

Your Basic Rights

Do the magic that's right for you. Ask yourself:

◆ Do/would I enjoy performing the trick? Why?

◆ It is a trick I'd enjoy watching?

◆ Is it a trick that the particular "street magician character" I'm creating would perform?

Sometimes a trick may be incredible, and it may be perfect for your audience. But if the trick doesn't rock your boat personally, there's no way you're going to be able to sell it. You have to find at least some segment of the trick that you really enjoy performing. The audience will pick up on your enthusiasm and be drawn in.

The Seven Basic Effects

With all of this in mind, what kinds of tricks are out there? Magicians tend to break tricks down by their basic *effects*—that is to say, what the audience thinks it sees. What does the audience thinks happens? Lists vary among experts as to number of different categories, but here's my personal list of the seven major effects, which I've based on the different ways in which a magician can defy the laws of nature:

◆ **Production:** making something appear.

◆ **Vanish:** making something disappear.

◆ **Transposition:** making something move or change places with another object.

◆ **Transformation:** making something change in shape, size, or other characteristic.

> **The Magic Word**
>
> In magic jargon, the **effect** is what the audience thinks happens during the trick or the basic law of nature that's magically broken.

◆ **Penetration:** making one solid object go through another without harm to either, such as Houdini's "Walking Through a Brick Wall."

◆ **Levitation:** making an object float. This category includes both levitations (where the item rises or falls) and suspensions (when an article hangs suspended in midair without any apparent means.)

◆ **Restoration:** breaking something into pieces and then making it whole (think the "Cut and Restored Rope" or "Sawing a Woman in Two").

In addition to this list of magical effects, I'd like to add another category: tricks that fall within the realm of the supernatural or paranormal. The effects themselves may vary, but these tricks would include apparent demonstrations of extra-sensory perception or mind-reading, telekinesis, ghost and spirit phenomena, and magic with occult or shamanic overtones.

Bizarre magick is sometimes listed as a subgenre of these types of tricks. (Magicians began to use the pseudo-archaic spelling of "magick" in the 1960s as a way to differentiate it from more mild-mannered, "normal" magic.) In addition to its subject matter, some (but not all) bizarre magick utilizes cabalistic props, such as pentagrams, incense, candles, or crystals. All of it emphasizes storytelling and an emotional connection with the audience. You have to use this type of material sparingly, but if you perform it for the right audience, you could find yourself getting some of the strongest responses you'll ever receive.

More Tricks!

At this point, you probably want to learn as many tricks as possible, and well you should. You'll want to gather as many tricks as you can to decide which ones you like most and which ones get the best response from your audience. Eventually, you'll hone your material to a few favorites that "speak to you" on a gut level, and these are the ones that you'll be inspired to make your signature pieces.

How big must your repertoire be? How many tricks do you have to know? When Al Goshman, a famous magician of the mid- to late twentieth century was considering becoming a full-time professional, he asked this question of Dai Vernon, who was considered so knowledgeable that other magicians had nicknamed him "The Professor." (You'll read more about Vernon in Chapter 12.) Vernon advised Goshman that if he could perform just five tricks better than anyone else, he'd have a successful, lifelong career in magic. Goshman took his advice and become internationally famous for a handful of trademark tricks. (You'll learn one of these as "The Conjuring Caps" in Chapter 10.) It doesn't matter how many tricks you do as long as you do them perfectly.

Get With the Routine

Most street magic that you've seen on the tube has been of the hit-and-run variety, with the magician performing a single trick seemingly impromptu for a group of total strangers. But you'll soon discover that a lot of people want to see more than just one trick. Then you'll have to worry about deciding, out of all the tricks you know, which ones to do for that particular audience and in what order they should go. Magicians call this *routining*.

Routining is usually thought of as a matter for stage magicians. After all, they're presenting full-blown acts that need to build to a big ending. Also, after each individual trick, the magician has to gracefully segue from one trick into the next.

The Magic Word

Routining is the process of deciding which tricks to perform and in what order to place them, starting with your first trick (the opener) to your final trick (the closer) of your "show."

Usually, that's not a concern for "wanna-see-something"-type street magicians. If they're only performing one trick, they don't have to worry about sustaining an audience's interest for very long. But if you're planning to do even two tricks back to back for the same people at one sitting, the concept of routining should play a big part in planning your street magic.

Your first trick (your *opener*) has to grab the spectators' attention and also has to tell the people something about the style in which you intend to perform. The trick must also be good enough to make them want to see more. You may wish to continue in the same vein with your next tricks, say, having all of them be pseudo-mind-reading or all demonstrations of skill with a deck of cards.

Of course, it's also possible to switch it all up and have completely dissimilar tricks follow one another. But you want to avoid having a "grab bag" feel to your "show"—with a little of this and a little of that but no real focus. The words you choose between tricks—what you say as you put one away and bring out the next one — should help make it sound inevitable that those tricks go together.

Some magicians try to assemble tricks in groups of three, using effects, props, or patter lines. This concept is known as the Rule of Three. It isn't unique to magicians, of course. Writers, comedians, and speakers often group three points or jokes on a single topic together for maximum impact. When used by a street magician, the first trick sets the groundwork, either by way of its theme, its props, or the mood in which you perform it. The second trick continues the premise, elaborates on it, and perhaps makes a twist. The third trick is the capper, with the strongest effect of the three, tying the three tricks together into a tight package.

The end of your routine has to have a Big Finish. I don't mean *literally* big: you don't have to have confetti shooting out of your butt. But for all practical purposes, your last trick should be the strongest one—magically, psychologically, and emotionally—in your "show," because that's the main thing the spectators are going to remember. The trick also has to have a sense of closure to wrap up your "act," and it definitely has to leave people wanting more.

It may take months of actual performance until you find which order of tricks just "feels right" to you. After a lot of trial-and-error—switching the order of the tricks and trying some as openers or closers—eventually certain tricks will just naturally want to follow one another. Even if they're totally unrelated tricks, if they feel like they belong together to you, you'll be confident when you present them as a routine.

Character Counts

A street magician dressed in black walks down an alleyway, steeped in dark and shadows. Moody music plays in the background. In three quick edits, he jumps from far down the street, then a block away, and then right in front of your face. The audience at home is captivated: what's that guy gonna do?

By the time you see street magicians on TV, their personas are already in place, reinforced by their stylists, background music, film crew, and editors. You don't have that advantage; you have to create all that for yourself. There's a lot to consider, so let's get started.

"As If"

As you're reading this book, you'll notice that I use the word "pretend" a lot. Magicians are in the business of pretend. We say we're doing one thing and we pretend to do it, but we're actually doing something else altogether.

Charms

As you establish a particular look or style, you may want to play "pretend" and try giving yourself various "as ifs" to help you discover clues as to how you should dress, act, and perform.

I also say "as if" throughout the book, especially when I'm trying to describe what something should look like. The magic "as if" has been an actor's tool for generations: it gives the performer a frame of reference upon which to build a character or perform an action. For example, if a director tells an actor to come through the door "as if" he'd been drinking all night, he gets an entirely different performance than if the actor chooses to enter "as if" he'd been to an AA meeting.

Who Are You Wearing?

The Devil may wear Prada, but what do *you* wear? Audiences make basic assumptions based upon how people dress. Before nineteenth-century magician Jean Eugene Robert-Houdin, magicians either wore long, flowing wizard gowns à la Merlin or they wore leggings, a troubadour shirt, and a shoulder bag like a strolling minstrel or mountebank. Robert-Houdin decided to dress in high fashion when he performed, which, in that day, meant top hat and tails. His magic was sensational, but it was in large part because of the way he dressed that society accepted him into their salons to perform. In the process, magic was finally accepted as a legitimate theatrical art.

In the 1970s, Canadian magician Doug Henning wore studded jeans and rainbow-colored tops in a sort of a hippy look. David Copperfield has always dressed fashionably and today goes in for high casual wear. David Blaine usually opts for jeans and a T-shirt. If you were only to see his wardrobe, Criss Angel could easily be mistaken for a rocker. (In his early years, pre-*Mindfreak*, you might have thought he shopped with Alice Cooper and Ozzy Osbourne.) People knew what they were getting with Henning and Copperfield just by looking at them as they walked onstage. Likewise, home viewers make certain assumptions the instant they see Blaine and Angel just by the clothes on their backs.

What look will you have? Consider these:

- Basic black, the urban guerilla magician's ready-for-all-occasions wear

- Goth, grunge, or other music-based wardrobe trend

- Trench-coat mafia

- Hooded jacket—gangsta rapper

- T, jeans, and layers—you're just an ordinary guy or gal with extraordinary power

What jewelry will you wear, if any? Finger rings? Ear loops or studs? Patches or badges? Paranormal or Satanic insignias? How about headgear, wristbands, and body art? Every piece says something.

All of these variables are valid choices. It all comes down to what message you want to give. Just put yourself in your audience's shoes: if a stranger walked up to you, dressed and acting the way you plan to present yourself, what would *you* think? How would *you* react? For better or worse, people will make their first impressions about you based in large part on how you look. And first impressions usually stick.

Should you dress with your planned audience in mind, or always stay true to yourself? For example, should you go with a different look if you'll be working in a trendy club area than at the food court in a shopping mall? That's a question only you can answer. Ask yourself what type of reaction you're trying to get and what final impression you want to leave behind. You're not "selling out" if you modify your extreme edges from time to time in order to be able to approach your audiences. After all, unless you, your props, and your accessories are in a form that people will feel comfortable watching, you'll never get the chance to share the incredible magic you have to provide.

Curses

Groom by the Golden Rule: "Do unto others as you would have them do." No one wants to stand close to a magician who smells bad.

Here Comes the Groom(ing)

This shouldn't have to be said, but good grooming is essential. I'm not saying that you have to wear a bow tie and have your hair neatly parted and combed. But no matter what "look" you're going for, people still expect your clothes to be clean and in good repair. There shouldn't be dirt under your fingernails. Brush your teeth and, if necessary, use a mouthwash. Smell good, but be careful not to overscent yourself.

Who Am I?

Although your wardrobe will cast a first impression, the audience's perception is really cemented by your attitude, the things you say, and the way you behave.

Let's start from the very beginning: how do you approach your potential prey? Shyly? Slyly? Wham-bam-pick a card, ma'am?

Once you've settled in to perform a trick or three, what's your demeanor? Are you an outsider? Do you come across as serious, evil, or mysterious? Maybe you're acting like an oddball or freak, just to keep the spectators on edge. Maybe you're comical or even acting clueless, as if you were just a normal person and all these weird things keep happening to you.

None of these styles is either right or wrong. But to be most effective, you have to make a choice and commit to it wholeheartedly. That way, the audience isn't just getting tricks; they're getting a whole street magic experience: you!

What's That in Your Hand?

You are what you hold. In the past, every magician carried a magic wand. In fact, according to legend, it was through the wand that a magician supposedly focused and channeled his or her powers. Even in the *Harry Potter* books, one of the student's first tasks before going to Hogwarts was obtaining the right magic wand.

> ### Tricky Tidbits
>
> Magicians have been wielding wands, rods, or staffs as emblems of their mystical authority since antiquity. In the Holy Bible, the Pharaoh's wizards turn their rods into snakes to demonstrate their power to Moses. The Druids, wizard-priests who populated Europe in the first millennium B.C.E., and, later, the alchemists of the Middle Ages, carried wooden wands to demonstrate their command over the earth's elements. No one knows when ordinary street conjurers adopted the magic wand. But a wand, they discovered, had practical uses. It's easy to hide something in your loosely closed fist when you're also holding a wand; and it's easy to secretly pick up or ditch things when you take the wand out of your pocket or put it away.

You probably won't see a street magician carrying a magic wand today. But take a moment to think about the props and accessories that you *will* take with you when you perform. When Harry Anderson was working as a street busker, he famously said, "Carry only what you can run with," because law enforcement doesn't look kindly on street performers in some communities. (They see street magicians as being just one level above the homeless.)

Will you be performing with only objects found on the table or where you perform? Or will you be carrying a deck of cards and other props? If you're taking stuff with you, where will you be carrying it? In your pockets? (And if so, will they bulge and look unflattering?) Or will you wear a side bag, fanny pack, or some sort of pouch on your belt? How will any of these accessories change the look of your outfit? Whatever props and accessories you carry, make sure they complement the rest of your "ensemble."

Word!

Ya gotta say *something*. I know: most of the street magicians you've seen probably started by simply saying, "Wanna see something?" But even that, minimalist as it is, was a conscious decision on the part of the performer. What you say when you first greet a group of strangers will affect how they perceive you and whether they'll even want to stick around. (I'll discuss how to approach a prospective audience more fully in the next chapter.) Magicians refer to what they say—the words and stories they use while performing their feats of prestidigitation—as their *patter*. But the word "patter" gives short shrift to what you're creating. Whether or not you actually write it down on paper, you're creating a script to follow as you perform a trick. In the course of the few minutes that you're performing, you can only say so many words, so each and every one of them has to count. Choose them wisely.

Tricky Tidbits

Some say the word "patter" has its roots in the Catholic rites, where the priests used to recite the "Our Father" or *Pater noster* in Latin. In medieval times, the words sounded like gobbydegoo to the uneducated masses and were impossible to understand. Likewise, the charms that medieval alchemists and wizards intoned as they cast their spells also sounded nonsensical. Both priests and sorcerers talked to spirits and demons. Did the two become confused and *Pater noster* become "patter" somewhere along the line? It's possible.

Get Buzzed

Believe.

That single word conjures up all sorts of images, doesn't it? It makes you ask yourself, "Just what *do* I believe?" It's such a powerful word that, before he died, Harry Houdini told his wife that if his spirit ever returned in a séance, he would use the word "Believe" to prove that it was really him.

Whether they're used in a question, a statement, or one of your stories, buzzwords immediately set your audience's mind flying. (Hence their being called "buzzwords.") So here's your assignment: make up an opening sentence or a question using one of the words out of the following buzzword list that could be used to introduce some street magic trick that you've already seen. It doesn't have to be one you may actually wind up doing. But this exercise will get you thinking in the right direction for when you're writing your script and patter.

Buzzwords, plot points, themes, and patter-lines points

Abominable Snowman	Graveyards	Pyramid power
Afterlife	Great Beyond	Reality
Alchemy	Guardian angel	Reasonable doubt
Alien abductions	Heaven and hell	Reincarnation
Alternate realities	Incubus	Resurrection
Angels	Indian fakirs	Role-playing
Apocalypse	Inquisition	Roswell
Astrology	Judgment Day	Satan
Atlantis	Karma	Séance
Auras	Last rites	Sex
Bermuda Triangle	Life after death	Signs and symbols
Bigfoot	Loch Ness Monster	Solitary confinement
Corpse	Matrix	Soul mates
Crystals	Medium	Spirit world
Cutting	Men in Black	Succubus
Danger	Nightmares	Superstition
Dark angels	Occult powers	Taboos
Dark Side	Opposites attract	Truth
Deathbed confessions	Other Side	UFOs
Demons	Ouija board	Undead
Doomsday	Outside the box	Underworld
ESP	Pallbearers	Vampires
Evil	Palmistry	Voodoo
Fate	Parallel universe	Witchcraft
Free will	Pentagram	X-Files
Ghosts	Powers of Darkness	Zombies

What Do *You* Think?

Consider starting out your patter with a question. By opening with a provocative question, you immediately connect with the spectator. When you ask, "Do you believe in the Dark Side?" trust me, the person can't help but become involved. What *do* they think?

Here are a few more examples of the types of stimulating questions that would grab your audience's attention:

◆ "Do you believe that people come into our lives when they do for a reason?"

◆ "If you could go anywhere in the world, where would you go?"

◆ "Do you believe in evil or that pure evil exists as an invisible force of nature in the world?"

◆ "If there were a war between good and evil, which do you think would win?"

◆ "Are you ever attracted to someone even though you don't want to be?"

◆ "Do you think that, on some level, identical twins can actually read each other's minds?"

◆ "Why do people who have been married for years sometimes die within days of each other?"

Questions don't have to be used just at the beginning of your patter, of course. They can be sprinkled throughout to keep the spectator engaged. Not only that, each new question leads the audience in a whole new direction. For example, let's say you decided to begin a trick by saying how happy watching your first magician made you. Just think what ways these questions might steer the trick if you scatter them throughout your routine:

◆ "Are you happy?"

◆ "What makes you happy?"

◆ "Do you believe perfect happiness is possible?"

When you're asking an open-ended question and it's not rhetorical—meaning you really *do* want the audience to respond—you're taking your performance into unknown territory. True, that's risky. It's not as safe as just saying the same old thing every time you do the routine. But it makes the trick immediate, important, and personal.

The Passion

Use emotion-laden words in your patter, ones that will grip your audience. Some words can even cause visceral reactions. Here's an example of how emotive key words or buzzwords might be used in a trick. In "Ashes to Ashes" (see Chapter 8), you'll be rubbing ashes onto the back of a person's hand. Let's say that while you're doing it, you talk about Ash Wednesday and how ashes are placed on people's foreheads at the beginning of Lent as a sign that they renounce their past sins and will forego sin in the future. When you start talking about sin, don't you think your audience is gonna perk up? You bet! And how about if you throw in a question or two like, "Do you have some sins you're really sorry for?" or, "Do you think there are any sins that are so bad that they can't be forgiven?" All the while, you're performing the same old trick, but now it's taken on a whole new dimension because it's infused with beliefs in religion and the Hereafter.

Myths and Legends

Myths and legends, timeless stories that have been passed down through generations, can act as springboards for your patter. For instance, the "effect" of several tricks in this book is Restoration, such as the cut and restored earbuds trick ("Cut and Restored Buds") in Chapter 15. You *could* just grab the person's earbud cord, saying, "Wanna see something?" Or, if you think your audience would be fascinated by tales of ancient Egypt, lost civilizations, and "secret wisdom," you might consider this patter, which has the benefit of supposedly being true:

The legend of a wizard named Dedi appears on an Egyptian scroll called the Westcar papyrus that was written around the eighteenth century B.C.E. While performing for the Pharaoh Khufu (also known as Cheops, the guy who built the Great Pyramid), Dedi cut off the head of a goose, reattached it, and then brought the bird back to life. He repeated the trick with another bird and then an ox. When the Pharaoh asked him to perform the trick on a human prisoner, however, the wizard refused, saying it was forbidden by the gods to practice on the "noble herd."

You could then offer to show your audience how freaky that trick must have seemed, minus the blood, using something a little more ordinary, like the earbuds to their iPod. (By the way, in case that story about Dedi sounds kind of familiar, David Blaine performed the same trick on a chicken in his television special *Magic Man*.)

The Least You Need to Know

◆ The tone of a trick changes considerably depending upon your attitude and demeanor when you perform it.

◆ A spectator's first impression of you generally sticks. Choose your wardrobe, props, and accessories carefully.

◆ The performance of your tricks should seem extemporaneous, but the words (or patter) should be carefully scripted.

◆ The best street magic is a complete package: your tricks, your style, and *you!*

4

The Magician Prepares

In This Chapter

- ◆ The three major rules of magic
- ◆ Practice versus rehearsal
- ◆ Tips and advice on performance
- ◆ Is the trick "too perfect"?
- ◆ Interacting with the crowd
- ◆ TV magic versus street magic

Can you keep a secret? You better be able to, because this chapter gives you some of the secret weapons that you'll be using to maximize the impact of your tricks on the unsuspecting public. If you follow this advice, they won't know what hit them!

The Big Three

People love lists. Top Tens. Top 100s. Even Top 500s! But I'm going to make it easy for you. I'm going to give you just three main rules that should always be in the back of your mind when you're practicing and performing. Three simple rules.

1. Never Reveal the Secrets

Never explain how a trick is done. You don't think it's just your pretty face and witty remarks that make people want to watch you, do you? No. They want to be fooled. At least half of the entertainment in magic comes from not knowing the secret.

And here's the weird part: even though people will beg you to tell them how the trick is done, deep down inside they really don't want to know. They *want* the mystery, because they want to believe in magic.

And here's another downside to revealing how the tricks are done. As you'll discover while working through this book, many of the methods are very simple. If you tell people how a trick is done and they were really duped by it, they'll hate you for making them feel so stupid.

Besides, why would you want to belittle all the hard work you've put in by deliberately telling someone how the magic works? Trust me, it doesn't make you cool. Any mystique that you might have had immediately disappears.

Bear in mind, there's another kind of exposure that's as bad as simply telling someone how the trick works: accidentally giving away the secret by performing the trick so badly that the audience can see how it's done. If you don't believe me, go to YouTube and watch the videos posted by up-and-coming street magicians. You'll see that many of the performers inadvertently expose the very tricks that they've paid good money to learn. The lesson is clear: it's easier to create a video than it is to learn, rehearse, and perform magic well.

2. Never Tell What You're Going to Do in Advance

There's a simple reason for this. If the audience knows what you're going to attempt to do, they have a better chance at catching you when you try to perform the secret move. They'll know what to look for. *You say you're going to make a card reverse itself in the deck*, they think. *Then I won't take my eyes off the pack.*

 Curses _____

Sometimes, despite all your rehearsal and preparation, the trick just doesn't work. If you've already told the spectators what to expect, they'll know something went wrong when it doesn't happen. Even if it's possible for you to steer the trick to some sort of satisfactory conclusion, if it's not the original trick you announced, the audience will see it as a failure.

3. Never Repeat a Trick

Although this rule isn't carved in stone, generally it's best not to repeat a trick to the same people at the same sitting. The reason goes back to Rule Number Two. Seeing a trick once is entertainment; twice is education. The second time they're not watching to see what you're going to do: they already *know* that. They're looking to see how you do it.

Some magicians keep repeating a trick until there's no question as to how it's done. For example, have you ever seen a magician do that trick where the metal rings link and unlink? At first it's baffling. Before long, you suspect there must be some sort of gap in at least one of the rings. If the magician performs a little longer, you'll try to figure out where the hole might be, and finally you'll notice that one hand never moves from a particular spot on one of the rings. Gotcha! The same can be said if you perform the same card trick over and over and over. Eventually, you'll be caught.

Of course, all rules are made to be broken. There are some tricks, called "sucker tricks" (which I'll discuss in the next chapter), in which you deliberately tell the spectators how a trick is supposedly being done so that you can fool them by using a completely different method. There are some tricks that are built around challenges, in which you tell the audience up front what you're going to attempt to do so they can try to catch you at it. (Needless to say, most of these routines don't involve difficult or secretive sleight-of-hand.) Finally, some routines gain in strength by their repetition because you're constantly changing the method: just when the spectators almost have it figured out, you change the trick just enough to fool them again.

Practice *Does* Make Perfect

Spontaneous street magic is anything but. Sure, you may not know exactly who you're going to be performing for, or when. But the tricks themselves have to be perfected through hours of practice and rehearsal.

First comes the practice. You must go through the trick step by step, learning the instructions and any required sleights. The secret moves may require even more intensive work. After you've learned the basic mechanics of the trick and practiced until you think you've got them down, set down the prop and walk away. Then, over the next few days, every time you walk by the prop, pick it up and try to execute the trick or the sleight just once. Once. Then put down the deck, or the coin, or the whatever. Why only once? Because when you finally do decide to put the trick into your repertoire and want to perform it in the real world, you won't have a chance to practice it over and over just before you do it for spectators. You'll have to hit it on the first strike.

Consider practicing in front of a mirror, because it allows you to see your hand and body movements from your audience's perspective. But you have to be careful not to rely on mirrors too much. Even if you use multiple mirrors, you're only seeing certain angles. Your spectators can always see more. It's also possible to become so dependent on watching yourself in the mirror that, in performance, it's hard for you to look up from your hands to the audience.

After you've practiced all the individual moments and then worked them through into a complete trick, it's time to begin rehearsal. Rehearsal is different than practice, because it attempts to recreate the actual performance situation that you'll be facing when you go out on the streets. To rehearse properly, you'll need the assistance of a trusted friend or family member. (Don't even ask about the living hell I put my mom and little sisters through when I was first starting out.) Remember, even the funniest comics and best bands needed someplace to be bad while they worked on their material. That's what the rehearsal room is for.

You need to rehearse the entire trick from beginning to end, without pausing, without starting over, as if you were actually performing for real people—the magical equivalent of a play's final dress rehearsal. If it's not ready, rehearse, and then rehearse some more. Never perform a trick for the public before it's ready. Only after several successful full rehearsals will you be prepared and have the confidence and ability to take to the streets.

The Devil Is in the Details

A magic trick is more than the sum of its parts. It starts when you decide what effect you want the spectator to receive. It takes into account all of the individual steps to get there. There's the selection of props, their condition, and the way in which you handle them. There's the way you approach your audience, your attitude, wardrobe, and style. Only after all of that does the actual performance come into play. Change any component or any moment, and the end result changes, too. Take every ingredient into consideration when you're planning, practicing, and performing your magic: make every moment in front of the spectator count.

Tell Ya What ...

Everybody has mannerisms that reveal his or her thoughts and moods. Psychologists call this "body language." Cardsharps and magicians call them "tells." You've heard about it in card games: when a person is dealt a good card, his eyes may widen or one of his eyebrows may unconsciously twitch, "telling" the other players what's in his hand. (That's why so many of them wear sunglasses.)

Well, unfortunately, we all have "tells" that we have to get rid of, or at least minimize, if we're going to get away with our secret moves. Even a momentary change in posture or tone of voice might let the audience know that something sneaky is going on. They may not see or know *what* you've done, but they'll know when it happened.

One of the most common ticks among magicians that you must avoid is blinking or looking away from your hands or the spectator's eyes just as you're performing your sleight. Perhaps your subconscious mind is telling you that if *you* don't see it, nobody else will, either. But instead, the "tell" is doing exactly the opposite.

Tricky Tidbits

Many times we become so afraid that our audience is going to figure out how the tricks are done that we go out of our way to prove that everything is above board. We not only show but also tell the audience that our hands are empty or that we're using an "ordinary, everyday" deck of playing cards. Stop it! Don't arouse suspicion when none exists. In the theater, where there's the deliberate artifice of performing on a stage, they talk about the audience's "suspension of disbelief." This exists in magic, too. As long as you're not challenging the audience by constantly making disclaimers, most spectators are willing to just "go along for the ride."

Be Natural

No, I'm not suggesting you perform magic in the nude—although that would raise a few eyebrows out on the street. What I'm suggesting is that none of your movements while you're performing should look unusual or raise suspicions in the spectator's mind. It doesn't matter whether you're doing a secret move or not. If the audience thinks you are, it's the same as if you actually were.

Now, what's natural to a magician is not necessarily the same as what's natural for a layperson. (That's what we call *them*.) For example, in Chapter 8 you're going to learn something called a *pass*, where you pretend to put a coin from one hand into the other, but you actually don't. To be natural when you perform the sleight, you'll have to make it look exactly the same as when you actually do transfer a coin from one hand to the other.

Of course, you can create your own naturalness. What does it look like when you perform the sleight? From now on, when you really do put a coin from one hand into the other, make it look the same as when you perform the secret move. Either way, the result is that you'll come out looking natural in all your movements.

With a Flourish

At this point, I should also address the issue of flourishes. A flourish is a deliberate show of skill. It might be the way in which you shuffle a deck, spread them on the table, or scoop them up. It's that special lilt or flair that lets the audience know you've done your homework. There's nothing wrong with a flourish or two. After all, it's kind of expected. The audience knows that you've handled this stuff before. They figure you've got to be an expert with cards and coins. In fact, they'd be surprised and disappointed if you were sloppy. But you don't want their awe at your technical prowess to overshadow the magic trick itself. You don't want them to see you do a flourish and think, "Well, if he can do that, he can do anything." Once the audience starts thinking along those lines, it's time to pack up the deck for the night. They won't think you're performing magic; they'll simply credit you with having manual dexterity.

The Magic Moment

There is, or should be, a meaning in every moment, every gesture, and every word when you're in front of an audience. Every moment should be carefully chosen to weave the spell or charm that's necessary to make the magic work.

But the magic itself happens in the blink of an eye. It's the split second that the spoon begins to bend. It's when the ghostly writing first appears on your arm. To focus all of the audience's attention on the instant that the magic supposedly takes place, you should provide a "magic moment." The cliché example of a magic moment, of course, is a tap with a magic wand. But in the case of a street magician, it could be a gesture, such as waving the hand or snapping the fingers. Perhaps a raised eyebrow or a sullen glare. Maybe an unnaturally long pause, followed by a staccato action. And, of course, there are magic words. As kids we learned "abracadabra" and "hocus pocus." They both seem pretty silly now. But what "magic word" could you come up with that would have relevance to you, your audience, and the situation in which you're performing?

Engage All the Senses

When you perform, try to involve as many of a spectator's senses as possible. Each sense adds to the overall feeling of magic, because it imparts different types of information to the brain. Suppose you were in a fish market: you see the fish lying on the ice, you smell them, you feel how rough their scales are, and you hear the fishermen hawking their wares as you sample a bite of sushi. Take any one of those senses away, and you're limiting the experience. Likewise in magic: the more senses you can involve in a single trick, the more intense and memorable your audience's experience will be.

Having a person write his or her name on a card personalizes it. Gently touching the back of a person's wrist draws him or her into the moment. Make the connection visceral—with as many senses as possible.

Don't be afraid to invade the spectator's personal space from time to time—both physically *and* mentally. Danger, unease, and uncertainty are important elements in successful street magic. In urban, guerilla-style magic, your very presence can be disturbing and unsettling. But as long as the audience knows that you're "an actor playing the role of a magician"—remember Robert-Houdin?—then instead of feeling threatened, they'll be willing to invite your "trickster spirit" to play.

The KISS Principle

KISS stands for "keep it simple, stupid." Never lose sight of the magic trick from the audience's point of view. You can be doing the greatest trick in the world, but if the audience can't figure out what the effect is supposed to be, then you're only entertaining yourself.

Magicians are fond of multi-phase tricks that (according to the way they're advertised in magic catalogs and websites) build to a stunning climax. You have four blue-backed Kings; they turn over one at a time, and as they do their backs change to red, and when you turn them face up they're now Aces. But what was the effect? How is a spectator going to remember, much less be able to describe to someone else, what he or she saw? How could that trick possibly be described as magic?

But how about these tricks:

- ◆ It floated!
- ◆ It disappeared!
- ◆ They changed places!

It all goes back to the basic effects in magic, tricks that can be described in a single sentence. Embroider your magic as much as you want with your stories, your props, your wardrobe, and your performance style. But keep the trick itself direct and simple.

Theft

This shouldn't even have to be said, but it's unethical to steal another magician's work. Period. The tricks themselves are fair game if they're purchased or learned from DVDs or through books like this one. If another magician shows you his routine and gives you permission to perform it, everything's copasetic. But otherwise, no. It's theft, pure and simple. You'd be trying to take a shortcut by co-opting all the hard work that another performer has put into perfecting his craft.

The Too-Perfect Theory

Believe it or not, sometimes a trick can be too unbelievable, too impossible. In 1970, magician Rick Johnsson first discussed a hypothesis in print that he coined the "Too-Perfect Theory." Succinctly stated, the Too-Perfect Theory says that a trick is "too perfect" when the only possible explanation is the actual explanation. The audience is able to figure out the trick because the only other option is that you really are magical—which they logically know is not true.

I'll give you an example of a trick that's "too perfect." You spread a deck of cards on the table. You allow the spectator to pick any card and return it to the deck. You never touch the pack. You show your hand completely empty, reach into your pocket, and pull out the one and only card that's there. It matches the spectator's freely selected card. Too perfect. The only possible explanation is that you're using a deck of 52 identical cards and you have a card that matches them already in your pocket.

In order to prevent spectators from figuring out the obvious, you have to give them magical options to explore. If they can immediately jump to the correct solution because it's the only possible solution, no magic can take place in their minds.

That's not to say that your tricks should be confusing. You just have to give the spectators some excuse to allow for the magic. You waved your hand: okay, they didn't see you touch the deck, but that's when it must have happened. You turned your back for just a second: that's when you did the secret something. By giving the audience some rational possibility, you actually allow them to take the magical journey with you.

Crowd Control

Practice, practice, and then practice some more. But at some point you're going to have to leave your room and go out to perform for people. And when you encounter live human beings, it's a whole new ballgame. How you interact with them and how you take charge of the performance situation makes all the difference in whether your magic is a success.

May I Come In?

One of the most important things you'll have to find out—and it's something you can only learn by experience—is knowing when and when not to approach people to perform for them. After all, do you like strangers coming up to you uninvited?

Before you spring out and throw yourself on some unsuspecting victims, take a look at the situation. Are the people in a deep conversation? An argument? Punishing a kid? Trying to close a business deal? Might one of them be about to spring a proposition of any kind? You never really know what you're getting into when you walk up to a group of people you don't know. For some street magicians, part of the thrill is being able to psych out the audience and know exactly when to pounce. (In fact, in street magic slang, the person whom the magician zeroes in on and decides to approach is called the "target.") It's a fine line between interrupting someone and proposing a unique experience to him or her. Make sure you're making the right offer.

Curses

You're a street magician, not a street jerk. Nobody likes a wise guy. If you come off with an attitude that suggests you're thinking, "I can fool you. I'm smart; you're stupid," nobody's going to want to watch or even be around you. Your audience's reaction to the magic—what they experience and get out of the encounter—is more important than you showing how clever you are.

Buzz Off!

I've cleaned up the title of this section for my editors. Don't be surprised if sometime you're greeted with language that's much worse. You just came out of nowhere, and now they're being asked to deal with you. Most likely, your magic will be very welcome. But—and perhaps this is common sense—if your prospective audience seems uncomfortable or uninterested when you first approach them, thank them and back off. That being said, if they agree or ask to see some magic, the floor should be yours.

Nevertheless, it's only human nature that at some point you're going to have to deal with drunks, hecklers, show-offs, and people who are bored or just plain not interested in what you have to show them.

What do you do when someone constantly interrupts, grabs at things, or insults you when you're performing? To make a long story short, confronting the person is a no-win situation. If you call out the offender, *you* come off looking bad. You also run the risk of upsetting his or her friends: they're probably already upset at their buddy for spoiling the unexpected performance, but if you insult their friend, they may turn their anger toward you.

Your first attempt should be to just ignore it. Often, the person is simply trying to stay the center of attention. Sometimes by acknowledging that, the person will settle down. But my best advice is to try to find a way to wrap up your trick as quickly and as gracefully as possible, thank the people, and get out of there.

However, if a spectator simply calls out, "I know how that's done" or "I've seen it before," it's not necessarily time to bail. They're just trying to let you know, though not very subtly, that they've been around the block a few times themselves. So don't challenge or belittle them. It will only pit you against the person's friends and also convince them that you've been caught.

Instead, if someone shouts out the secret, just tell them that you've heard about that method, too, but that you do it a different way. That's right: just lie to them. My favorite way to handle the situation is to give a sneaky smile and or a conspiratorial wink and say, "You're right. Let's keep it our secret." The heckler will shut up and realize that he or she is in on something special, some sort of conspiracy of silence—even if the rest of the audience knows that you're just humoring the person.

The comments you're going to hear most often, however, won't be menacing at all. They'll just be feeble attempts at humor, like …

- "If you were a real magician, you could …"
- "Can you make my wife [or that food] disappear?"
- "Boy, I wouldn't want to play cards with you."

Sad to say, over the next few years you'll be hearing those words hundreds of times, but remember: it's the first time they've ever thought the joke up. Grin and bear it.

Who Was That Masked Man?

According to the lyrics of an old Cy Coleman song, "It's not where you start, it's where you finish." Let me add to that: it's also *when* you finish. Already a cliché in vaudeville, the saying is just as true today: always leave them wanting more. Walk away with them thinking, *Did I just see what I think I just saw?* not, *I thought he'd never leave.*

What to Do When ...

Admit it. We magicians are control freaks. We always like to be in command of a situation. But things do go wrong. It's a law of nature. No matter how good you are, no matter how careful you are, eventually and perhaps when you least expect or want it to happen, you're going to screw up. The trick doesn't work.

Never blame the audience, no matter if it was their fault. No, they didn't take the wrong card. Yes, they should have been allowed to shuffle. But you're supposed to be a magician. You should be able to do anything, despite the best efforts of mere mortals to mess you up. Do whatever you must to come up with an alternate ending. Then move on to your next trick. Since you haven't told people in advance what you were trying to do, most people won't even notice when you suddenly change gears.

When something happens around you in the room or the environment and it distracts your spectators, you have to acknowledge it. You can't just keep on performing as if nothing had happened. Didn't you *hear* that? The audience will wonder whether you're deaf and blind. Ignoring the situation only makes it worse because it keeps people from refocusing on your magic. You don't have to make an amusing aside or stop to help fix the problem, but you have to at least let the audience know that you're not performing on cruise control. Just by acknowledging the situation, you and your audience can forget it and move on.

The Curse of TV Magic

I can't leave the final chapter of this section without discussing the difference between real street magic and TV magic—what you can actually perform versus what is seen these days on television. When Mark Wilson pioneered the use of magic on television on his weekly series *The Magic Land of Allakazam* (1960–1964), he was acutely aware that audiences at home might think that when he made his wife Nani Darnelle disappear or he sawed her in half, he simply stopped the camera and took her out of the box to make the magic work—which is exactly what they *did* do on the sitcom *I Dream of Jeannie*. So for decades, television magicians lived by the creed that once the actual "trick" started, there would be no camera cutaways or edits.

But because today's audiences are used to—in fact, demand—very short shots and multiple edits to keep their attention, television magic has had to go along with the trend. Just a decade or two ago, viewers would have been very aware if the camera cut away to an audience reaction shot or a different camera angle. Today, most people don't even consciously notice that an edit or a change to a different camera has taken place.

I know from experience. I was once taped for NHK television in Japan, performing a trick in which I held a ball in one fist and it jumped into my other hand. I performed the trick using a standard magician's sleight, but when the show aired, the trick that the home audience saw was actually impossible. The editor, who wasn't a magician, happened to change camera angles just when I was performing the move, and because the motion seemed irrelevant, he simply eliminated it to tighten up the shot. But the edit was so imperceptible that it looked as if I had performed *real* magic!

Besides the need for editing, another reason that some of the magic performed on television can't be performed live is, for lack of a better term, the forced perspective of the camera. Yes, if your eyes were exactly where the camera lens has been placed, you would have seen what shows up on your TV screen. But if you were anywhere else on the set, perhaps only inches to the left or the right, you would be able to see exactly how the trick is done. Most times this is forgivable; after all, when we perform certain sleights or tricks, we hold our hands or bodies at the best possible angle to deceive the public. But a TV camera has the advantage of being able to focus the trick within a very tight frame, one that would be impossible to achieve in a live performance situation.

Add to that the ability to shoot the performance multiple times, manipulate the images, and include shots that were not part of the actual performance, and you have the possibility of creating magic specifically for the home viewer.

Finally, there's sometimes a nagging suspicion that some of the spectators at the performance are, in actuality, working for the magician. Could some of the audience members see how the trick was done but didn't say anything? Could someone have been hired to block a camera angle or slip a chosen card somewhere that the magician couldn't possibly get to? Well, it is a possibility.

Isn't that cheating? As you'll see later in this book, the use of *stooges* is a time-honored tradition of the magical art. Perfect examples of this are "Ascension Undercover," which you'll learn in Chapter 6, and "Meet Mr. Wizard" in Chapter 14, both of which require a secret assistant to help you pull off the trick.

Bottom line? There's no easy way to say this, but there are some tricks that cannot be done anywhere other than on television. They were conceived to be performed one or two times in a particular setting, sometimes in front of a mixture of regular and hand-chosen people, and to be shown in an edited form on the small screen.

The Magic Word

A **stooge** (also known as a secret assistant, confederate, plant, or shill) is someone you've let "in" on the secret and usually rehearsed on the trick in advance, and then placed among the regular spectators in the audience.

So where does this leave you? In the long run, no matter how good you become as a street magician, you're always going to be judged by some of the stuff that the audience has seen on television. Unfortunately, there's nothing to be gained by telling your spectators that a particular TV trick looks impossible because it actually *is*. Your only recourse is to be so imaginative, so entertaining, so convincing that whatever you do put into your repertoire is every bit as amazing as what they've seen on TV or the web—and all the more so because they see you, one-on-one, flesh-and-blood, live and in person.

Well, there you have it. Tips, suggestions, ideas, and advice, all to help you become the best and most powerful street magician you can be. It's probably more than you thought you ever needed to know about street magic. But it's only the beginning. Now it's time to go on to the tricks.

The Least You Need to Know

◆ Remember the Big Three: never tell how the tricks are done, never explain what you're going to do in advance, and never repeat them.

◆ Practice a trick to learn the sleights and the routine, but rehearse to find out what it'll feel like performing the trick for a real audience.

◆ Magic is in the details, from your body language to the use of the senses, creating "magic moments" and keeping your effects simple but direct.

◆ A trick is "too perfect" when the only possible explanation is the real explanation. The effect is actually improved by giving the spectator some other excuse, however implausible, to allow for the magic.

◆ Your success as a street magician depends on your ability to interact with people, turning strangers into eager participants in your kamikaze conjuring.

◆ Much of what you see on TV purporting to be street magic is actually "television magic," created as a one-time event to be viewed at home on a small screen.

Part 2

Defying Gravity

Humans have always dreamt of being able to fly. Ancient myths of people levitating abound, of course, but can it actually be performed? Well, from the streets of India to the Vegas Strip, magicians have been giving it their best shot for centuries.

It's time that you got into the act! First, we'll warm up with a few tricks in which you levitate inanimate, everyday objects. You'll learn how to make things float from your fingertips using ordinary items such as a dinner roll, a steak knife, a wedding ring, and a playing card.

Then we'll get into the hardcore stuff. After a couple of quick gags, you'll learn how to float from a park bench while lying underneath a cloth or rise a foot off the ground using only your jacket for cover. Then, the trick that's worth the price of the book: the Balducci Levitation. This is the trick that laid the groundwork for the self-levitations currently being performed by such master street magicians as David Blaine and Criss Angel.

Ready to fly?

Chapter 5

Levitate This!

In This Chapter

- Floating dinner rolls
- The Clinging Knife
- The Rising Card trick
- Levitating finger rings

It's not just people that magicians make rise into the air. Indeed, once magicians started levitating ladies, it was only a matter of time before they started floating all sorts of things. Sometimes it seems as if anything they touch can be made to float. Let's look at some other stuff that streetwise sorcerers—and that means *you*—can levitate.

The Floating Roll

One of the most popular stage tricks in the early twentieth century was the Floating Ball. As its name suggests, a large, silver sphere soared above the stage all by itself and in full view of the audience. The trick was created by the British magician David P. Abbott, but it was made famous by the Dutch-born illusionist Theo Bamberg, who, performing in disguise as an Asian magician named Okito, first presented it in London in 1921. It went on to become a standard illusion in the repertoire of magicians worldwide and was popularized in the United States by master stage illusionist Howard Thurston, among many others.

The problem was, the method was very complicated. It required strings (gasp!), special lighting, and an elaborate set-up. Many versions also required secret assistants off-stage. Added to that, it couldn't be done in every theater.

There *had* to be a better way to accomplish this miracle! Can you imagine what would happen if someone hired you and expected you to perform your most famous trick, a levitation, and then you had to beg off because the conditions weren't right for you to do it? Lame excuses like "the spirits aren't with me tonight" just wouldn't cut it.

Well, one magician rose to the challenge to come up with a practical method to per-form the Floating Ball illusion. In 1940, Joe Karson patented a practical one-person, self-contained way to make a ball float underneath the cover of a scarf. (Yes, it was so new and different that he actually received a U.S. patent for it!) The ball would dart about the stage, sometimes dragging the magician along after it. The ball peeked out from under the cloth and seemed to fly in a complete circle around the performer. Karson called his creation "Zombie," and it's still one of the most popular tricks per-formed by magicians throughout the world.

Although not as complicated as the Okito or Thurston floating balls, Zombie still requires special apparatus. But not so in the trick I'm about to show you. It's per-formed completely impromptu at the dinner table. And while it may not be quite as impressive as having a lady float over your head, handled properly it can still be a fun little mystery.

Effect

As you sit at the table, you cover a dinner roll with a napkin. The bun rises and floats under cover of the cloth.

Preparation

None, really, but you'll need a dinner roll, a cloth napkin that you can't see through, and a fork. When you're ready to perform, make sure that the fork is nearby, posi-tioned on the right side of your plate.

Performance

Set a dinner roll in front of you on the table. If there's a basket of buns, all the better: ask your spectator to hand you one of them. This'll prove that you haven't prepared the roll in any way.

Open a cloth napkin, and hold it by two adjacent corners, with one corner in each hand. The cloth will drape down between your hands like a curtain. Show both sides of the napkin.

Cover the dinner roll with the napkin, making sure that it spreads out enough to also cover the fork. Reach under the napkin to reposition the bun, and, as you do, stick the tines of the fork securely into the roll. Don't take a lot of time or make a big deal out of stabbing the bun with the fork. Remember, you're supposedly only straightening out the cloth and preparing the roll for its unearthly ascent.

As you pull your hand out from under the napkin, position the fork so that the end of its handle is at the corner of the napkin closest to your right hand.

So the other day I was baking cookies. What? You don't think it's possible that someone like me could bake cookies? Well, I have a sensitive side, too, you know.

Okay, so I wasn't exactly baking them from scratch. I was making them in the microwave from one of those tubes of cookie dough. But I was watching them puff up while they were, uh, cooking.

And it made me wonder. Could I use magic to make the cookies or anything else—say this dinner roll—rise?

An exposed view showing the position of the fork under the napkin after you've stabbed it into the bread roll.

Pick up the two corners of the napkin closest to your side of the table, one in each hand, with your thumbs on top and your fingers underneath the napkin. As your right hand picks up its corner, also grab the handle of the fork and press it against the cloth between your right thumb and fingers.

Tilt your hands as you raise them off the table. A round bulge appears under the cloth. Something appears to be rising. As soon as the napkin clears the tabletop, the spectator will realize that it's the dinner roll that's "floating" under the cloth.

Make the dinner roll levitate by tilting the fork upward under cover of your napkin, exposed view.

By pushing your arms forward, you'll create the illusion that the dinner roll is trying to fly away from you. By simply raising or lowering your arms or moving the ball back and forth, you can make the dinner roll seem to rise up, float downward, or pull you from side to side. If you stand up and turn in a circle, you can make it appear that the dinner roll is spinning you around. (If you do this last move, make sure that the fork remains hidden underneath the cloth out of the spectator's view.)

The bun also rises! The dinner roll appears to levitate under cover of your napkin.

By maneuvering the fork and moving your arms, you can make it appear as if the bun is trying to fly away from you.

There are a couple more fancy maneuvers you can try once the dinner roll has taken flight. In the first, you can make the bun play "peek-a-boo" from beneath the cloth. Hold the napkin taut in front of you between your two hands. Slowly tilt the angle of the fork upward behind the cloth so that the dinner roll peeks out over the top horizontal edge of the napkin. By tilting the fork, you can make the bun seem to bob up and down behind the napkin.

The bun peeks out from behind the napkin.

And here's a "rock-a-bye baby" kind of move. Tilt the fork upward until the bun rests on the top edge of the cloth, which should be held horizontal and taut between your hands. (You have to be very careful that the tines of the fork remain hidden from the audience as you do this.) Bring your hands slightly together, which will make the napkin droop, but as you do, keep the bun resting against the edge of the cloth. Swing your hands back and forth. The bun seems to be riding on the edge of the slackened cloth as it rocks between your hands.

The bun balances on top of the napkin as you hold it slack between your hands.

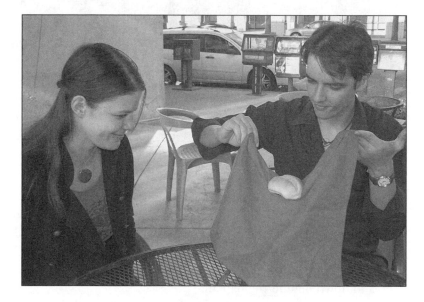

Finally, lower your arms until the bun "floats" down and rests once more on the table. To separate the bun from the fork, let go of the inner left corner of the napkin. Place your left hand on top of the napkin, and press gently against the bun. At the same time, pull the inner right-hand corner of the napkin (as well as the fork) slightly to the right until the fork is free from the roll. This whole action should look as if you're using your left hand to help settle the bun into place.

Basically, this is the end of the trick. You could simply lift the napkin to reveal the dinner roll. After all, the fork is back where it started. But someone might be suspicious of it, so here's what I do. I reach under the napkin with my left hand, grasp the dinner roll, and then whisk the napkin (along with the hidden fork pinched beneath it) away from the roll. As all eyes look at the dinner roll, I casually place the napkin into my lap. Later, when I put the napkin back on the table, I either let the fork fall to the floor (if it's carpeted or the restaurant is noisy enough to cover the sound) or slip it into my pocket and return it to the table later.

You can toss the dinner roll out for examination if you want, but you should either break it in half, squeeze a hole into it, or take a bite out of it to get rid of the holes from the fork tines.

Curses _____

Even if you treat this trick as a gag, don't expose how it's done. It's similar enough to the actual Zombie Ball that magicians who perform it will be upset, even though the methods are not identical. Besides, it goes without saying that once the spectators know how the trick works, they won't think much of you as a magician.

The duration and the pacing of the trick depend completely on you. Remember, you want to create the illusion that the bun is floating freely, but if you're too stiff or perform the trick for too long, people will figure out where and how you're connected to the dinner roll.

Bottom line? Just have fun with it. It should be performed as a snappy, visual throwaway that will have people scratching their heads afterward.

Static Cling

While you're at the table, you might as well make use of some of that cutlery. In this next demonstration, you claim to use your "electrical" personality to make a knife float—well, actually, stay suspended in place—by static electricity. Even after you expose the secret, though, you'll still be able to fool your spectators.

The Magic Word

A **sucker trick** is any routine in which a magician performs a trick, shows how it is done, and then repeats the trick using a different method to fool the audience again.

This is a perfect example of a genre of magic known as a *sucker trick*. No, you're not calling your audience "suckers." At least not to their faces. But sometimes you're able to fool the people more easily if they already think they know how the trick is done. All you have to do is use an entirely different method. It proves the old adage that "a little knowledge is a dangerous thing."

Effect

You set a knife on your palm and raise your hand, but the knife doesn't fall. It remains in place, clinging to your palm. You expose the secret, showing how you're secretly holding it in place. You then offer to repeat the trick, but this time the knife seems to remain suspended against your hand for real.

Preparation

Slip a pen (or pencil, knife, heavy swizzle stick, or any other similarly shaped object) up your left shirtsleeve. Tuck one end of the pen under your watchband to hold it in place against your inner forearm.

Performance

Don't you hate it when you pull your socks out of the dryer and you can't get them apart? Or you try to brush your hair and it sticks to your comb? The culprit, of course, is that evil villain, static cling. Let me show you what I mean.

Hold out your left hand, palm upward, over a table. Pick up a knife with your right hand, rub it one or two times against your left sleeve, and then set the knife on your left palm so that it's perpendicular to your forearm. Turn your left hand palm down. The knife, naturally, falls to the table. Appear to be puzzled.

Pick up the knife, and rub it a few times against your left sleeve again. This time, press your palms together with the knife squeezed between them. Tilt your hands perpendicular to the table, so that your thumbs are pointing upward and the back of your left hand is toward your spectator. Separate your hands. Once again, the knife drops to the table.

Frustrated, pick up the knife one more time. Rub it back and forth against your left sleeve several times, and set the knife on your left hand. Close your left fingers around the knife. Clasp your right hand around your left wrist, as if to steady your left hand. Your right thumb should be against the back of your left wrist, and your right fingers should encircle it.

Tilt your left hand so that it's perpendicular to the table and the back of the hand is toward the spectator. Slowly open your left hand. Extend and separate your left fingers. Miraculously, the knife clings to your palm. You can shake your hand, but the knife doesn't fall. It remains suspended there.

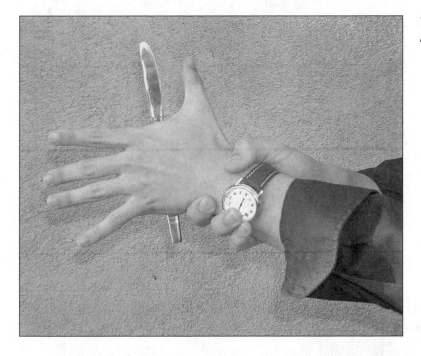

The knife clings to your left hand, audience view.

What the audience can't see is that your right forefinger is holding the knife in place: as you tilted your left hand into position the last time, you extended your right forefinger along the underside of your left wrist, into your left palm, and pressed the knife against your hand. When you opened your left fingers, the right forefinger held the knife in place.

The knife clings to your left hand, your view.

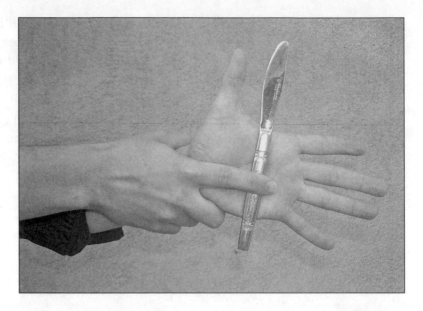

Offer to show how the trick is done. Still holding the knife in place with your right forefinger, turn your left hand palm upward. Suggest that this trick is a cute gag that the spectators might like to show their friends. Let them try it.

While they're attempting the trick, casually reach under your wristband, and pull out the end of the pen so that it extends into the middle of your left palm. The rest of the pen should remain held in place, pressed against your left wrist by the watchband.

Let me try it again. Maybe this time I can get it to work for real.

Hold your left hand open, with your palm facing the floor. Take back the knife with your right hand, and rub it back and forth several times against your left sleeve. Then place the knife against your left palm, slipping it underneath the pen.

Close your left fingers into a fist and, like before, encircle your left wrist with your right hand. Deliberately hold your right hand in such a way that your right forefinger is hidden under your left fist, away from the audience's view.

Tilt your left hand so that it's perpendicular to the floor, with the back of your hand toward the spectators. Slowly open your left fingers. The knife seems to cling to your left hand just like it did before. The audience, of course, assumes that your right forefinger is holding the knife in place.

It's not what you think. The knife is stuck there, suspended in place. It really is!

Slowly move your right forefinger so that it's next to your other fingers encircling your left wrist. After it registers to the spectators that your forefinger isn't holding the knife against your left palm, let go with your right hand completely and move it away from your left arm. The knife still stays stuck against your left palm.

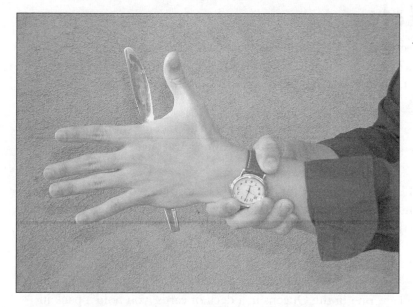

The knife appears to cling to your left palm by magic.

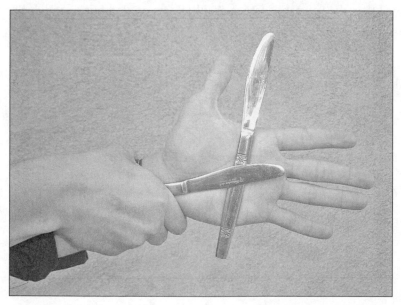

An extra knife secretly holds the one that the audience sees in place, your view.

To finish the trick, grab the knife with your right hand, and slip it out from under the pen. Set the knife on the table or hand it to the spectator. As they examine the knife, push the pen back under the watchband so that it's hidden up your sleeve.

I guess I must have an electric personality!

The Levitating Lady

Speaking of static electricity, do you think that "static cling" could really be used to make something float? Of course it can. Or at least it can *seem* to. You're going to use it to make a lady float. Okay, not a live person exactly, but it *is* one of four Queens in a deck of playing cards.

As you'll see, I like to give my spectator a choice of which Queen I should levitate, because it gives me a chance to talk about fortune telling. And that seems to interest everybody!

In fact, many times I'll get more credit for talking about fortune telling than for performing the trick. And you know what? That's okay with me. Captivating the audience's imagination is, perhaps, the most important part of being a street magician.

Effect

Offering to levitate a lady, one of the Queens in a deck of cards, you hold a pack in your left hand. The card that the spectator names visibly floats up and out of the deck.

Preparation

None. You'll need a deck of playing cards.

Performance

We're going to make a lady float in midair—in miniature. We have four lovely female assistants in a deck of cards. Should we use the Queen of Hearts, the Queen of Diamonds, the Queen of Clubs, or the Queen of Spades?

What's that, you say? An interesting choice. Because, as you probably know, in fortune telling ….

Cartomancy—fortune telling using a deck of cards—dates back to the time of the earliest playing cards in the fourteenth century. Some *readers*, as those who use cards to tell fortunes are called, work with regular playing cards. Others prefer special decks, such as Tarot cards, that have designs that differ from a standard pack. In every type of deck, each suit and value has a symbolic meaning for fortune telling.

Using the most generally accepted interpretation for the four suits, you might want to try one of these patter lines, depending upon which Queen the spectator chooses:

◆ *… Hearts represent the Emotions, so the Queen of Hearts is the passionate, romantic lady in the deck—no doubt already used to flights of fancy.*

◆ *… Diamonds represent Wealth, so the Queen of Diamonds is a "Material Girl." Be careful: this ride is going to cost you!*

◆ *… Clubs represent Power, so the Queen of Clubs will try to take charge during this trick. It's our will against hers. I'm going to have to force her to levitate whether she wants to or not.*

◆ *… Spades represent the Intellect, so the Queen of Spades will spend her whole time up in the air trying to figure out how it's done.*

For more information on divination using playing cards, check out these great books:

◆ *The Complete Idiot's Guide to Fortune Telling* by Diane Ahlquist

◆ *The Complete Idiot's Guide to Tarot, Second Edition* by Arlene Tognetti and Lisa Lenard

◆ *Max Maven's Book of Fortunetelling* by Max Maven

Whichever Queen the spectator has chosen, place it face down on the top of the deck, and hold the pack face down in your left hand. Tilt your left hand upward so that the back of your hand is toward the spectator.

Make a fist with your right hand. Stick out your right forefinger. Touch your right forefinger to the top, short edge of the cards, and lift your finger about 2 inches.

Rise!

Nothing happens. The Queen doesn't move. Look puzzled and try again. Still no luck.

I know! What we need to make the Queen jump is a little magical jolt of electricity.

Rub your right forefinger against your left sleeve, as if you were building up a static charge. Once again, rest your right forefinger against the top edge of the deck. This time, however, also stick out your right little finger, and press it against the top card of the deck (the Queen). If you've angled yourself properly, the deck will completely hide your little finger from the spectator's view.

Preparing to make the card rise, audience view.

(Photo courtesy of Titus Photography.)

Preparing to make the card rise, your view.

(Photo courtesy of Titus Photography.)

Raise your right forefinger, and as you do, let your little finger drag the Queen upward. The card appears to cling to your right forefinger.

Slowly continue to lift your right hand. At the instant that the bottom of the Queen clears the deck, pinch the card between your right thumb and forefinger. At the same time, curl your right little finger back into your fist, hiding the method of the rising card.

The lady levitates, audience view.

(Photo courtesy of Titus Photography.)

The card rises, your view.

(Photo courtesy of Titus Photography.)

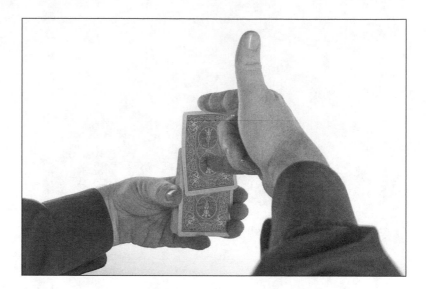

The Rising Ring

Let's try one more levitation of an ordinary object before we move on to the real deal. Using people's personal property in your magic tricks always commands their attention. First of all, they'll watch closely to see if you're gonna make their stuff disappear. And there's an added advantage: they know their own things aren't *gimmicked* in any way.

That's why you'll be borrowing the finger ring you'll be using for this next trick. Sure, you'd love to be able to make its owner float. But instead, let's go for something a bit more manageable.

The Magic Word

A **gimmick,** sometimes called a gaff, is an item that's been prepared in some way to allow the trick to work. Some gimmicks are allowed to be seen by the audience because they look ordinary. Others are pieces of special apparatus that have to remain hidden from the audience's view. An object that's been altered or prepared in order to accomplish a trick is said to be gimmicked or gaffed.

Effect

A finger ring is threaded onto a rubber band, which you then stretch between your hands. As you hold the band at a steep angle, the ring visibly rises upward along the length of the band.

Preparation

None. You'll need a rubber band.

Performance

Ask your spectator to remove his or her ring. You can use any ring, of course, but a wedding ring is the perfect weight and size.

You ever see that trick where a magician makes a girl float in midair? Then, just to prove there are no wires, he passes a big ring all around her? What if it's the ring that's actually doing the magic and not the magician? Can I take a look at your finger ring?

Although it may not be your style, there are several standard—meaning old—jokes that comedy magicians commonly use when they examine a borrowed ring. Among them are …

◆ *I see your ring's imported. It's French, from J.C. Penné!*

◆ *And look: it has a place for a stone and everything.*

◆ *Oh, and it's inscribed. Thanks for the night ….* (Needless to say, the way you complete this last joke is limited only by your good taste and sense of decorum.)

Thread the ring onto a rubber band. You can use any size rubber band, but for visibility's sake, I generally use one about 3½ inches long and no wider than ⅛ inch.

Pinch one end of the rubber band between your right thumb and forefinger. Pinch the center of the rubber band between your left thumb and forefinger. The ring should be in the area of the band between your two hands. Curl your hands into loose fists.

Stretch the rubber band about 6 inches. Note that half the length of the rubber band is hanging over the back of your left forefinger and is hidden inside your left fist.

Charms

Some magicians prefer to break the rubber band first, so that the ring travels along a single elastic "thread." I personally think that the trick seems more impromptu if the band remains unbroken. Also, you don't have to use a finger ring to perform this trick. In fact, many magicians simply use a second rubber band.

Stretch the rubber band, with the ring threaded on it, between your hands. Note that half the rubber band is hidden behind your left fingers.

(Photo courtesy of Titus Photography.)

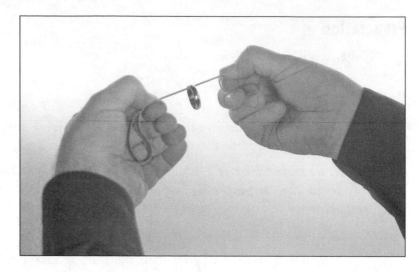

Hold your hands so that the band is horizontal, parallel to the floor. Let your spectator plainly see that the ring is on the rubber band. Raise your right hand a few inches so that the rubber band is held at an angle of about 30° to 45°.

The ring will naturally fall by gravity to rest against your left thumb and forefinger.

Now watch. Concentrate on the ring. Believe it or not, it will start to rise!

Slowly—very slowly—release the tension on the part of the rubber band that you're holding between your left thumb and forefinger. As the rubber band relaxes, its movement will be imperceptible; but it will carry the ring upward, giving the perfect illusion that the ring is rising on its own. (If the ring *doesn't* rise or if it falls back down to your left fingers, decrease the angle at which you're holding the rubber band.)

Hold the rubber band at an angle as the ring "rises" upward.

(Photo courtesy of Titus Photography.)

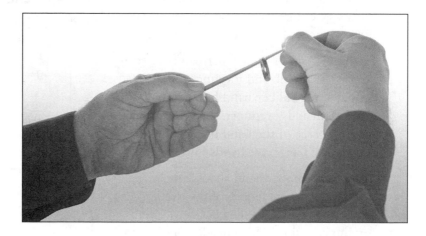

When the left end of the rubber band reaches your thumb and forefinger, don't let it fall out of your hand. Stop. Remove the ring from the rubber band, and hand it back to your spectator.

Just be careful when you put that ring back on. If it starts to float away, you're connected to it. You could be next!

Well, so far in this part we've taken a look at several novelty levitations, and you've learned how to float a bunch of common items you might run into when you're out on the street. Now it's time to move on to what you've been waiting for: how to levitate yourself, just like you've seen the street magicians do on TV.

The Least You Need to Know

- ◆ Joe Karson created Zombie, the most popular version of the Floating Ball trick, in 1940.

- ◆ Don't repeat a trick too often. Each viewing gives the audience another chance to figure it out.

- ◆ Sucker tricks fool the audience because the magician first exposes a believable way in which the trick could be done. This causes the spectators to miss the actual method.

- ◆ Cartomancy, fortune-telling with a deck of cards, probably dates back to the invention of playing cards in the 1300s.

- ◆ Sometimes in street magic, the patter and the mystical experience are as important as the trick itself.

- ◆ Using someone's personal property heightens the mystery and ensures the interest of the spectator.

Chapter 6

Up, Up, and Away

In This Chapter

◆ Funny flotations

◆ An unusual levitation, rising from the ground or a park bench

◆ A one-person self-levitation, with only a coat or jacket for cover

◆ The Balducci Levitation

Here's the chapter many of you have been waiting for: how to make yourself levitate.

Descriptions of people being able to fly date back at least 2,000 years. Most of these accounts center on religious figures, such as Simon Magus (mentioned in the Book of Acts in The Holy Bible), Saint Theresa (the original Carmelite "flying nun"), and Tibetan monks and yogis of urban legend. Even Sheshal, the "fakir" magician who you met in Chapter 1, was actually a member of the higher Brahmin priest caste.

Well, to perform the levitations described in this chapter, you don't have to be a monk, a yogi, or a saint. Not even a "fakir." But you do have to be able to "fake it."

Fly By

This is the first of two really crazy ways to magically float into a room. They're sight gags rather than tricks, but most people won't be able to explain exactly how you performed them. And they're both great optical illusions in the truest sense of that phrase: the audience is seeing one thing, but what's really happening is something else entirely.

Effect

You appear to float horizontally into a doorway, about 5 feet off the floor.

Preparation

You'll need a sturdy chair. You'll be standing on its seat, but you won't be bouncing up and down on it.

Performance

The group that you want to surprise should be in the room next to the one you're in, and the two rooms should be separated by a doorway. On your side, set a solid chair against the wall next to the open door, and step up onto the chair.

Stick your arms out in front of you in your best "Superman" pose. Lower your head so that you're looking down at the floor. Bend at your waist and lean forward, slowly and smoothly. You can increase your balance by standing on one foot and raising your other leg so that it's parallel to the floor. You can also lean your torso against the wall for extra support.

Charms

You don't have to perform this prank standing on a chair. However, the extra height afforded by the chair makes the stunt seem even more incredible.

To the spectators in the next room, it looks as if you're floating in a prone position about 5 feet off the ground. Turn your head toward them and smile or say hello. Wave.

To float back out of the room, simply lean back slowly. Be careful that your upper body stays parallel to the floor until it's completely out of sight. Step down off the chair, walk into the other room, and take your bow.

Floating into the room, audience view.

(Photo by Claude Piscitelli. Photo courtesy of David Goldrake.)

Floating into the doorway, exposed view.

(Photo by Claude Piscitelli. Photo courtesy of David Goldrake.)

Crawl Space

If you've ever wanted to make a grand entrance into a room—in even a more impressive fashion than in our last routine—then this is the trick for you. And trust me, if you fooled 'em with the last gag, they'll never figure out how you can keep yourself up in the air long enough to do this stunt.

Effect

Your arms and then your head appear along the edge of a doorframe or wall about 5 feet off the floor. You start to claw your way around the doorframe and into the room where the spectators are standing. You lose your grip and slide back into the room you came from.

Preparation

Again, no special preparation is essential, but the gag is more effective if you perform it while standing on a solid chair.

Performance

This trick basically works the same way as "Fly By." You start in a room that's separated by a doorway from the one in which your audience is standing. Set a sturdy chair against the wall next to the doorframe so that it's out of sight of the people in the next room.

Stand on the chair. Face the wall separating you from the next room. (You can actually lean flat against the wall for balance and support, if you wish.) Bend at your waist, sideways to your left, until your upper torso is horizontal and parallel to the floor; but don't lean out so the spectators can see you just yet.

Suddenly, poke your right hand into the doorway, fingers spread and palm toward the spectators. Curl your fingers around the doorframe and grasp it tightly. Extend your left arm out into view, straight and parallel to the floor. Swing your arm around the doorframe so that your left palm slaps the wall on the other side. Spread your fingers, and curl them claw-like, as if you're trying to get a hold on the wall. Finally, pop your head into view, and grin like a Cheshire cat. Carefully balancing yourself, lean out as far as possible into the doorway without falling. Wrap your arms as far as you can around the doorway, and press them against the wall on the spectators' side. Don't be afraid to grunt and groan while you're doing this.

To the audience it'll look like you're floating on your side about 5 feet off and parallel to the floor. With a little bit of imagination on the audience's part, you'll look like a giant bug, trying to crawl along the wall from one room into the next.

Clawing your way into the spectators' room, audience view.

(Photo by Claude Piscitelli. Photo courtesy of David Goldrake.)

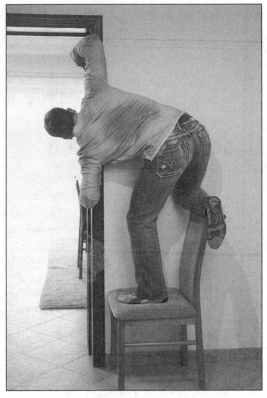

Clawing your way into the spectators' room, exposed view.

(Photo by Claude Piscitelli. Photo courtesy of David Goldrake.)

After you're sure that the other people have noticed you—how couldn't they?—raise one of your hands to wave to them. Pretend that you've lost your grip and that you're starting to slide backward. As you "slip" back into the room from which you emerged, show real panic in your face. Struggle to keep your grip. Maybe cry, "Uh oh" or even "Oh, no!" Keeping the visible part of your body as parallel as possible to the floor, lean back until you've completely disappeared into the room from which you started.

If you want to have a comic ending to this stunt, have some nonbreakable items that'll make a lot of noise if they're spilled set up in advance near the chair. As soon as you've gotten out of sight of the spectators and regained your balance, jump off the chair with a big thud. Then drop or scatter all of the noisy objects you've preset nearby. From the next room, it'll sound as if you've fallen off the wall and crashed onto a pile of junk. After a few moments, stagger into the spectators' room and collect your Oscar.

Once again, you don't have to stand on a chair in order to pull off this prank. But it's all the more startling when you start your creepy crawling from that high up along the doorframe.

Now, if that accolade's not enough for you, here's a rarely performed but baffling levitation that can be performed lying on a park bench or the ground.

Undercover Ascension

There's a comedy levitation that's become a standard among clowns. Even though you'd never perform it as a street magician, it's worth mentioning because anyone who's seen it will be especially fooled by this next levitation.

In the old circus gag, a clown lies down on a cot or small bench and is covered with a cloth, with his or her head sticking out from under one end and the shoes out of the other. The clown rises to a height of about 5 feet. Suddenly, the cloth gets snagged, or falls off, or is whisked away by another clown, revealing the performer simply tilting his or her head back and holding out a pair of stilts with shoes on the end. Yuk, yuk, yuk.

But what if you could float like this and it wasn't a gag? The beauty of this next trick is that it can be performed on the floor, on the ground, or on the pavement. You can even perform it on a park bench if you can find one that doesn't have railings or a back and is long enough for you to stretch out on.

Effect

You lie down on a flat bench, the floor, or even the ground, and an assistant covers you with a blanket or cloth. Under cover of the cloth, you're seen to rise straight up about 2 feet off the ground.

Preparation

None, except that you'll need a large opaque blanket or cloth. You'll have to experiment to find the proper size. The blanket has to completely cover you, from head to toe, when you are "floating" about 2 to 3 feet off the floor and extend all the way down to the ground—with a little extra so that no one in the audience can peek underneath. You'll also need the help of a friend or secret assistant who has practiced this with you.

The "stilt" levitation isn't always played for laughs. Here, two young street magicians perform it in front of the Red Fort in New Delhi, India, in the mid-1980s.

Performance

Have you ever seen the trick where a magician covers a girl with a cloth and she rises up into the air? Whenever I've seen it, it's been performed far away on a dimly lit stage. You just know that there are wires or something somewhere. Wouldn't it be amazing if I could do it right here, right now, out in the open?

Find a clear, level area at least 4'×6' in which to perform. The audience can examine the ground if they wish to make sure that there's no hidden apparatus anywhere. Spread out the blanket, and let the audience look it over as well.

Lie down flat on your back. Have your assistant lift up the cloth like a curtain in front of you and then drape it over your entire body. As soon as you're completely out of the audience's view, roll over on your stomach. Bend your arms at your side, in position to do a push-up. This should only take a second or two, and there should be no telltale movement or sound as you turn over. To the audience, it should simply look as if your assistant has spread a sheet over the top of you and stepped back.

Now it's time for the gymnastics. Keeping your head pointed face down, very slowly extend your arms into a push-up. At the same time, raise yourself up onto your left shin, so that your left knee to left foot is resting on the ground. Lift your right leg, straight and extended back. Your body should "rise" as a straight line, from your head all the way to the end of your right foot, level and parallel to the ground.

From outside the cloth, it'll look like you've floated upward. If the trick's performed well, it's very believable because people know that you can't move your body into that position when you're lying face up.

After a few seconds, slowly ease yourself back down to the ground. As soon as your assistant begins to remove the cloth, roll over onto your back so that you're lying face up again. As you stand up, you may want to act as if you're exhausted from all the energy you expended levitating.

You seem to float under cover of a large cloth.

Your position underneath the cloth to perform the covered levitation, exposed view.

Okay, they've seen you seemingly float behind a doorway, crawl your way around the doorframe, and float under a blanket. Isn't it about time that they got to see you just stand there—and levitate?

Got Ya Covered

There are many versions of a levitation in which you first have to cover either part or all of your body in order to get into a special position or to put a secret gimmick in place. This trick is no different, except that it seems very casual because you use your own trench coat or jacket. But, as in all magic, there's more than meets the eye!

Effect

You start the trick as a joke by holding your jacket in front of your leg. When you raise the jacket, your right leg seems to have disappeared. You lower the jacket, raise it up, and the leg is back. You repeat the sight gag with your left leg. Finally, as you hold the jacket in front of you, you seem to float straight upward for several inches, tilt to the side, then return to earth.

Preparation

You need to be wearing a jacket of some kind, as well as shoes that can be easily slipped off and on. (Dress loafers are ideal.) You also have to prepare these shoes in advance in a special way.

Take a long strip of Velcro and pull it apart. Glue one side of the Velcro along the inner sides of each of the shoes, from the heel up to about the base of the big toe. When you're wearing the shoes, if you touch the inner sides of the shoes, the Velcro strips should stick together. (This method dates back to the 1970s and is credited to Karl Fulves or U.F. Grant.)

You'll have to experiment how best to attach the Velcro. Most Velcro comes with sticky pads backing the strips, but, depending upon the weight of the shoes, this may not be strong enough to hold the shoes together when they're being lifted in the air. It's best if you can dedicate a pair of shoes to this trick: that way, you can use an epoxy or Superglue to permanently attach the Velcro to the shoes.

Attach a strip of Velcro to the inner sides of both of your shoes, exposed view.

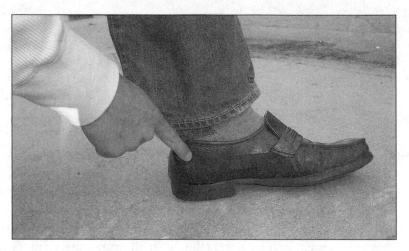

Performance

When you're ready to perform, position the spectators about 3 feet directly in front of you. Remove your jacket. Hold the jacket between your two hands along the seam between the collar and the sleeves as if the coat were a curtain dangling in front of you. The bottom hem of the jacket should be just touching the floor.

I always wanted to be able to make myself disappear. Watch! First, I'm going to make my right leg vanish.

Behind the coat, bend your right leg and hold it up in the air behind you as you balance on your left foot. Raise the jacket to just below your right knee. From the audience's view, your leg is gone! Lower the jacket and your right foot. Lift the jacket to show that your right leg has returned.

And it's back! Now for the left leg!

This time behind the jacket, bend your left leg and hold it in the air behind you as you balance on your right foot. Raise the jacket to just below your knees. Your left leg seems to be missing! Lower the jacket, drop your left leg, and then raise the jacket once more to show both feet standing on the floor.

And it's back! I know what you're thinking. Big deal. I'm not so good with this disappearing stuff. So maybe I'll try my hand at levitation instead.

Once again, hold the jacket in front of your legs so that the bottom hem just brushes the floor. Move your feet together. Press your two shoes against one another so that the Velcro holds them together. Slip your right foot out of its shoe and take about one step back with it, leaving your left foot and the shoes in place.

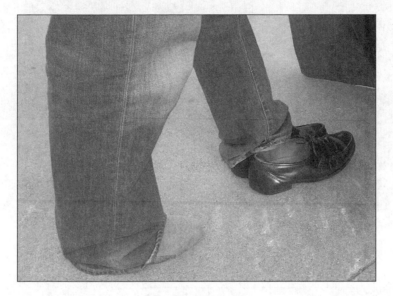

Remove your foot from your right shoe, and take a step back with your foot.

Either move your left foot slightly forward or move the jacket closer to your body so that the audience can see the toes of both shoes slightly protruding out from under the bottom of the jacket. From the spectator's point of view, you are simply holding your jacket in front of your legs, with your shoes slightly visible under the jacket.

Ever so slowly, lift your left foot straight upward a few inches as you balance yourself on your right foot. Because your two shoes are connected, they'll be lifted together. Raise your jacket as well so that its bottom hemline remains resting against the top of the shoes. From the audience's perspective, you're not only floating but they can see the ground beneath both of your shoes as well.

You can even do aerial acrobatics if you're able to stay balanced on your right foot. If you tilt your left leg upward to the left at the same time as you lean your upper torso to the right, it'll look to the audience as if your whole body is slanting to one side. (Although it's a bit trickier, it's also possible to tilt your body in the opposite direction by leaning your upper body to the left at the same time as you move your left leg upward and to the right.)

Push the toes of your shoes under the bottom hem of the jacket.

To the audience, you appear to self-levitate in a nearly vertical ascent.

By leaning your upper torso as you tilt your leg, you can create the illusion that you're floating sideways.

You can also seem to float backward. Instead of tilting your body to the side, lean backward at your waist as you slightly lift your left leg forward and upward. This will look to the audience as if you're starting to rise up into a horizontal position.

Needless to say, any of these levitations will only be effective as long as you're able to keep your balance and your shoes stay together. Angles can be a problem, so you'll have to have a trusted friend help you experiment when you rehearse to find the optimal distance to place between yourself and the spectators so that they can see the floor beneath your shoes but not far enough back to catch a glimpse of your right foot.

After you're finished floating, lower the jacket and your left leg. Place your right foot back into its shoe. Pull your two feet apart. (Hopefully there'll be enough noise wherever you're performing to cover the sound of the Velcro ripping apart.)

Remove your coat from in front of your legs to once again let the audience see that there were no special apparatus or hidden gimmicks to help you float. Some magicians recommend making a big deal of sweeping the jacket away from in front of their legs, sort of the way a matador snaps his cape, as they separate their feet so that the distraction helps hide the sound of the Velcro tearing apart.

The Balducci Levitation

Finally: the secret that everyone has been looking for! How do David Blaine, Criss Angel, and a host of other street performers levitate themselves in view full? Get ready for this underground method that's been kept super-secret for decades.

The Balducci Levitation, as it's become known, was first described by Ed Balducci in a magazine for magicians called *The Pallbearer's Review*. (It appeared in the July 1974 edition, under the straightforward name "Impromptu Levitation.") Balducci didn't claim that he invented the trick. On the contrary, he said that he'd been shown it by a member of a famous harmonica group of the time, the Harmonicats. Nevertheless, Balducci's name has been associated with the levitation ever since.

Effect

You step a few feet away from a small group of people and turn your back. Slowly, you appear to levitate several inches, hover a moment or two, and then drop back down to the ground.

Preparation

None. The advantage of this levitation is that there's no preparation required. Because of the essential angles involved, however, it does require extensive rehearsal until you've gotten it down pat. You'll have to find a trusted friend to help you practice while you're learning the trick.

Performance

In one sentence, I'm going to tell you the *secret*. It'll seem so simple and obvious that you won't believe the method will fool anybody. That's why I'm then going to take about three pages to tell you how to get away with it: all you do is stand on tiptoe on your right foot, which the audience doesn't see because it's blocked by your other foot.

This success of this levitation depends almost *entirely* on presentation. Before you begin, you must first psychologically prepare your audience into believing that they're actually going to see you levitate. This has to be subtle. It can't just be, "Hey, gang, look at me float!" If you're lucky, someone will start talking about one of those magicians who float on TV. Otherwise, if they already know you do street magic, it shouldn't be hard to turn the conversation in that direction.

Regardless, you warily admit that sometimes—not always, but sometimes—you're able to "do something like that." Or you confess that sometimes you feel yourself starting to float: it just happens. Emphasize that it doesn't always work when you try to do it, and that it's always very difficult and exhausting. You can mention that "most of those guys you see on TV use wires" or are wearing something special under their clothes. (True or not, this emphasizes that your levitation will be spontaneous—and *real*.) By now, you've got your audience hooked.

The spectators can only watch this trick from behind. If they're in front of you or to one side, they'll see how it's done. So this requires very precise stage management.

Curses _____

The danger of being "known" for being able to levitate is that people may challenge you to do it at any time, even when conditions aren't right. To forestall this, from the very first time you perform the trick you should preface the feat with disclaimers, such as "This doesn't always work" or "Sometimes the energy just isn't right," and so on. This gives you a reason later if you can't or don't want to perform it.

Also, because your spectators have to stand in a fairly tight group, you can only do it for a half dozen or fewer people at a time. Ask them to stand close together. Now here comes a very important psychological point: tell the people to extend their arms and to be prepared to catch you in case you fall.

Step about 2 to 4 feet away. Walk around a bit, taking some time to pick the exact place where you're going to stand, as if you were trying to feel the best "vibes." Settle on one spot, turn your back to the spectators, and then slightly to the left, positioning yourself at about a 45° angle (or 10 o'clock position) with respect to your audience. The spectators should be able to see the entire length of the left side of your left shoe (as well as its heel and toe) but only the heel of your right shoe.

(The most effective angle and correct distance to stand from the spectators are two of those things that your friend can help you work out. When I first saw the Balducci Levitation performed, the magician stood in a doorway, which perfectly framed him and covered his angles.)

You want those watching to think that this'll take intense concentration and that you have to mentally psych yourself, so you might want to shake out your arms or roll your neck back and forth on your shoulders as if you were limbering up for a sporting event. Finally, stand up very straight and still, with your arms held loosely at your sides.

Keeping the sides of your feet and your ankles pressed together, slowly, very slowly, push yourself up on your right tiptoe. At the same time, lift your left foot about 3 to 5 inches off the ground. It's very important that your left foot remains flat, parallel to the ground as you lift it. Because your right foot can't be seen and its heel is pressed against your left heel, the audience assumes that your right foot is likewise level and floating off the ground.

To increase the illusion of levitation, slightly raise your arms up and out from your body as you "rise." (An interesting variation might be to bend your arms at the elbows, make two fists with your hands, and hold them at chest level as if you were in position to do a chin-up. If you lower your arms as you "float," it'll look as if you're somehow pulling yourself upward.)

Stand with your back to the spectators at about a 45° angle.

(Photo by Claude Piscitelli. Photo courtesy of David Goldrake.)

Raise yourself onto your right tiptoe to perform the Balducci Levitation, audience view.

(Photo by Claude Piscitelli. Photo courtesy of David Goldrake.)

You'll get an audible reaction the moment you start to rise. "Hover" for only a few seconds. (Not only is it hard to keep your balance, but if you "levitate" any longer, it'll probably give the audience time to figure out the method.) Drop both feet hard onto the floor as if you're crashing to the ground. This subtly suggests to the audience that you've fallen a greater distance than you actually rose. In fact, you can increase the illusion by slightly bending your knees as you "drop." Stagger (that is, pretend to fall) slightly backward toward your audience. Some of them will probably extend their arms out even farther to keep you from falling down.

The audience assumes that both feet are floating off the floor during the Balducci Levitation, audience view.

(Photo by Claude Piscitelli. Photo courtesy of David Goldrake.)

A close-up of your feet during the Balducci Levitation, exposed view.

(Photo by Claude Piscitelli. Photo courtesy of David Goldrake.)

You've apparently just achieved the impossible, so don't ruin the mystery of the moment by basking in your achievement. Don't brag, "Great, huh?" Instead, when you turn back to the audience, pretend to be a bit tired and still a little woozy and off-balance. By all rights, this feat should have taken a great deal out of you.

Here's a way to lead them even further down the garden path: hold out your hands, one above the other and about a foot apart, and, in your most sincere voice ask, "How high did I go?" (This is the magical equivalent of the old fisherman's tale—holding the hands apart and claiming that "the fish was this big.") You aren't asking the spectators to confirm that you floated, only to tell you how *high* you levitated. And, as is human nature, every time they retell the story of what they saw, that distance will grow higher and higher.

Charms

You may want to experiment with what some magicians have called a "reverse Balducci." The performance and the angles are the same, except that you face the spectators instead. The spectators see the toe, length, and heel of your right shoe but only the toe of your left shoe. To "levitate," you lift yourself up on your left heel while raising your right foot a few inches, level to the floor.

If someone is unconvinced and challenges you, remember what I said in Chapter 4 about handling such situations. I usually register surprise or puzzlement, and then acknowledge that, yes, I suppose it *could* have been done the way the person suggests—but that's not the way *I* did it.

Perhaps the bigger problem with performing the Balducci Levitation is that some television and web magicians have added trick shots to their performances so that it looks like people are able to see completely under the street magician's feet. It sets an almost impossible bar for the live street magician. But don't let this deter you: if you've done your homework, the experience of seeing someone levitate live and in person will more than compensate for any expectations the spectators may bring from watching street magicians on TV or the Internet.

Well, there you have it—about a half dozen ways to create the illusion that you're able to levitate, suspend, or otherwise float yourself in the air. For many of you, this chapter alone was proverbially "worth the price of the book." But don't stop now. There's much more! In our next section, we'll be looking at powerful street magic performed with everyday objects such as playing cards and things you'd find on the table at a restaurant or a bar. And better yet, there's also a bunch of tricks that make it look like you're really hurting yourself for the audience's entertainment pleasure.

The Least You Need to Know

◆ Truly effective illusions of flight can be achieved by simple methods.

◆ People can be more readily fooled if they erroneously think they know how a trick is done. Case in point: the old clown gag using stilts versus similar-looking levitations without gimmicks.

◆ One of the most popular versions of the levitation, the "Asrah," in which a lady covered by a cloth floats and then vanishes in midflight, was introduced by Servais LeRoy in 1914.

◆ The Balducci Levitation, first described in 1974, is the inspiration for most modern one-person levitations, including ones performed by David Blaine and Criss Angel.

Part 3

Unnatural Acts

In this part, roll up your sleeves and flex your fingers to learn some honest-to-goodness sleight-of-hand. With practice, the secret "moves" that you pick up in these pages will always be there for you to use at a moment's notice.

You'll learn how to do strange and astounding things with stuff found at the restaurants, cafés, food courts, and bars where you'll be holding court. We'll move on to the kinds of weird and disturbing feats that you'd expect to see a street magician perform. In some you play with fire; in others you endure great pain; in all of them you perform unexpected astonishments—truly unnatural acts.

And, yes, you'll find out how to astound people with a deck of playing card tricks. I know what you're thinking. Card tricks suck. Yes, many do. But not these. It's no accident that more than half of the tricks that David Blaine performed in his first TV special were card tricks. Out of the thousands of card tricks out there, the ones in this part were selected for maximum impact, shock, and awe.

Chapter 7

Extreme Card Magic

In This Chapter

- ◆ Some basic playing-card history
- ◆ Basic card technique
- ◆ How to find a freely selected card using a key card
- ◆ How to force someone to take any card you like
- ◆ Unusual ways to reveal the name of a chosen card
- ◆ Tricks where no one has to "pick a card"

Card tricks? Why do I have to learn card tricks? Didn't I have to put up with pick-a-card tricks when I was in the third grade? Well, yes, you probably did. Bad card tricks. But if you check out any of the recent magic specials and series on TV, you'll see that tricks with playing cards are a staple of the street magician's repertoire. The difference is that their tricks are amazing!

There are literally thousands of card tricks to choose from. Dozens of books on the market teach nothing *but* card tricks. But too many card tricks are based on mathematical principles, require you to deal off or count down playing cards, or just take forever to get to the climax. Boring!

The tricks I've chosen for this chapter have one thing in common: they are real mind blowers, with endings that have maximum impact. Not only does each of these tricks start out with an attention-grabbing premise, but it also has a startling, sometimes eerie revelation.

I'll start out by teaching you two of the basics of card handling—how to find a freely selected card and how to force people to pick any card you want them to. Then we'll look at lots of neat ways you can reveal the card to the audience. And finally, we'll take a look at some of the best tricks where people don't have to pick a card at all. They can just sit back and be entertained—and astounded.

In the Beginning ...

First, a little history. (No, it's fascinating. Really. And you might be able to use some of it in your patter.) Ever wonder where playing cards came from? And why magicians are so attached to performing tricks with them? Playing cards were created in the late 1300s, and they weren't used merely for games of chance. There were secret signs and symbols built into them—and this was long before *The Da Vinci Code*!

A deck of playing cards was a miniature almanac, spell book, and "Who's Who" of feudal society all rolled up into one. Every value and suit in the deck had an astronomical, historical, or occult reference. Consider these points:

- The two colors, red and black, supposedly represent the most primal elements of all: Day and Night, Light and Dark, Good versus Evil.

- There are four suits, because there are four seasons in a year. (Some say they also represented the four major kingdoms in Europe at the time.)

- There are 13 cards in each suit, because there are 13 lunar cycles in a calendar year.

- There are 12 court, or face, cards because there are 12 months in a year.

- There are 52 cards, because there are 52 weeks in a year.

- If you add up all of the spots, or pips, assigning a value of 11 to the Jacks, 12 to the Queens, and 13 to the Kings, and add in one more for the otherwise unnecessary Joker, the total is 365, the number of days in a year.

Alchemy, that mystical blend of science, magic, and religion, was in its heyday in the 1300s, and no doubt every wizard and enchantress carried a deck of playing cards in his or her bag of tricks. The connection between magicians and playing cards has continued ever since.

Pick It and Stick It

Almost every card trick is some variation of the old "pick a card, any card, any card at all." You may surround the trick with something clever or even a weird story, but the basic plot line runs like this:

- The spectator picks a card.

- The card is "lost" in the deck.

- You find the card.

There are just endless variations. Well, before you learn how to make this cliché of a card trick exciting, you have to learn the basics. How do you find the card in the first place?

The simplest method makes use of what's known as a *key card*. All you have to know is the location of one card in the deck, and that's your key. If you know where the chosen card is in relation to the key card you already know, you can find the selected card.

The Magic Word

A **key card**, also known as a **locater card**, is any card whose identity and position you know in a deck of playing cards. You can locate a selected card by knowing its position in the deck in relation to your key card.

Effect

Someone picks any card out of deck, remembers it, and returns it to the deck. The deck is mixed, but you find the card.

Preparation

None. You'll need a regular deck of playing cards.

Performance

Hand your spectator a deck of cards, or let him use his own. Have him shuffle the deck so that he knows the cards are in a random order.

Spread the cards between your two hands. Ask the person to select one card, look at it, and remember it. If there are other people watching, it's always a good idea to have them look at the card, too, just in case the spectator forgets the card or—to try to screw you up—lies about the card's identify at the end of the trick. (Unfortunately, this happens more often that you'd think!)

Now, for those of you who've never really handled cards before, spreading the cards smoothly between your hands might be a big deal, so here's a little tip. Start with the cards in your left hand, as if you were ready to deal the cards. (Magicians call this the "dealer's position"). Hold your right hand palm up. With your left thumb, push cards from the top of the deck onto your right fingers. As you do, slowly separate your two hands a few inches until there's an even fan of cards between your hands.

Spreading the cards from hand to hand to enable the spectator to pick a card.

(Photo courtesy of Titus Photography.)

If you prefer, you could spread the cards on a table. If you want to look like a professional gambler here—and with all the poker tournaments on TV right now, it's kind of expected of you—here's how to spread them out in an even, straight line. Set the deck on the table so that one of its short ends is parallel to the edge of the table. Arch your hands over the deck, with your right thumb resting along the short end closest to you and your right middle, ring, and little fingers resting on the outer short edge. Place your right forefinger on the top of the deck. Press down lightly on the deck, and move your hand in a straight line to the right, dragging the deck with you. Your forefinger will help control the evenness of the spread. (This style of spreading the cards in a straight line on the table is called a ribbon spread.)

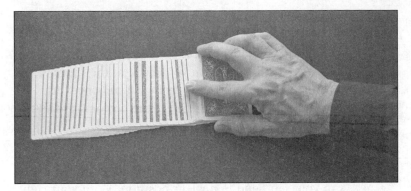

The ribbon spread on a table-top.

(Photo courtesy of Titus Photography.)

After you've mastered spreading the cards in an even, straight row, you can vary the display by moving your hand in a rainbow-shaped arc as you spread the cards. All three methods—the hand-to-hand spread, the straight table spread, and the fan-shaped spread—are effective, professional-looking ways to offer the deck to have a card selected.

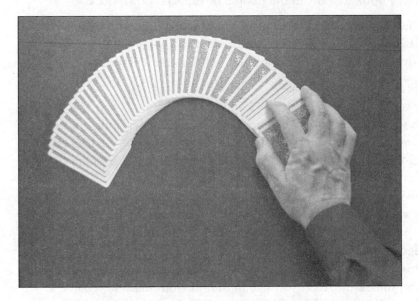

Using handling similar to the ribbon spread, you can fan the cards in an arc on the table.

(Photo courtesy of Titus Photography.)

So your volunteer picks a card. While the person is looking at it, you're going to do the sneaky bit. You have to find out the identity of the bottom card, because this is going to be your key card. Now, you can't be obvious about this. Here's one way to do it: simply tilt the deck upward slightly as he hands you the deck after he shuffles and

The Magic Word

A **peek** is a quick, secret glance to give you some sort of special information, usually the identity of a playing card. Magicians also sometimes use the word **glimpse**.

you're squaring up the deck. Look down at the deck and take a quick *peek*. If you don't think you can get away with something that obvious, say, "Don't let me see your card," and turn your back to the spectator. While you're facing away from the audience, just turn the deck over and look at the bottom card. It's bold, but it works!

Once you know the key card, you're ready to have the chosen card returned to the deck. Hold the deck in your left hand in dealer's position. With your right hand, remove the bottom half of the deck. Extend your left hand toward your spectator, and ask him to return the selected card to the top of the stack in your left hand. Drop the cards in your right hand on top of the cards in your left hand, and square the deck. Although the spectator doesn't know it, this has placed your key card on top of the selected card, and both are now in the middle of the face-down deck.

Before I go on, let me warn you: a lot of people know about the bottom key-card method, and they'll be looking for it. So here's another way to obtain a key card without looking at the bottom of the deck. This is much subtler and will fool even those in the know.

After your spectator selects a card, hold the deck in your left hand. Lift up the top half of the deck with your right hand, with your thumb along the left long edge and your right middle, ring, and little fingers along the right long edge of the packet. Tilt the cards in your right upward as you use your right forefinger to point to the cards in your left hand. If you're following along with a deck of cards in your hands, you'll notice that in this position you can look down and quickly peek the bottom card of the packet (which is what magicians call a small bunch of playing cards) in your right hand. This will be your key card. Tell your volunteer to return the selected card to the "middle of the deck," still gesturing to the cards in your left hand. As soon as the spectator puts the chosen card on the packet in your left hand, drop the cards in your right hand on top, and square the deck. Just like in the previous method, you now know the name of the card on top of the chosen card that's buried in the middle of the deck.

You can now casually cut the cards a few times, if you wish. Your key card will still be on top of the selected card. (Just don't shuffle the deck, which might separate the key card from the selection. And don't make a big deal out of cutting the deck or say something like "now we'll mix the cards," or the spectator might want to shuffle.)

Peek the key card at the bottom of the right-hand packet while telling the spectator to return the selection to your left hand.

(Photo courtesy of Titus Photography.)

Now you know *where* the chosen card is. How do you find out *what* it is? There are many ways to do this. The tedious way is to deal the cards face up, one at a time, until you come to your key card. The next card after your key card is the person's selection. But I promised you: no countdown tricks.

So here's a simple and direct method to find the card, and it never fails: you just turn the deck over and look. How can you get away with something like that? Easy! After the cards have been cut a few times, turn the deck face up and spread them between your hands or on the table as you say something like …

◆ *Your card isn't in my hands or up my sleeve, so it must still be somewhere here in the deck.*

◆ *Is your card still in the deck? Check. I'll turn my head so you don't think I'm trying to see where you look.*

◆ *As you can see, I'm only using the 52 cards. There are no Jokers.* [Optional bad joke: *I'm not playing with a full deck.] And the cards are completely mixed, in no special order.*

As soon as you turn the cards face up, quickly scan through the cards with your eyes and locate your key card. The spectator's chosen card is below the key card, so if you've spread the cards from left to right, the selected card will be the right of your key card. (If you happen to have cut between the cards—a 1 in 51 chance—your key card will be the bottom card of the deck, and the spectator's card will be on the top.)

Once you know the name of his card, close up the deck and turn it face down. Believe it or not, after the trick is over, no one will even remember that for a few seconds you had the cards face up.

Yes, this is audacious, but it is a 100 percent effective, surefire way to locate the chosen card without any fancy finger work. To the audience, it looks as if you're just proving to them that the card is still in the deck, not that you're looking for it.

Now comes the big finish. All you have to do is tell the person the name of his card. But wait! It's not that simple. If you just blurt out the name of the card, there's no drama and no suspense. It's just not interesting. You have to find a way to make the *revelation*—the way you announce the name of the chosen card at the end of trick— exciting and memorable.

The Magic Word

The way in which a magician announces or displays the identity of a chosen card is called the **revelation**.

Here's my favorite method: I ask the person to just think of the name of the chosen card, to draw a mental picture of it. I pretend to mentally receive the information slowly, a bit at a time. (Remember, mind-reading isn't supposed to be easy. If it were, everyone would be doing it.) For example, I might say: *Your card is a black card. Yes? A club. It's a face, no, wait, a number card. Yes, a number card. A low number. It's a three, the three of clubs. Is that correct?*

Is *This* Your Card?

J.G. Thompson Jr., a famous twentieth-century magical inventor and author, once pointed out that if you have 100 different ways to find a card but only one way to reveal it, to the spectator it looks like you only know one card trick. But if you only know one way to find a card but 100 ways to reveal it, it looks like you know 100 different card tricks.

So you can use the same key-card method over and over, even for the same audience, as long as you find a new way to display the card at the end. Each time it will seem like a new trick. With that in mind, let's look at some really cool ways to say, "Is this your card?"

CSI: Magic

Go through small packets of face-up cards, claiming that you're looking for fingerprints. Tilt the cards this way and that in the light, as if you're trying to catch a glimpse of a smudge. Narrow down your choice to three or four cards, and then settle on the selection.

The Vulcan Mind Meld

Place your fingertips on your spectator's temples and pretend to be able to see into her thoughts using a Vulcan-like mind meld connection.

The "Magic Mirror"

You say that what a person sees is often burned into his eyes. You stare at your spectator's face, hoping to catch a snapshot of the chosen card in his eyes. And, of course, you do.

Flashpoint

Ask your spectators to just concentrate on the chosen card. Ask them to draw a picture of it in their minds. Pretend to be puzzled, then unsure, and then suddenly name the card as if it has suddenly flashed into your mind by telepathy.

The Voice Detector

Tell your spectator you can recognize stress in a person's voice. Have your volunteer call out the names of the cards in the deck, in order, one at a time. When she names her card, say, "That's it!"

The Lie Detector

Tell your spectator you can tell when a person is lying by the tone of his voice. Call out the names of the cards, in order, one at a time, and after each card, ask, "Is that it?" Tell the person that he can lie or tell the truth. It doesn't matter; you'll be able to tell regardless. (For both "Voice Detector" and "Lie Detector," I'd suggest starting with the same suit as the selected card that you already know. Otherwise, this revelation could get really boring fast!)

The Airdrop Turnover

In this classic revelation, you drop the deck face down onto the table or floor, and the selected card magically appears face up on top of the deck.

To perform this, you have to be able to get the chosen card to the top of the deck. (Magicians call any method that allows them to move a specific playing card or cards to a known position in the deck a *control*.) How can you do this? When you glimpse the key card and the selection, the cards will be spread face up either between your hands or on the table. Normally you would simply square up the cards. Instead, as you gather up the cards, casually cut the cards so that your key card returns to the face of the reassembled deck. Your audience won't be suspicious, because they don't know the name of your key card. Turn the deck face down.

With your right hand, hold the deck from above, with your thumb at the inner short edge and your four fingers along the outer short edge of the deck. With your left thumb, push, or *jog*, the top card about an inch to the right. This *side-jog* is hidden by the back of your right hand and the fingers at the front of the deck.

The Magic Word _____

A playing card is **jogged** when one of its sides is deliberately extended out of the deck. A **side-jog** protrudes from either side of the deck. An **out-jog** protrudes from the outer or front side of the deck (the edge held toward the audience), and an **in-jog** sticks out of the inner or back side (the edge toward you).

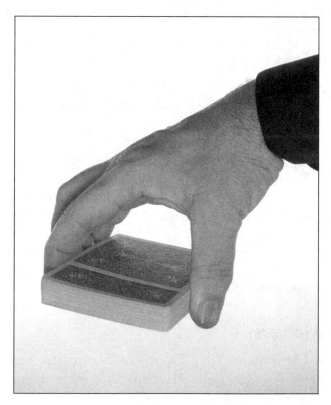

Holding the cards in preparation for the Airdrop Turnover, exposed view. This way of holding the cards is known as the "Biddle Grip," named for Elmer Biddle, a twentieth-century American magician who popularized the distinctive hold in his trick "Transcendent," published in Genii Magazine *in April 1947.*

(Photo courtesy of Titus Photography.)

Hold the deck about 15 inches above the table or the floor. Drop the deck straight down. Because the top card is side-jogged, air pressure will flip it over.

Unfortunately, this doesn't work 100 percent of the time. Some magicians get better results by giving a very gentle push when they drop the deck. You might also experiment with the height from which you drop the pack. But don't worry. If the card doesn't flip over, you still have an effective ending: just turn over the top card yourself and say, "The force knocked your card all the way up through the deck to the very top."

The Clapper

Do you remember that old lady on the TV commercial who turns the light in her bedroom on and off by clapping her hands? Well, in this next revelation, you clap your hands over the deck, and the top card flips over, face up. It's the selected card.

Once again, you must secretly position the chosen card on the top of the deck as you gather up the cards. Then set the deck on the table in front of you so that one of the long ends of the deck is parallel to the edge of the table. Cover the deck with both hands, as if you were squaring the cards. Using both thumbs, give a slight upward bend—what magicians call a *crimp*—all along the length of the top card. (This should be only a curl, not a full crease.)

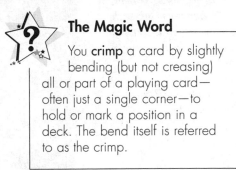

The Magic Word

You **crimp** a card by slightly bending (but not creasing) all or part of a playing card—often just a single corner—to hold or mark a position in a deck. The bend itself is referred to as the crimp.

Your card is an acrobatic card. And it likes to work to applause. Not a lot of applause. Just a little.

Hold your hands about 6 to 8 inches apart, just above the tabletop and positioned between the playing cards and the edge of the table. Clap your hands together with one firm, quick scoop of air. The air pressure will catch under the curled edge of the top card and will flip it over, face up. The card flies off the deck, sometimes looping once or twice, before it falls onto the table. Even though the card is only coming from the top of the deck, because the spectator didn't know it was there, it's a very startling revelation.

Use both thumbs to put an upward crimp along the inner edge of the top card, your view.

(Photo courtesy of Titus Photography.)

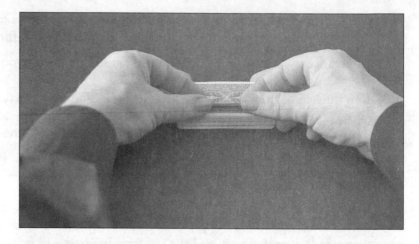

The air pressure from one strong clap is enough to flip over the top card. Note that your hands do not actually touch the deck.

(Photo courtesy of Titus Photography.)

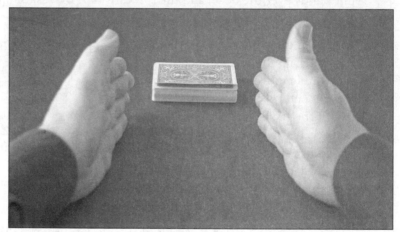

May the Force Be with You

Wouldn't it be great if you could make people think they have a completely free choice of any card in the deck, but you actually make them pick the card you want them to? Well, not only is it possible, but magicians do it all the time. They call it a *force*, or forcing a card.

The advantage of knowing the card beforehand, of course, is that there are many more ways—some that would otherwise be truly impossible—in which you can reveal the name of the card at the end of the trick. Entire books have been written on how to force

The Magic Word

A **force** is used to make a member of the audience perform a desired action without him or her knowing it. In card magic, it usually refers to making a person select a particular playing card.

playing cards on unsuspecting members of the audience, but many of the methods involve very difficult sleight-of-hand that takes years to perfect. I'm going to share just two ways to do it that are guaranteed and easy to do. One involves nothing more difficult than cutting the cards; the other only requires you to be able to shuffle the deck.

The Cross Cut Force

The Cross Cut force, also widely known as the Criss Cross force, was invented by early twentieth-century magician and publisher Max Holden. It is perhaps one of the subtlest and most convincing ways to force a playing card. To get ready, out of sight of the audience, place the card you want to force on the top of the face-down deck. For the sake of explanation, let's say it's the Ace of Spades.

Set the deck on the table in front of your volunteer. Ask him to cut the cards. He will take off about half the cards from the top of the deck and set them to one side. Pick up the bottom half of the deck and place them on top of the others, as if to complete the cut, but instead of squaring the deck, place them at a 90° angle on top of the cards that used to be the upper half of the deck. The two halves of the deck will be criss-crossed (which gives the force one of its names), forming an "X."

The bottom half of the deck is set on the top half, marking the "free selection" in the Cross Cut force.

(Photo courtesy of Titus Photography.)

The card you wish to force (the former top card of the deck) is now the top card of the lower portion of this unsquared deck. For the card force to work, you must momentarily take the spectator's attention, either psychologically or physically, away from the deck. (Believe it or not, it'll only take a few seconds for the audience to lose track of which half of the deck was which.) I usually remind the volunteer that the cards could have been cut at any point, as high or low as he wanted in the deck. (If you talk to a spectator, he or she will usually look you in the eye, which gives you the momentary distraction you need.)

Draw his attention back to the deck. Remove the upper block of cards (the original bottom half of the deck) and say, "Take a look at the card you cut to." Have the specta-tor pick up the top card of the stack remaining on the table. This is, of course, the card you already know. At this point, the deck can be reassembled, the card can be placed anywhere in the deck, and the deck can be shuffled by anyone. It doesn't matter to the outcome of the trick. All you have to do is reveal the name of the "freely selected" card.

The Hindu Shuffle

The Hindu Shuffle is the name of a particular shuffle that's seldom seen in the United States and other Western nations but it is very common in the Middle East and throughout Asia. This is a legitimate shuffle, but magicians like it because it can be performed in the hands without the need for a table. It looks flourishy and it also enables the magician to force the bottom card of the deck.

To perform the Hindu Shuffle, hold the deck in your right hand by arching your hand over the top of the deck, with your thumb along one long edge and the fingers along the other long edge. Some magicians also like to rest the right forefinger on top of the deck to stabilize it.

Hold your left hand palm up, with your thumb and fingers raised upward to form your hand into a sort of U shape. With your left fingertips, grab the top five to ten cards of the deck, holding them together as a small block.

Release tension with your left thumb and fingers, and let the packet of cards fall onto your left palm. Repeat this series of moves: each time, pull off another small packet from the top of the deck with your left hand, and then let them fall on top of the cards already on your left palm. Eventually, all of the cards will have been shuffled off the deck into your left hand.

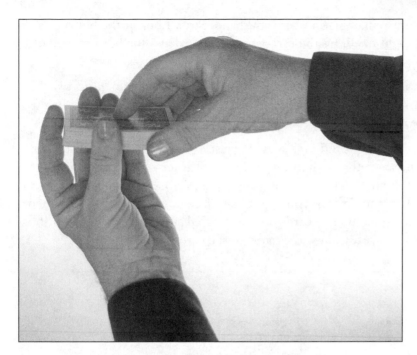

The hands in position to perform the Hindu Shuffle.

(Photo courtesy of Titus Photography.)

As you shuffle, you may want to stretch your left forefinger out and around the outer short end of the cards so they don't fall out of your palm. If it will help to visualize what your left hand should look like, think of it as the tray that catches the copies as they come out of a photocopy machine.

Charms

Here's a tip to make you look like an expert card handler when you perform the Hindu Shuffle. As you remove cards from the top of the deck, either move your left hand away from your right hand *or* move your right hand, pulling the deck back away from your left hand. But don't move both hands at the same time. The shuffle will look cleaner, and the cards will be easier to control if you move one hand or the other. I know that, as a street magician, you don't want to look too slick, but you also don't want to look sloppy.

Okay, so what's the big deal with this shuffle? How can you use it to force a card? Try the Hindu Shuffle again, but this time before you do, look at the bottom card of the deck. Start to shuffle off small packets into your left hand until, like before, you only have a dozen or so cards remaining in your right hand. Stop. Look at the bottom card of the packet in your right hand. It's the card you just looked at—the bottom card of the deck. Right?

So, knowing this, let's use this secret knowledge to mess with someone's head. Unbeknownst to the spectator, you already know the bottom card of the deck. Begin to Hindu Shuffle the cards. Ask the spectator to call "Stop!" at any time.

As soon as he or she does, stop shuffling, pause for just a second, and then raise your right wrist to show the spectator the bottom card of the packet in your right hand. (This is the original bottom card of the deck, your force card.) Ask the person to remember the card. Turn the cards in your right hand face down, and then drop them onto the cards in your left hand. The cards can be shuffled again, either by you or by anyone else, because you already know the name of the card you just forced.

Forcing the original bottom card of the deck using the Hindu Shuffle, your view.

(Photo courtesy of Titus Photography.)

"Why does this fool people?" you may ask. The spectator's train of thought is interrupted when you abruptly stop shuffling. The short pause I recommended is also important, because if you immediately turn over your right hand, it might be obvious that you're simply showing the person the bottom card of the deck. The volunteer's mind is also confused because you change the way you hold the cards during the shuffle. At first, they're being shuffled horizontally, but you display the chosen card vertically, and then you lower the cards again to square the deck.

For completion's sake, I should point out that the Hindu Shuffle can be used for a key card location as well as for forcing a card. Let's say you know the bottom card of the deck. Spread the cards and ask a spectator to pick a card. Square the deck, and start to Hindu Shuffle the cards from your right hand into your left hand. Tell your spectator to say "stop" at any time. Stop shuffling when he or she calls out, and have your volunteer drop the chosen card on top of the cards in your left hand. Drop the cards in your right hand (with your key card on the bottom) onto the selected card, and square the deck. Your key card falls on top of the chosen card. You can now peek the selected card using any of the methods described in the earlier section "Pick It and Stick It," and then finish up using your favorite revelation.

Revelations

Speaking of revelations, now that you can make a person pick any card you want to, the way in which you reveal the name of the card is up to you. You're limited only by your imagination. For example, you could …

◆ Bring out a second deck of cards in which you had previously placed a duplicate of the force card face up in the face-down deck. For added mystery, have the person hold this prepared deck while you're forcing the same card in the regular deck.

◆ Have the force card drawn, printed, or airbrushed onto the back of the T-shirt you'll be wearing while performing. When you're ready to reveal the card, just turn around. If you think someone might see the back of the shirt before you're ready, wear it under another shirt or jacket. Depending upon your audience, no one's gonna object if you have to peel off some clothing to show the back of your T.

◆ Before performing the trick, use a felt-tip marking pen to create a temporary tattoo somewhere on your body of the card you're going to force.

◆ You could have previously planted a duplicate of the force card literally anywhere—in your shoe, in your wallet, in your shorts. Well, let's not go *there*.

◆ Refer the spectator to your MySpace page, on which one of your Top Eight friends is a mysterious, hooded person holding the force card. Better still, create a fictional MySpace page in which the person in the main photo appears in shadows, but the force card is clearly visible.

Here are four more revelations that require you to force a card, but the preparation for them is a bit more involved.

Could You Put That in Writing?

Many, many years ago, back before texting, kids actually used to pass handwritten notes back and forth to each other in class. And if the teacher intercepted them, sometimes they'd read the embarrassing notes aloud in class. How mortifying! If only there had been something like invisible ink.

Well, there actually *is* such a thing as invisible ink. In fact, there are amateur, commercial, and industrial grades of invisible ink—even inks that are used in intelligence gathering and espionage. But they all have one thing in common. When the liquid is initially applied to a surface, it can't be seen. It doesn't show up until it's "developed" by use of some sort of chemical reaction, heat, or special (often ultraviolet) lighting.

The most practical "ink" to use for the purposes of street magic is one that'll show up when it's heated. The most common substances to use as inks are diluted lemon, apple, or orange juice, but any of these organic substances will work, as long as they're watered down enough that no noticeable color remains in the liquid:

◆ Milk

◆ Onion juice

◆ Sugar

◆ Honey

◆ Cola

◆ Vinegar

◆ Wine

◆ Soapsuds

Once you've prepared your "ink," use a toothpick, small paintbrush, or even your finger to write the name or make a drawing of your force card on a piece of paper. Let the writing dry completely.

Here are a few warnings: don't use coated (that is, shiny, glossy, or photographic) paper, because the invisible ink won't be absorbed and will smear or run off. Even if the ink does dry in place, it might reflect in the light. Also, try not to scratch the paper when you're writing the secret message. The nicks might be noticed even if the invisible writing isn't.

It doesn't matter whether the paper is blank or not. In fact, if you write on a page of text or write something in regular ink on top of the invisible design after the fact— what's called a cover message—it'll ensure that your spectators won't examine the paper itself too closely. They'll only be interested in reading what's already visible on the paper. Just be sure to use a ballpoint pen or pencil if you're writing the cover message. The ink in fountain pens or felt-tips might "run" when they try to write on top of the invisible ink.

When the paper is ready, stick it in your pocket. Don't worry if it gets wrinkled or you have to fold it. In fact, if the paper's a bit messed up, it'll arouse less suspicion than if it looks brand new.

When you're ready to perform, force the playing card that's already written in invisible ink. Bring out the prepared piece of paper, and casually show it to your spectator. Say that you think there might be some sort of clue hidden in the message on the paper but you can't decipher the code (or, if the paper's blank, hidden in the weave or threads).

To make the invisible message appear, all you have to do is hold the paper over some sort of heat for a short period of time. You might wave it a few inches above a candle flame, or you can pass it over the flame of a cigarette lighter. Now, don't be stupid and hold the paper still long enough or close enough to the flame to catch it on fire. But as you wave the flame under the paper, almost immediately you'll start to see the hidden message appear as the invisible ink oxidizes and turns brown.

You don't have to wait until the revelation is fully developed to let the spectator see it. In fact, it's actually kind of spooky to watch the mysterious writing appearing from nowhere. Especially if it's underneath some other, visible message on the paper.

For this trick, if you can find an aged, off-white parchment-style paper, all the better. Also, you might consider using a deck of Tarot fortune-telling cards that can be found in many New Age bookstores or gift shops instead of regular playing cards. The unusual deck will add another shroud of mystery to an occult-themed card trick.

By waving a flame underneath the prepared paper, the secret writing appears in brown lettering.

(Photo courtesy of Titus Photography.)

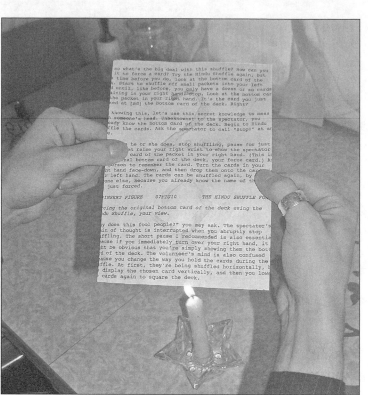

The message fully revealed.

(Photo courtesy of Titus Photography.)

Disarming

This is a stunning card revelation, and it also enables you to show off a little flesh because the name of the card appears on your bare arm or upper torso. Sound pretty hot?

To set up for the revelation, you're going to need some soap, and when you perform the trick you'll need a deck of cards, a piece of paper, something to write with, an ashtray, and matches or a lighter. Any of these last items can be borrowed when you do the trick.

Let me warn you in advance, you're going to be rubbing cigarette ash on your body to make the writing appear, so keep in mind that you're going to have to clean up afterward. And the skin has to be hairless. Most magicians use the inner left forearm or upper arm. For the sake of explanation, let's say you go for the forearm.

Decide what card you want to force. Because you're going to have to draw the initials of this card on your forearm to have it show up later, I'd recommend forcing one of the cards that will take very few strokes to write its abbreviation. I'd suggest either the Ace of Hearts (AH), Ace of Clubs (AC), Seven of Hearts (7H), or Seven of Clubs (7C). If you must go with one of the Diamonds, draw a diamond shape rather than a D (which could come out looking like an O) for the initial.

Take a small slice of soap and dampen it. Using this piece like a pen, draw the initials of your force card on your bare inner arm. Press hard and make the lines very bold. Make sure that no flakes of soap remain on your arm; also, the soap should not be too wet, or the writing will run. (If you have tattoos on your inner arm, write the initials at some empty space. It will actually look pretty cool if the writing later appears written between "other" tattoos.)

Allow the writing to dry completely. You can cover it with a shirt or other clothing if you want, but the outerwear shouldn't be so snug that it smudges or rubs off the lettering.

Curses

In a pinch, you *can* use lip balm instead of soap to write the secret message on your arm, but if you're wearing a shirt over the writing, the lip balm can be easily smudged. Also, before you rub on the ashes, the balm can glisten under direct lighting, giving away your method.

Until you bathe or unless you sweat profusely, the "invisible ink" should remain set for a few hours. But to be on the safe side, you should probably plan to do this trick shortly after you set up. In fact, if you're performing this trick while you're on the run or you're repeating it throughout the evening, you can draw the letters on your arm using the liquid soap found in many public restrooms.

(By the way—not to gross you out or anything, but when this trick was first performed, long before the invention of soap, magicians apparently used urine for their "invisible ink." I'm told it works quite well, but I'll take the magical historians' word for it.)

Force your spectator to select the card that you've already secretly written on your arm. Ask the person to remember the name of the card and to write it down on a piece of paper. (If you're in a bizarre magick mood, this gives you a perfect opportunity to talk about rituals and ceremonial fires.)

Have your volunteer bunch the paper into a loose ball, set it in an ashtray, and set it on fire. Let the flames completely consume the paper all the way down to ashes. (If you prefer, you can have the spectator burn the actual selected card, but it may not produce enough ash to complete the trick.)

Show your bare inner arm, making sure the spectator sees that nothing is written on it. Scoop up a handful of ash in your right hand. (Be very careful that the ash is completely out, with no glowing embers in it.) Let the spectator watch as you rub the ash back and forth on your inner arm. The ash will cling to the unseen soap residue and will form the abbreviation of the chosen card. Call out the initials, followed by the full name of the selected card. The name of the chosen card has appeared on your arm!

As I suggested at the beginning of this trick, the name of the card doesn't have to appear on your arm. A good alternative—especially if you have a "special friend" to help you clean it off—would be to have the writing appear on your chest or abs. In fact, because your volunteer can't see or feel the dried soap, if your spectator is willing, he or she could even rub the ash on you to make the letters appear.

Karate Kard

Have you ever come out of one of those crazy martial arts movies and just wanted to go around kicking, punching, and chopping things up? Well, here's your chance, and the only thing that's gonna get hurt is one of your playing cards. But don't feel too bad. The trick is so freakish that it's worth the sacrifice.

Effect

A selected playing card is returned to the middle of the deck. You set the cards on the table and make a karate chop across the back of the deck. With a flourish, you reveal that the chosen card has magically been karate chopped in two.

Preparation

You'll need a duplicate of the playing card you want to force. For the sake of explanation, let's say it's the Queen of Spades. To set up for the trick, place one of the Queens on the bottom of a stack of about a dozen playing cards. Take the other Queen and cut it in half widthwise (across the midsection of the Queen).

Reassemble the cut card and lay the two sections face down on top of the small packet on the table. Then take the remaining cards of the deck, place them on top of the gimmick card, and square the deck. What you'll now have is a deck of cards with one Queen on the bottom and a duplicate card cut in half, positioned about three quarters of the way down in the deck. To keep the gaff card in place until you're ready to perform, you'll probably want to carry the deck in a card box.

Performance

Take the cards out of their case, and set the box to one side. Ask the person to call "stop" to select a card as you shuffle the cards, using the Hindu Shuffle to force the Queen of Spades on the bottom of the deck. Make sure that you shuffle slowly enough that you don't pass and, in the process, disturb the gimmicked duplicate Queen. (That's why you have it located so close to the bottom of the deck.) You also have to be careful that when you raise the right-hand portion of the deck to show the force card on the bottom that the loose sections of the duplicate Queen don't fall out of the stack. After you've shown the force card on the bottom of the deck, drop the cards in your right hand onto the cards in your left hand. This will bury both the force card and the gimmick card in the middle of the deck.

Square the pack and set it on the table in front of you, so that the long side of the deck is parallel to the edge of the table. Tell your spectator that you've been studying karate, and that you'll use the venerable Japanese martial art to find the chosen card. Raise your flattened hand over the deck, and give one swift karate chop to the middle of the deck, as if you were trying to cut the deck in half along its width. (Feel free to make the stereotypical "Hi-ya!" grunt as you strike the deck. If you're old enough to remember Miss Piggy on *The Muppet Show*, you'll know what I mean.)

The Karate Kard gimmick.

(Photo courtesy of Titus Photography.)

The Karate Kard gimmick set in place in the deck before adding the upper half of the deck, exposed view.

(Photo courtesy of Titus Photography.)

Place your left hand over the top of the deck, with your thumb pressing down on the long edge at the table's edge and your middle, ring, and little finger pressing down on the other long edge of the deck. Place your left forefinger on the middle of the deck, and press down to hold the deck in place. Hold your right hand palm up, and slip your right fingers under the right short end of the deck.

Quickly riffle upward through the cards with your right fingers, allowing the cards to fall back down onto the table. Air pressure will cause the right portion of the slit duplicate card to pop out of the right short end of the deck. It won't fly free of the deck; it will still be embedded in the deck with half of its length protruding out.

Grasp the deck with your right hand, with your right thumb pressing down on the inner long edge of the pack, your right middle, ring, and little fingers pressing down on the outer edge, and your right forefinger pressing on the center of the deck. Slip your left fingers under the left short edge of the deck. Briskly riffle your left fingers up through the deck, letting the cards fall back down onto the table. The left portion of the gaffed card will pop about halfway out of the left short edge of the deck.

Riffle the cards upward to make the karate card appear.

(Photo courtesy of Titus Photography.)

Pause to let the audience plainly see the two halves of a playing card, apparently cut by a magical karate chop, sticking out of the ends of the deck. Grasp one half of the cut card in each hand, pull them out of the deck, and turn them over with a flourish. It's the selected card! The revelation will be so surprising—and entertaining—that you won't need to show whether or not there's another Queen of Spades in the deck.

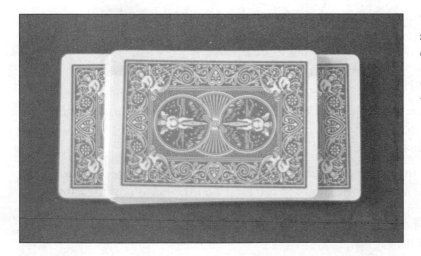

The two portions of the gimmicked card pop out of the ends of the deck.

(Photo courtesy of Titus Photography.)

The Singed Card

Like the Karate Kard, this trick starts with a gimmicked duplicate of the force card in the deck, but at the end of the routine, the revealed card appears to be burned around all four edges instead of being chopped in half.

You'll need to prepare a special gimmick card. Again, let's go with the Jack of Spades as the force card. Take one Jack of Spades and, using a cigarette lighter or matches, lightly singe the card around all four edges. Be very careful while you're doing this that you don't burn yourself. Flick away any excess ash around the gimmick, and it's ready to use.

The singed card gimmick.

(Photo courtesy of Titus Photography.)

Following the same set-up as you did for Karate Kard, place the burned card three quarters of the way down in the deck, face down. The duplicate Jack of Spades, your force card, is placed on the bottom of the deck.

When you're ready to perform, begin a Hindu Shuffle and ask your spectator to call "stop." When he or she does, show the force card on the bottom of the cards in your right hand. Drop this right-hand portion of the pack onto the cards that you've already shuffled into your left hand. This buries both the force card and the gimmick in the middle of the deck.

Ask to borrow a cigarette lighter or matches. (If you're in a location where there's a lit candle, this makes a great substitute for the lighter.) Hold the deck in one hand as you light the cigarette lighter with your other hand. Slowly pass all four edges of the deck over the flame, being very careful not to actually get the cards close enough to the fire to singe them for real.

Spread the cards slowly between your hands or on the table. A burnt card can be seen in the middle of the deck. Allow the spectator to remove the card and turn it face up. It's the selected card. (Again, the impact is so strong that there's no need to prove that there's no other Jack of Spades in the deck.)

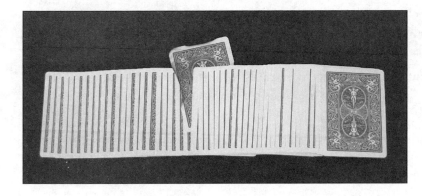

The burnt card is revealed in the middle of the deck.

(Photo courtesy of Titus Photography.)

To finish out our chapter on card conjuring, let's take a look at a trick that doesn't require anyone to pick a card—unless they really want to. The audience can just sit back and admire your prowess with a deck of cards.

The Slop Shuffle

This simple yet amazingly effective card trick was invented by twentieth-century Canadian magician Sid Lorraine. It was first published way back in 1937 in Stewart Judah and John Braun's *Subtle Problems You Will Do*. It's been a staple of the card magician stock-in-trade ever since.

Effect

You mix the deck in small packets of face-up and face-down cards. With a final cut, the cards are once again all facing in the same direction.

Preparation

None. You need a deck of playing cards.

Performance

Hold the deck face down in your left hand in dealer's position. Hold your right hand palm up, flat like a tray, to the right of the deck. With your left thumb, push about eight to a dozen cards onto your right fingers, and then press down on the cards with your right thumb to hold them in place.

Still holding the block of cards against your right palm, rotate your right wrist and hand toward your body, turning the small packet face up. Your right thumb is now underneath the cards, and your fingers are on top.

Using your left thumb, push off a few more cards from the top of the deck, and shove them between your right thumb and the cards it's pressing against. Your right hand will now hold a packet of about 20 cards.

Rotate your right wrist away from you, so that your right hand is palm up. With your left thumb, push another small block of cards off the top of the deck, and slip them between your right fingers and the packet already in your right hand.

Continue to flip-flop your right wrist back and forth, each time picking up another packet of about 10 cards from your left hand. Eventually you'll be left with a stack of about a dozen cards in your left hand, with the remainder of the deck, split in half, back to back, in your right hand. Place the cards in your left hand face down under the cards in your right hand, and square the deck.

A small point before we move on, however: while you're mixing the cards back and forth, don't keep the cards squared. The cards look more mixed up if you keep them sloppy. In fact, that's what gives the trick its name, the Slop Shuffle.

Have you ever seen someone who's had a little too much to drink try to shuffle cards? The cards get pretty messed up, with some of the cards going face up and some of the cards going face down, every which way in the deck.

The audience believes that the cards are randomly mixed in small bunches of cards, with some face up and some face down. It looks so convincing that you might believe it yourself the first time you try it! Actually, the deck is almost equally split, with the top half of the cards face up and the bottom half of the cards face down.

Now comes what magicians call a "convincer move"—a subtle gesture or action that convinces the audience that everything is in the condition you claim it to be. In this case, you're going to convince the audience that the cards are all jumbled up without actually having to prove it.

Hold the deck in your left hand. With your right hand, lift up about 15 cards. Where you cut, the audience sees a face-up card on top of the left-hand stack. Drop the cards in your right hand back onto the cards in your left hand.

Cut deeper into the deck, picking up about 35 cards with your right hand. The audience will see a face-down card on top of the stack in your left hand. Again, drop the cards in your right hand back onto the cards in your left hand. These two quick cuts before you do the "move" convinces the audience that the deck really is randomly mixed.

Now you have to cut the cards between the two back-to-back cards, which will be somewhere near the center of the deck. Most decks of cards acquire a natural bend in them after they've been used for a while, so you might be able to detect a small break between the two back-to-back sections. (I usually give the entire deck a slight upward bend before I do this trick so I know that a break will be there at this point.)

When you locate the two back-to-back cards, lift up all of the face-up cards in a stack with your right hand. Turn them over and drop them onto the face-down cards in your left hand. Square the deck.

Some of the cards are face to back, some are back to face, and some of them are back to back. All mixed up. But if I just pass the shadow of my hand over top of the deck, the cards are all facing the same way once again.

Make a magical gesture over the deck. Then spread the cards between your hands or ribbon spread them on the table to show that miraculously they're all now facing in the same direction.

Remember I said that you could make this a "pick a card" trick if you really wanted to? Well, the Slop Shuffle can be used to reveal a chosen card. Start the trick by having a card selected and returned to the deck. Then, secretly control the card to the bottom of the deck. (By now, you should be able to do this using either a force card or a key card.)

Perform the Slop Shuffle until you have only one face-down card (the chosen card) remaining in your left hand instead of a whole packet. Set this single face-down card on top of the rest of the deck in your right hand. Transfer the deck to your left hand.

You'll have a deck consisting of two back-to-back sections with a single face-down card on top.

Locate the two back-to-back cards. With your right hand, cut off all of the cards above the lower face-down stack of cards. Turn over all of the cards in your right hand, and drop them onto the face-down cards in your left hand. Spread the cards. Surprise! All of the cards will be face down except for the chosen card, which will be face up in the middle!

Tricky Tidbits

Here's an alternate patter line for the Slop Shuffle. As you mix the cards, compare the deck to your computer hard drive. Your applications and extensions keep creating conflicts, and if you don't do something fast, the whole system might crash and you'll lose all your data. Fortunately, you've backed up everything, and all you have to do is "restart" your computer. By this time, you've completed the Slop Shuffle and secretly restored the deck. Hold the pack in your left hand and press and imaginary "Restart" button in the middle of the back of the top card. (Some brands of playing cards, such as Bicycle and Aviator, actually have a small circle in the middle of their back designs.) Spread the cards to show that they're once again all facing in the same direction.

Magic with playing cards isn't particularly hazardous to your health, with the possible exception of a paper cut now and then. But now we're going to learn some tricks that add the element of danger—in the form of fire, matches, cigarettes, and maybe even secondhand smoke. You're warned!

The Least You Need to Know

◆ Though you don't want to look like a card shark, a street magician should still handle playing cards with some visible expertise.

◆ Street magicians should be familiar with such card handling as crimps, glimpses, jogs, peeks, convincer moves, and the dealer's position.

◆ You can discover the identity of a freely selected card, know where it is in a deck, and control it to the top or bottom of the deck by use of a key (or locater) card.

◆ You can use the Cross Cut force or the Hindu Shuffle to make a spectator pick any card you want him to.

◆ The way you identify the chosen card is known as a revelation.

Chapter 8

Light My Fire

In This Chapter

- ◆ Playing with fire
- ◆ Serious sleight-of-hand: the Standard Vanish and the thumb palm
- ◆ Gimmicks and gaffs, moves and passes
- ◆ Cigarette, ash, and matchbook trickery

Probably one of the most inherently dangerous substances on earth is fire—not only because it can burn, but because of its unpredictability. You just never know what it's going to do next. Any firefighter can tell you that sometimes it seems to have a mind of its own.

Any trick that uses fire or objects associated with fire, therefore, is going to naturally rivet the attention of a wary audience. Your mother may have told you not to play with matches, but that's just what you're going to do as you check out some fire-related sorcery.

Heads or Tails

You wouldn't think that a trick with a single paper match could be so effective, but it is! Perhaps it's because it's so straightforward, and there doesn't seem to be any monkey business: everything's out in the open.

The trick's been around forever—probably since shortly after Pennsylvania lawyer Joshua Pusey invented book matches back in 1889. In his 1978 book *The Encyclopedia of Impromptu Magic*, Martin Gardner, a prolific writer on magic, credited the trick to Fred Peterson, who published several original magical effects in *The Phoenix*, a magic magazine in the 1940s and 1950s.

To have the most impact, this trick has to seem completely spontaneous. So, unless you're known to carry matches with you, wait until you can borrow someone else's or are at a location where you know you'll find them, such as at a bar, a restaurant, or where cigarettes are sold.

Effect

You break the head off a match and have a spectator hold the rest. The match head disappears. When the spectator opens his or her fist, the match is back together.

Preparation

For the purpose of explanation, I'll call the small red tip of the match the "head" and the remaining paper stem of the match the "tail."

During this trick, you'll use an extra head from a paper match. You can carry one in your pocket, of course, so that you're ready to do this trick on a moment's notice. But it's more practical to wait until just before you're ready to perform, and then rip the head off a match from another folder. If you're really sneaky, you can do this under a table or behind your back. I find it's easier to find an excuse to briefly go into another room to get ready. (I've discovered no one *ever* questions you if you excuse yourself to go to a restroom—whether you need to use it or not.)

Charms _____

To perform this trick, you'll need a pack of matches. I'd recommend using a matchbook from the bar or restaurant you're at, or borrow one from your spectator because audiences are naturally suspicious of any props the magician provides.

After you've gotten the match head, discard or pocket the rest of the match and the matchbook. You won't be needing them anymore, and they might arouse suspicion if anyone sees them. Pinch the extra match head between your right thumb and forefinger, and you're ready to go.

Performance

Have you ever broken something and wished you hadn't? A date? A promise? A heart? Didn't you wish you could take it back, fix it, and start all over?

Pick up or ask to borrow a book of paper matches. Ask someone to rip one of the matches out of the folder and hand it to you. Take the match with your left hand and hold it between your thumb and forefinger, so that the head of the match just peeks out past your fingertips and the tail is hidden behind your slightly curled left fingers.

Bring your two hands together so that the thumbs and forefingers touch. As you do, secretly rotate the match in your left hand 180° so that the tail end of the match is now pinched between your thumb and forefinger, and the other end is hidden by your curled left fingers.

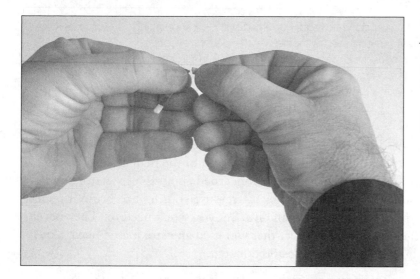

Bring both hands together as you pretend to rip the head off the match. Note that the match is reversed in your left hand.

(Photo courtesy of Titus Photography.)

Pretend to tear the head off the match. As your hands separate, slide the match head that's between your right thumb and forefinger forward a bit so that the spectators can see it. At the same time, use your left thumb to slide the tail of the match forward, too, so that the end of the match can be seen between your thumb and forefinger. Ask your volunteer to hold out his or her right hand, and drop the head of the match onto the spectator's open palm.

Which do you prefer? The head or the tail? The head? All right, we'll use the head. You hold on to the tail.

With your right thumb and fingers, pick up the head of the match from the spectator's hand. Lay the tail end of the match on his palm, and ask your spectator to close a fist around it. Be sure that you don't let go of the match until after the match is completely covered, or the person might notice that the match still has its head attached. If the person replies "Tails," go through the same actions. Simply say, "All right. Hold on to the tail end tightly so that the match can't escape—and so that I can't get to it."

There are two reasons for this ruse. By asking a question and letting the spectator think she has a choice, the person becomes actively involved in the trick. But even more important, by allowing the person to visibly see and feel a detached match head, it psychologically proves that the match has been torn in half without your having to say so.

Curses

> As a general rule, you don't have to—and shouldn't—say anything to reinforce what the spectators can already see for themselves. A perfect example would be "I have an ordinary, everyday, household deck of playing cards." In the case of "Heads or Tails," don't point out things like "This really is the head of the match" or "See, this is where I broke it off." Verbally stating the obvious will raise suspicion rather than prevent it.

Ask your spectator to hold out her closed fist. At the same time, momentarily let your right arm drop to your side and simply let the head of the match fall onto the floor. That's right: Just drop it! If you're really concerned about the spectators finding the match head on the floor after the trick is over, use your foot to brush it under the table or far away from where you're standing. But you won't need to. They never look to the floor because they don't suspect that you used an extra match head. (And besides, they're too busy examining the restored match.)

I've broken the match. Let's see if we can start over. You're not going to believe this. But you might just feel it happen.

Raise your right hand, with the thumb and fingers pinched together as if you were still holding on to the head of the match. Either make a tossing gesture toward the spectator's fist or, if you prefer, tap (or even slap) the back of her fist with your right hand. You might even stick your thumb and forefinger into the side of the spectator's closed fist as if you were trying to slip the match head inside.

Open your right hand to show that the head of the match is gone. Ask the spectator to open her hand slowly. The match has restored itself inside the spectator's hand!

Amazing! And if you can do something that astounding with just a single match, just think what you could do if you had an entire book of matches! Read on.

Under Cover

This is one of the most puzzling tricks ever devised with an ordinary book of paper matches. Although it takes a bit of preparation, the trick seems to be completely spur of the moment. The best part is that everything can be completely examined at the end.

The trick, originally called "Match Stickler," dates back to the 1950s and is credited to Milbourne Christopher, a magician, author, and magical historian. Since it first appeared, many variations of the trick have been published, but the original is, perhaps, still the best.

Effect

You tear a paper match out of its folder, and the pack is closed. You light the single match, blow it out, and then make it disappear. Finally, you open the matchbook to show that the burnt match has returned to the folder.

Preparation

You'll need to prepare a book of paper matches in advance. Bend one of the matches in the front row forward away from the rest of the row, and ignite it using a second match. (Be careful not to accidentally set all of the matches on fire.) After the burnt match has cooled, fold it back into place. Close the book of matches, and place the gimmicked match folder in your pocket.

In order to perform this routine, you'll also have to perform a versatile piece of *sleight-of-hand*, or *move*, known as a *pass*.

There are several ways to perform a pass, but the most common technique is probably the handling that J.B. Bobo called the Standard Vanish in his classic book *Modern Coin Magic* (see Appendix B). (He called the move a "vanish" because the sleight is most often used to make a coin disappear.)

The Magic Word

Sleight-of-hand, from an Old Norse word for slyness, is a general term for any manual action performed to accomplish a magic trick. A **pass** is a type of sleight (or **move**) in which you pretend to place (that is to say, pass) an object from one of your hands into the other while you secretly retain it in the first hand.

Burn a single match in the front row of a book of paper matches.

(Photo courtesy of Titus Photography.)

Although the move can be performed with any object small enough to be concealed in your hand—and in "Under Cover" we'll be performing it with a match—I'll describe the sleight with a coin, because it'll make the move a bit easier to learn, practice, and master.

The pass is performed in one nonstop fluid motion, but I'll break it down into three basic steps:

1. Hold the coin between your right thumb and forefinger. Show the coin to your audience. Open your left hand, palm upward, and begin to place the coin onto your left palm.

The Magic Word

Secretly hiding an object in your hand is known as **palming.** The sleight sometimes has different names, specific to the area of the hand in which the item is held. Concealing an object in a loose fist with the fingers curled around it is known as a **finger palm.**

2. As your right fingers touch your left palm, curl your left fingers around your right fingers, as if you were grabbing hold of the coin. Your raised left fingers will hide the coin as well as your right fingertips from the audience's view.

3. Now comes the really sneaky part: with your right thumb, slide the coin about an inch back toward your right palm. Let the coin drop to the base of your middle, ring, and little fingers, which then slightly curl around it. (This is known as the *finger palm* position.)

There should be no detectible motion in the fingers of your right hand, however. As you're *palming* the coin, continue to curl your left fingers into a fist around your right fingertips. Then, move your fist to the left, away from your right hand. After a few moments, let your right hand casually fall to your side, with the coin resting at the base of your loosely curled fingers. This whole action should simply look as if you transferred the coin from one hand to the other.

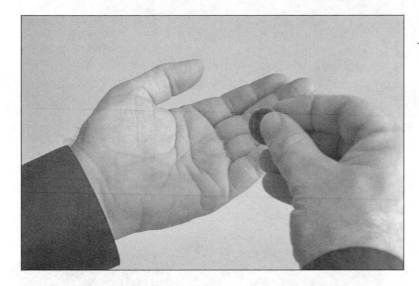

Show the coin at your right fingertips, and begin to place it onto your left palm.

(Photo courtesy of Titus Photography.)

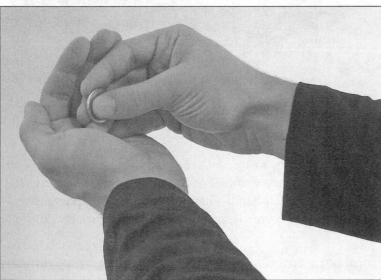

Cup your left fingers to hide the coin, your view.

(Photo courtesy of Titus Photography.)

Your left fingers, raised to cover the coin, audience view.

(Photo courtesy of Titus Photography.)

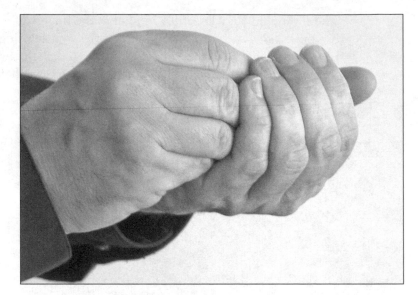

The coin held in a finger palm position.

(Photo courtesy of Titus Photography.)

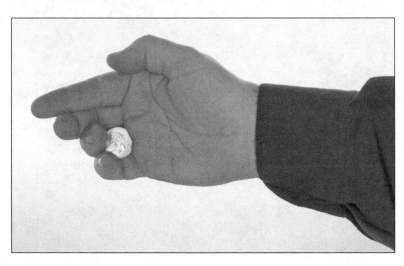

Think of the action as taking place along an arc, with the coin being moved from one end to the other: the right hand makes the first half of the journey. Halfway through, supposedly it passes the coin into your left hand. Then the left hand completes the motion. If you've performed the move correctly, the audience will believe that the coin is now in your left hand.

Now, armed with the matchbook that you've gimmicked and the ability to perform a pass, it's time to perform our trick.

Performance

Bring out the matchbook and hold it so that its back cover is facing the audience. With your right hand, open the cover. Immediately place your left thumb on top of the burnt match and fold it down toward you. Transfer the folder to your left hand so that you're holding it between your left thumb (which conceals the burnt match) and your left fingers. Openly tear out a single unburned match and set it on the table. Ask your spectator to count the remaining matches left in the folder.

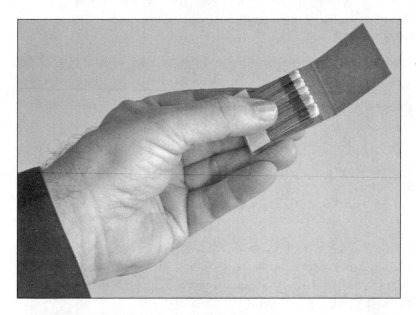

The burnt match is folded down and hidden underneath your left thumb.

(Photo courtesy of Titus Photography.)

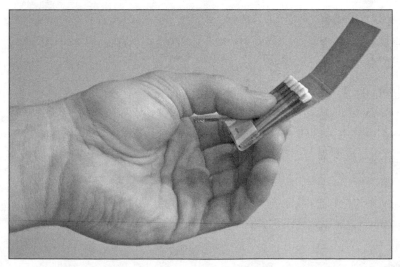

An exposed view of the burnt match hidden underneath your thumb.

(Photo courtesy of Titus Photography.)

Close the match folder. As you do so, secretly fold the burnt match upward and back into its original position. You have to take special care to make sure that the audience doesn't catch you doing it. They should only see the back cover of the matchbook as you close the folder, not the matches themselves. (Fortunately, the larger motion of closing the matchbook cover will conceal the smaller motion made by your left thumb as it pushes the burnt match into place.)

Pick up the single match from the table, light it using the striker on the back of the matchbook, and hand the folder to your spectator. If you trust the person not to open the matchbook, you can place it on his open palm. Otherwise, have the person hold the matchbook in a closed fist.

When I was little, my mom told me "don't play with matches, or you'll get burned." But did I believe her? Like a moth to a flame, I found the fire impossible to resist.

After you're certain that the audience knows the match you're holding is actually burning, blow out the match. (Don't let it burn too long, however, or at the end of the trick it won't look the same as the match hidden inside the folder.)

Now you're going to make the match disappear! Display the burnt match in your right fingertips. Perform a pass, pretending to place the match into your left hand but secretly retaining it in your right hand. Casually drop your right hand to your side as you look at your left fist.

Make a tossing motion toward the matchbook with your left hand. Open your left hand. The match has disappeared! (Because everyone is concentrating on either your left hand or the pack of matches, this is a good time to drop the match that's in your right hand onto the floor.)

Does the matchbook feel any different? Do you feel it getting warmer?

Open the matchbook. Show that the vanished burned match has reappeared inside the matchbook. Tug on the match a bit to demonstrate that you haven't just slipped it into the folder somehow; it's actually fastened in place. Finally, tear out the match and pass out everything for examination. The audience can count the matches to prove that the same number are there as when the trick began. (In case you're wondering, I remove the burnt match at the end of the trick because otherwise it's possible that a sharp spectator could notice the crease at the bottom of the match and figure out how the trick was done.)

Charms

Here are three tips to help you be more deceptive when you perform a pass:

- When you move your left hand away from your right, follow your left hand (which is supposedly holding the coin) with your eyes. The audience will follow your eyes with their own.
- Don't clench your right hand into a fist after performing the pass. This is a telltale giveaway that you're hiding something in your hand.
- As you separate your hands, don't move them at the same time. The audience won't know which hand to follow. It'll look like you're playing a game of "Guess Which Hand Is Hiding the Coin."

According to the old saying, "Where there's smoke, there's fire." And where there's fire, eventually we're going to be left with ashes. So let's put that ash to good use.

Ashes to Ashes

They also say that seeing is believing, which is why street magic right in front of a person's eyes is so powerful. But you'll get an even stronger reaction if the spectator can also *feel* the magic happen. Let's say you made a flower appear. The spectator may see it or even smell it. But if the person pricks a finger on one of its thorns, the reaction is visceral. The person has been touched—literally and figuratively—by your magic.

In this next trick, you make a mark appear on a person's palm inside his or her closed fist. Trust me, people are floored by this trick because there are only two ways the trick could be done: either your hands are so fast that you're able to touch them without their knowing or feeling it, or it's real magic. Either way, the prospect is unnerving.

Effect

You rub a bit of ash from a cigarette onto the back of one of your spectator's fists, claiming that it will go through the back of the hand. But the trick doesn't work as planned. Instead, the ash appears on the palm of the other hand.

Preparation

You'll need an ashtray with some cigarette ash in it, but otherwise, none.

Performance

Find an ashtray containing some ash that's no longer hot. Pick up the ashtray with your right hand and move it to one side, as if you're clearing space to perform your trick. As you do, dip your right forefinger into the ashes and pick up a bit of ash on the pad (the fingertip part) of your finger.

Needless to say, your audience shouldn't notice this. The good news is that it doesn't take much pressure or time to pick up a few specks of ash, and you don't need a lot of ash on your finger.

Dip your forefinger into the ashtray to pick up a bit of ash.

If your fingertip is very dry, you might want to get the tip of your finger damp before you pick up the ashtray. The obvious way to do this is to lick your finger, but that's a bit conspicuous. You could dip your finger into your drink as you casually move the glass; or, if the exterior of the glass is moist, you could simply rub your finger along it.

There's an unusual phenomenon in which open sores or lesions appear for no reason on people's bodies, feet, or palms. And, to some, these holes look like the wounds of the crucified Christ. Psychiatrists call the individuals who have these symptoms "stigmatics," and they're often diagnosed as being religious hysterics. Some clerics believe that the marks are true holy manifestations, however. Maybe the answer lies somewhere in between.

Hold out both of your hands in front of you, open and with palms down. Ask your spectator to do the same. (Don't worry: no one will notice the ash on your fingertip.)

Reach forward and grasp the spectator's right hand with your left hand and, at the same time, take the spectator's left hand with the your right hand. Your thumbs should rest on the top of the volunteer's hands and your fingers should naturally curl underneath her palms.

Spread your helper's hands about a foot apart. As you do, lightly press your right forefinger against the person's left palm. It should take just a moment for some of the ash to transfer from your finger to her palm. Close both of your hands into fists, and ask the spectator to do so as well. (Not only does closing your fists demonstrate what you want the spectator to do, but it also hides any remaining ash on your right fingertip.)

Ask someone to hand you the ashtray. Openly stick your right forefinger into the ashtray, and pick up some ash on the pad of your finger, covering any remaining ash that might still be there.

Set the ashtray to one side. You won't be needing it for the rest of the trick.

Now, this part is really gross.

Reposition yourself so that you're standing to the spectator's right, as far as possible from her left hand. The reason is psychological: later, the volunteer believes that you were nowhere near that hand. Smear a dab of the ash on back of your spectator's right hand. Wipe off any ash remaining on your own hand.

Now comes the freaky part. Believe it or not, as I rub the back of your hand, the ashes don't disappear. They actually penetrate the back of your hand.

As you say this, lightly rub the back of the person's hand in a circular motion. Although it won't be obvious, this action will simply brush the ash off the person's hand. (I know: you're lying when you say it's going through her hand. But magicians make an art out of deception. Get used to it.)

As you move the spectator's hands apart, transfer a bit of ash to his or her left palm.

An exposed view of adding the ash to the spectator's left palm.

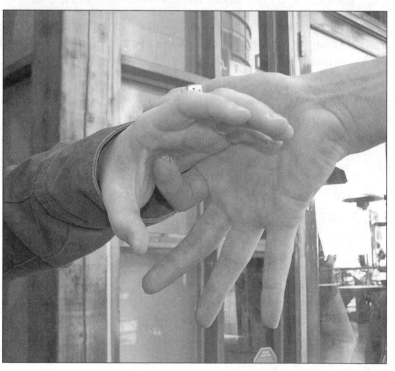

Ask your volunteer to open her right hand. Look for the ashes on the person's palm. There's none there! Something seems to have gone wrong.

No ashes. That's odd. I know: try the other hand.

Point to the spectator's left hand, which, remember, is now some distance from you. Ask the person to open her left hand and check the palm. Your volunteer will see the ash on her palm—which you seemingly never touched—and freak!

Your volunteer will freak out when the ash is discovered!

Before we finish up with the fire and ash tricks, let's look at a couple of tricks that can be done with cigarettes. Don't start smoking in order to perform these two tricks! In fact, I've deliberately chosen tricks where you make the cigarettes disappear. Who says you can't be an edgy street magician and still be a do-gooder?

Snuff Happens

Everyone knows you shouldn't smoke. But once you've started on the evil weed, it's almost impossible to quit. It's that d*#n nicotine! I wouldn't be surprised if some addicts' biggest complaint is that it simply takes too long to smoke a whole cigarette to get their fix; why isn't there some way they could inhale the toxins and carcinogens all at once? Can't you street magicians do something about that? Well, yes, we can. Here comes magic to the rescue.

Effect

You appear to shove a cigarette up your nose. With a final snort, it's gone! If you wish, instead of making the cigarette completely vanish, you can make it reappear between your lips.

Preparation

You'll need a cigarette; otherwise, none.

Performance

Pinch one end of a cigarette between your right thumb and fingers. Hold the cigarette up in a vertical position to display it. Most of the cigarette should stick out past the ends of your fingers.

Ya gotta admit it: smoking is a quick and easy way to get toxic chemicals into your system. You grind up a few leaves of tobacco, sprinkle the tar and nicotine onto a piece of paper, roll it up like a tortilla, light it on fire, and presto: a cigarette.

Before the invention of cigarettes and pipes, some people used to use snuff—little bits of ground-up tobacco leaves that they'd just snort up the nose.

Hold the cigarette between your right thumb and fingers, your view.

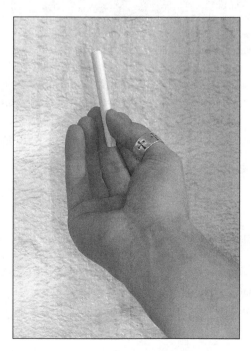

With the back of your fingers facing the spectators, raise your right hand to your face. Press the exposed end of the cigarette against the fleshy area between your two nostrils.

Hold the exposed end of the cigarette against the space between your nostrils, audience view.

Tilt your head slightly backward. As you take a deep sniff, slide the fingers of your right hand upward along the length of the cigarette. The cigarette, anchored against the nose, won't move. Instead, your fingers will slide over the shaft of the cigarette as your hand travels upward. Continue to move your fingers all the way up until your fingertips touch your nose. To the audience, it looks like the cigarette is going up your nostril.

This shouldn't have to be said, but don't actually stick the cigarette up your nose.

Curses

If you perform this trick with one of those cigarettes that has a colored filter or a gold band around one end, make sure that the unmarked end is the one you place against your nostril. Otherwise, the illusion will be spoiled when the audience notices that the ring of color doesn't move.

It might get stuck there and require medical attention—I mean, even more medical attention than you'd need after years of smoking.

The cigarette is hidden by the fingers after you slide your fingers along its length, your view.

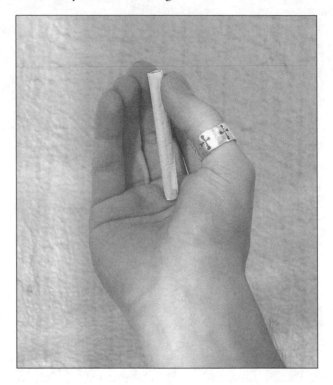

As soon as it mentally registers to the audience that you've seemingly inhaled the cigarette, lower both of your hands to the edge of the table or your sides, making sure that the cigarette remains hidden behind your right fingers. If you're seated, relax your right hand and let the cigarette drop into your lap or fall onto the floor. Otherwise, wait until the attention is no longer on your right hand, and then stick the cigarette in your pocket. (If you're in a hurry to get rid of the cigarette or are nervous about getting caught with it, reach into your pocket to retrieve a tissue to wipe or blow your nose and leave the cigarette behind.)

As a final convincer move, after you've ditched the cigarette you might want to gently press your fingers against the outside of your nose, as if to see if you've done any damage or to ease the discomfort. (After all, you've supposedly just snorted an entire cigarette. Even if it didn't hurt, it must have felt mighty odd.) Or, hold your right thumb against your nostril or squeeze it, as if your nose were starting to run.

An alternate ending to this trick is to have the cigarette reappear between your lips. After you've supposedly "snorted" the cigarette, keep the cigarette palmed in your right hand. Almost immediately, move your right hand to your mouth and clip the end of the cigarette that's at your fingertips between your lips. Now, slide your fingers away from your mouth along the length of the cigarette. (This is basically the same move you used to *vanish* the cigarette, except in reverse.)

Stop when your fingers get to the end of cigarette. Pause a moment for the "reappearance" to be seen by the audience. Then let go of the cigarette, and move your hand away from your face so that the cigarette can be seen clearly. If the "vanish" and "reappearance" are performed in one continuous motion, it'll look like the cigarette's gone up your nose and popped out of your mouth.

As a final note, I should point out that you can do this trick with other objects besides a cigarette, such as a pencil or a tube of lipstick. Major illusionist Kevin James has done the trick with a soda straw and chopsticks, and Las Vegas comedy magician Mac King's been known to perform it with a french fry.

But since I've taught the trick with a cigarette, it's only fair that I also teach you a trick where you can make all of that the tar and nicotine—in fact, the whole cigarette—disappear.

Don't Butt In

Whether they admit or not, almost everybody is addicted to something. Maybe not the usual suspects—drugs and alcohol. But how many times did you check your MySpace last week? How many pairs of shoes do you own? How many times did you listen to "that song" over and over and over? But at least that's not hazardous to your health.

You want to help your friends quit smoking, but you know that just the thought of losing their cigarettes will put them into nicotine fits. Well, here's a trick for you that's a small first step for that all-important intervention you've been considering. But don't worry. If your friend starts to go crazy when you make the cigarette vanish, you can always conjure up another cancer stick. Leave the 12 Steps for another day.

Effect

You grab a friend's cigarette from between his lips, toss it to the ground, and grind it under your foot. When the person objects, you reach out into the air and produce another coffin nail.

Preparation

None.

Performance

Ask to borrow the cigarette that your spectator is smoking. Or, if you have the *chutz-pah*, simply reach up and snatch it out of his lips.

You know, you really shouldn't smoke. It's bad for you! And for everyone else—including me. All that secondhand smoke!

The Magic Word

The **thumb palm** is a way of concealing an object in your hand by holding it at the crotch of your thumb, pinched between the base of your thumb and fore-finger.

Hold the cigarette between your right forefinger and middle finger as if you were about to raise it to your lips to smoke it. Curl your fingers, making a loose fist. As you do, the unlit end of the cigarette will naturally come in contact with the fleshy part of the hand at the base of your thumb where it meets the forefinger. Pinch your thumb against your forefinger, clipping the cigarette in place. This move is called a *thumb palm*.

Pretend to throw the cigarette to the ground. As you do, release the burning end of the cigarette from between your forefinger and middle finger but keep the unlit end pinched in a thumb palm. Uncurl your fingers, almost flattening your palm, with the back of your hand toward the spectator. If you don't spread your fingers, the cigarette will remain completely hidden from view.

As you close your hand into a fist, the unlit end of the ciga-rette touches the base of your thumb.

(Photo courtesy of Titus Photography.)

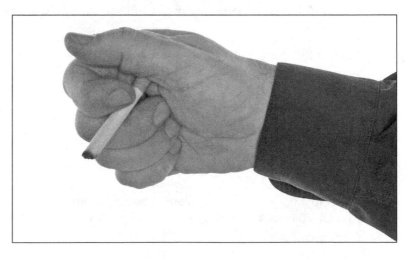

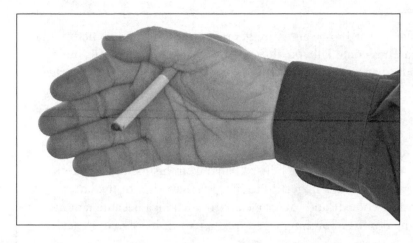

*Your left fingers hide the cig-
arette that's clipped between
your thumb and forefinger,
your view.*

*(Photo courtesy of Titus
Photography.)*

Look down at the spot where you've supposedly thrown the cigarette. Remember: the audience will follow your eyes with theirs. Imagine that you see the cigarette on the ground, cover the spot with your foot, and pretend to grind out the cigarette. Most likely your spectator's reaction will be one of shock and disbelief. How could you throw away a good cigarette?

Curses _____

You have to keep your hand in motion throughout this trick. If you hold it in one place too long, the spectator will be able to follow the trail of smoke back to the cigarette and discover where it's hidden.

Now pretend to see something invisible floating in the air in front of you, and thrust out your right hand to grab it. As you do, reverse the motions of the thumb palm: curl your right fingers into your palm and clip the cigarette about an inch from its lit end between your forefinger and middle finger. As you open your right hand, release the unlit end of the cigarette that's pinched between the base of your thumb and forefinger. A lit cigarette seems to appear at your fingertips. Hand it back to your spectator.

Of course, if your want to smoke it's your choice. If you're an addict, you're an addict. Why give it up now? Besides, you have to die of something.

By the way, this trick is especially effective if you're performing it while you're walking. When you pretend to toss down the cigarette and grind it out with your foot, just keep walking. The spectator won't have time to stop and look for the cigarette.

Cigarette manipulation used to be an entire genre of stage magic, and before the discovery that cigarettes could kill you, dozens of professional magicians built their entire acts out of an endless succession of producing and vanishing lit cigarettes, cigars, and pipes.

Perhaps the most famous of the lot in the mid-twentieth century was Cardini, who perfected the character of a slightly befuddled magician dressed in monocle, white gloves, top hat, and tails. In his act, he would toss aside a stream of lit cigarettes (as well as playing cards and billiard balls) from his hands, only to have them continually reappear at his fingertips to his great surprise. In the latter quarter of the century, comedy and bar magician Tom Mullica became famous for seemingly eating dozens of burning cigarettes as part of his signature act.

Needless to say, most cigarette magic is out of fashion today. But as long as people still smoke, cigarette tricks won't disappear. And politically correct or not, cigarettes are perfect props for roving street magicians.

Well, that's about it for tricks with fire and brimstone. I hope you were careful and didn't get burned. I need you in good shape, because now we're going to move on to some tricks that—if they weren't magic—would really hurt to perform.

The Least You Need to Know

- Using a spectator's personal items proves that they're not gimmicked.

- Large movements will help divert a spectator's attention away from smaller hand motions.

- Touching spectators during a trick directly involves them and forces them to pay attention. (Just be careful not to take it too far or venture into the inappropriate.)

- A spectator's eyes will naturally follow where you look.

- Calling an object "everyday" or "ordinary" raises the audience's suspicion instead of reducing it.

Chapter 9

That's Gotta Hurt

In This Chapter

- ◆ Tricks with your fingers, arms, and neck
- ◆ More "palming"
- ◆ The Bobo Switch
- ◆ Tricks that look painful but aren't

Don't worry: the stunts in this chapter are really magic tricks. Perhaps it's the fact that they seem to cause incredible pain that makes them so darn entertaining to the street sorcerer's audience. Which is kinda kinky when you think about it.

Now, not all of the tricks in this section are sadistic. Some of these gags are just plain gross. I'll leave it up to you to decide which is which.

By the way, I'll give you these warnings now so I don't have to say them again and again throughout the chapter:

- ◆ Don't try any of these tricks without carefully reading all of the instructions first.
- ◆ Follow the instructions as written when you're learning to perform the tricks, or you're going to hurt yourself.

◆ If you're starting to feel any kind of pain or discomfort when you're trying any of these tricks, stop! None of them is worth hurting yourself over.

Have I made my point? Now that the disclaimer is taken care of, let's begin.

Stretching a Point

Have you ever wanted to grab something that was just out of reach? What if you were one of those superheroes like Mr. Fantastic in the Fantastic Four or Elastigirl from that movie *The Incredibles*? It would be no problem then! Well, here's your chance to display your own superpowers of flexibility and elasticity.

Effect

You stretch your right arm until it appears to be twice its normal length.

Preparation

None, although you should be wearing a loose jacket. This trick actually will work with just a long-sleeved shirt, but it's infinitely more effective if you're wearing a coat, especially if your shirt sleeves are rolled up underneath.

Performance

This is an optical illusion rather than an actual physical feat, which makes it a little hard to explain. To begin, position your body so that the person you want to fool is standing in front of you or on your left side. The trick is least effective if the person is standing to your right.

I think I hurt my arm the other day. It's a little out of joint.

Press your right arm lightly against your side. Bend your right arm, and extend it toward your spectator. Reach over with your left hand, and grab your right wrist between your left thumb and fingers.

With your left hand, give a slight tug on your right wrist. Keeping your sleeve pressed against your right side, slightly extend your right arm. Your sleeve should stay in place, but your arm will extend an inch or two out of your cuff.

Allow your sleeve to ride up as you extend your right arm to give the illusion that your arm is stretching.

(Photo by Brad Ball. Photo courtesy of Alba.)

Continue this action, stretching out your right arm farther and farther each time you tug on your right wrist. Each time you will also be straightening out your arm a bit more until, eventually, it will be straight out in front of you. Because you've allowed your coat sleeve to ride up your arm, your arm should extend several inches past the cuff of your jacket.

Pause for a moment for it to sink in that your arm has "stretched." To return your arm to its regular length, shake your arm as you allow your sleeve to fall back down into place.

Here's an alternate handling that somewhat simplifies the action. Set your right foot up on the seat of a chair or one of the rungs of a stool. Bend slightly forward, and rest your right forearm on your right thigh. Grab your right wrist with your left hand, and tug on your right arm, as I've already described. Because there's a lot more friction on your coat sleeve when it's resting on your leg, the sleeve shouldn't move at all. This will make it look like your arm is stretching ever farther.

You can also perform the trick with your foot resting on the seat of a chair.

And now that you've gotten that stiffness out of your arm, it's time to work upward. How about that crick you have in your neck? A simple, quick twist, and everything will be fine. Or will it?

Thumb Tack

We've all seen the trick where a magician sticks a girl in a big box or a woven basket and starts shoving in swords. But what's supposed to be happening? Are we supposed to be amazed that the girl isn't being stabbed to death? Or are we supposed to be thinking that the girl has disappeared and therefore isn't being hurt? There's a lesson to be learned here: when you perform, you have to keep the "effect"—what the audience is supposed to think is happening—clear in everyone's mind.

The effect in this next demonstration couldn't be clearer. You're not making your thumb disappear. You're just subjecting it—and yourself—to an unbelievable amount of pain.

Effect

After covering your thumb with a handkerchief or napkin, you stick it with pins and needles—or maybe even chop the end off.

Preparation

Get about a half-dozen pins or needles. If you want to go for the "big ending," you'll also need a knife or scissors. In addition, you have to prepare a special gimmick to substitute for your thumb.

Take a small carrot that's about the circumference of your left thumb, and let it sit out for a few days. Funny thing about carrots: they don't rot, exactly. First, they get kind of rubbery. When you can bend the carrot back and forth, and it's as flexible as a pencil eraser, it's ready to use for this trick.

With a knife or scissors, cut off a piece of the carrot that's about as big around as your left thumb and about an inch longer. Trim the carrot so it's the same general shape as your thumb. No one expects you to be Michelangelo here, but the carrot has to pass for your thumb when it's felt through a napkin. Let the carrot dry, stick it in your pocket along with the needles, and you're ready to rumble.

Performance

Do you know anyone who's ever tried acupuncture? Do you think it really works? Don't you think it would hurt?

While people at the table are discussing this, slip the carrot under a paper napkin on the table. Keep the napkin close to you. You don't want anyone picking up the napkin and seeing the carrot before you're ready to do the trick.

My aunt just had acupuncture, and they let her keep the needles! Pretty cool, huh? Let's try it!

Toss some sewing needles, straight pins, or short hatpins onto the table. If you want the needles to look even more authentic, you might want to bring them out wrapped up in a piece of medical gauze.

Pick up the napkin with the carrot hidden beneath it. Make a fist with your left hand, with the thumb side upward. Cover your fist with the napkin. As you do, tuck your thumb into your fist, and shove the straight end of the carrot into the end of your fist, with the rounded end pointing upward. Gather the paper napkin loosely around the carrot. This should all be done in one continuous motion. It should simply look as if you covered your fist with the napkin and stuck out your left thumb.

Substitute the carrot for your left thumb as you cover your fist with a napkin, exposed view.

(Photo courtesy of Titus Photography.)

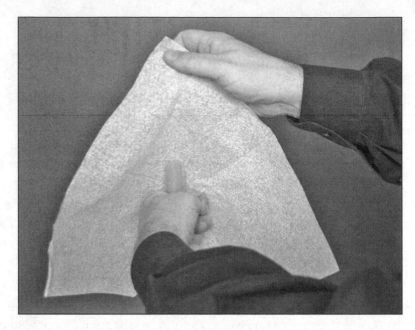

Ask one of the spectators to hold the end of your thumb gently. They will actually be grabbing the end of the carrot through the napkin, but because of its flexibility and texture, the carrot will feel like your thumb to them.

Pick up one of the pins. Poise it over top of the napkin, and then stick it into your thumb—I mean, the carrot. Close your eyes. Wince a bit. Stick in another pin. And another, and another.

A small gory detail: I shouldn't have to say this, but don't actually stick your thumb or hand with the pins. Stick them in the carrot through the napkin. People only *think* it's your thumb. *Capisce?*

For the big finish, ask someone to pass you one of the sharp knives on the table. Ask the spectator to continue to hold on to the end of your thumb as you lower your left hand onto the table. Take the knife in your right hand, rest it against the side of carrot—*making absolutely sure that you are far away from your actual thumb and the rest of your left hand*—and, then, in one swift move, chop your way straight through the napkin and the carrot. Be prepared to have your helper drop the napkin-wrapped digit or even throw it across the room in horror!

Charms

There are some advantages to using scissors instead of a knife: you don't have to lay your hand on the table to steady it, and scissors make more a squishy cut as they snip their way through the carrot. If you want to make sure that you can always perform this really shocking ending, you may want to carry a pair of scissors with you or only perform the trick when you know that there will be scissors nearby.

Pin Head

Speaking of pins and needles, what starts out here as a gag seems to end up as a test of your pain threshold. The trick also introduces you to a new sleight that can be used to great advantage whenever you want to switch one small, hand-held object for another. Once you've mastered the move, you can pick up something, and when you set it back down, it's completely changed. Imagine the possibilities!

Effect

You press a nickel against your forehead, and it stays there. When your friends scoff, saying that it's not sticking there by magic, you confess that they're right: peel off the coin and hand it to them to show that it has a huge nail attached to its back side.

Preparation

You have to make a gimmick coin for this trick. You'll require a nickel, a small tack or nail, and some Superglue. I use a ¼" galvanized roof nail. Set the nickel face down on the table and superglue the head of the tack to the back of the coin. Let it set until the glue is hard.

By the way, the government's been messing with our money again, so there are all sorts of designs on the nickels out there. Some have the regular Jefferson profile on the front that's been there for years. Now there's a "new and improved" nickel that has Jefferson facing at a different angle. And don't get me started on all the different designs on the back of the nickel. That's why I use an old-style nickel to make the gaff: the odds are better that it'll match the nickel that you borrow when you perform the trick. Place the gaff in your pocket along with a regular nickel with a matching face design, and you're ready to go. It's always better if you borrow the ungimmicked nickel, but I carry the extra nickel with me if I know I'm going to perform the trick—just in case no one has a nickel or if the face design doesn't match.

Glue a nail to the back of a nickel to produce the "Pin Head" gimmick.

(Photo courtesy of Titus Photography.)

Be very careful where and how you carry the gimmick around with you. The point of the nail could very easily poke a hole through your pants or shirt. I usually press the end of the nail into a cork when I want to carry the gimmick in my pocket.

Insert the head of the nail into a cork to carry it with you safely.

(Photo courtesy of Titus Photography.)

Performance

Before you're ready to perform, finger palm the nickel in your right hand, holding it in a loose fist with your slightly curled right middle, ring, and little fingers.

Borrow a nickel from your friend or use one of your own. Pick it up between your right thumb and forefinger, and press it against your forehead so that Jefferson's face is pointing outward. Let go of the coin. Because of the moisture on your forehead, the coin will cling there.

And now, with no regard for personal safety, I will hammer this coin into my forehead. Gee, this smarts!

Pause for a couple of seconds, and then act surprised that you're friends aren't impressed.

You think it's easy? You try it!

Pluck the coin off your forehead between your right thumb and forefinger. (Remember, the gimmick coin is still finger palmed in your right hand.) Open your left hand, palm up.

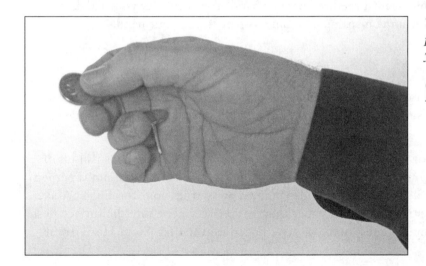

The hands in position to perform the Bobo Switch, your view.

(Photo courtesy of Titus Photography.)

You are now going to perform a Bobo Switch, a sleight described by J.B. Bobo in his book *Modern Coin Magic* (see Appendix B), to switch the nickel with your fingertips with the gimmick hidden in your hand. Pretend to toss the nickel at your right fingertips onto your left palm, but never let go of the coin. Instead, slightly open your curled right fingers to allow the finger palmed gimmick to fly into your left hand. As soon as the gaff hits your left palm, close your left hand into a loose fist, hiding the gimmick. At the same time, use your right thumb to slide the coin at your fingertips back into your right hand. Let the ungaffed nickel in your right hand fall into a finger palm.

Hand the nickel in your left hand to the spectators. When they look at it, they'll find an inch-long nail sticking out of the back of the coin.

No wonder it hurt so much!

Pin-etration

If you can hammer a nail into your forehead, it should be no big deal to stick a pin into the back of your hand, right? But how about slamming it all the way through? Are you starting to see an S&M theme running through the street magic tricks in this chapter? Even if you don't, some of your friends certainly will!

Effect

You slap a straight pin against the back of your hand. You turn over your hand, and then extract the pin from your palm. The pin has penetrated your hand.

Preparation

First, here's the insurance disclaimer: if you're under 18, only practice and perform this trick under the supervision of your parent or adult guardian. Promise? Okay? Then read on.

Take a straight pin or needle and carefully—*carefully*—push it through a small bit of skin on the pad of your right thumb. It should be positioned so that the pin is perpendicular to your thumb and the sharp end is pointed away from your forefinger. Make sure that when you stick the pin into your thumb, you only penetrate the surface flesh. If you experience any pain or blood, you have poked it in too far. Stop! Heal! Try it again later.

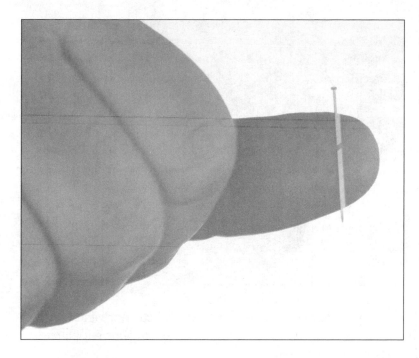

The straight pin stuck through the pad of your right thumb.

(Photo courtesy of Titus Photography.)

Performance

Pinch your right thumb and forefinger together. It will look as if you're holding the pin between your fingers. Hold out your left hand, open and with the palm downward. Scratch or poke the point of the pin against the back of your left hand one or two times, as if you're trying to decide on the best spot to use.

This is gonna be quick. And it's gonna hurt a lot, so I can only do it once. Don't blink or you're gonna miss it. ... Now!

As you raise your right hand, separate your right thumb and forefinger. Slap your right fingers hard against the back of your left hand and *at the same* time wrap your right thumb around and under your left hand. (Don't slap the pin against the back of your hand or it really *will* hurt a lot!)

Pause briefly to allow the spectator to realize that you have (seemingly) smacked the pin into the back of your hand.

Slap the back of your left hand with your right fingers as your right thumb moves underneath your left hand, exposed view.

(Photo courtesy of Titus Photography.)

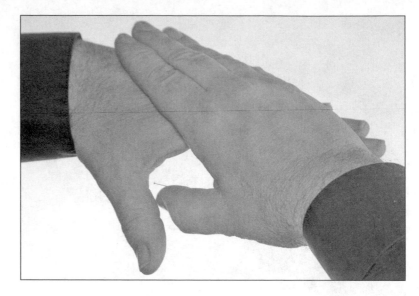

Turn over your left hand. As your left palm comes into view, pinch your right thumb and forefinger together again, holding the pin against the center of your left palm. The pin appears to be sticking through your hand.

Pinch the right thumb and forefinger together to make it appear as if the pin is sticking out of your left palm.

(Photo courtesy of Titus Photography.)

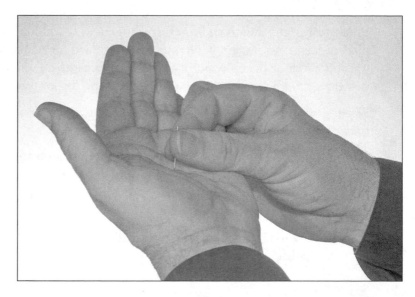

Jerk your right hand upward, as if you were pulling the pin out of your left palm. Use your left thumb and forefinger to pluck the pin out of your right hand. What you're really doing, of course, is removing the pin from your right thumb.

Curses _____

If they want, your audience can examine the pin (or your hand) to their heart's content. I'd advise against letting them try to perform the pin penetration in your presence, however. Let them try it at home when they're alone so you're not responsible for their pain and injury.

Pierced!

"You did what?!" How many kids have heard that from their parents after coming home with an ear, nose, or who-knows-what-else pierced and sporting a brand-new stud or ring? Having anything more than your earlobes pierced used to be a guaranteed way to freak people out. These days everyone's getting pierced—and some of them are in really weird parts of the body. Places you don't necessarily want to see or even need to know about.

Well, you don't have to worry with this one: the piercing is only temporary but it looks pretty darn real—and gross at the same time, which is only a plus. This "trick" has circulated for years and has become a popular sight gag among Japanese school children—which means it probably wouldn't make a big stir if Cyril performed it on the streets of Tokyo—but (as demonstrated here by Vegas-based magician Jeff McBride) the stunt can still create considerable impact.

Effect

You stick the end of your thumb through your ear. (If you wish, you can shove a chopstick, pen, pencil, soda straw, or swizzle stick through the hole as well.) Your ear then instantly heals.

Preparation

None.

Performance

Facing the audience, poke the your right thumb against the back of your ear, visibly suggesting that you're planning to poke your thumb through your ear.

I've always wanted to get pierced, but I'm kinda afraid of the pain. And what if I change my mind later? I'd be stuck with holes in my whatever.

(Because the reaction to this trick comes from its surprise factor, you may want to forego any patter, simply mumble, "Watch," and then just do it.)

Turn your body so that the left profile of your face is toward your audience. Raise your open right hand, and turn it so that the back of your hand is toward your right cheek and your palm points outward. Extend your right thumb so that it crosses the middle of your ear, covering the ear canal. Lay your right forefinger above your ear, as if it were a pencil perched behind your ear. Clip the upper half of your ear between your thumb and forefinger, as far down into the crotch of the thumb as possible.

Curl your right index finger down and around your thumb. Stretch your forefinger down past your thumb, and then curl it underneath your earlobe. Use the pad of your right forefinger to press your earlobe up against your thumb. Spin your body so that you're once again facing the audience. The tip of your thumb appears to be coming through the flap of your ear.

Place the back of your right hand up to the right side of your head and clip the upper part of your ear between your thumb and forefinger, exposed view.

(Photo by Paul Draper. Photo courtesy of Jeff McBride.)

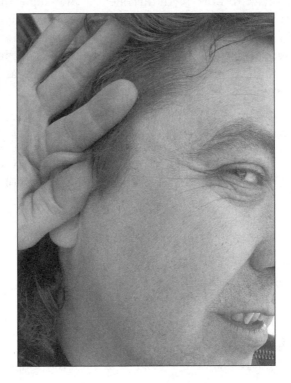

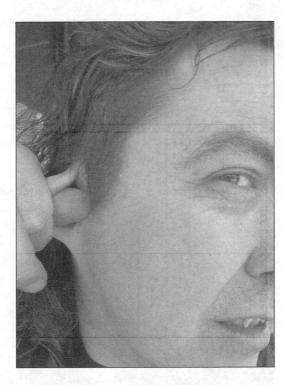

Curl your right forefinger all the way around your thumb to press your earlobe up against your thumb, giving the illusion that your thumb is sticking through a hole pierced in your ear.

(Photo by Paul Draper. Photo courtesy of Jeff McBride.)

The spectators react in shock and disbelief as you force your thumb through your ear.

(Photo by Paul Draper. Photo courtesy of Jeff McBride.)

You can add to the appearance that you're pierced by wiggling your thumb or thrusting it forward (all without letting go with your forefinger, of course). It'll also increase the effect if you move your right hand away from the side of your face, pulling at your entire ear.

Moving your right hand slightly away from your head (which gently stretches your entire ear) increases the pierced effect.

(Photo by Paul Draper. Photo courtesy of Jeff McBride.)

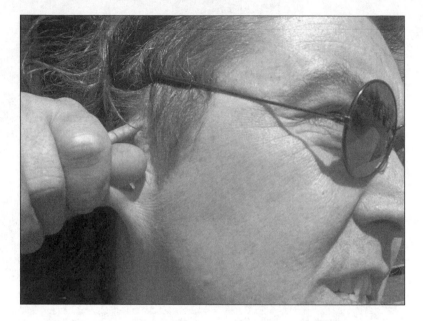

To release the secret hold on your ear, you can simply turn your right side away from the spectators. Or cover your ear with your left hand, and then remove your right hand out from under it. Rub your ear a bit. After a slight massage, move your hand away from your ear to show that it's as good as new.

Here's an extra bit you might try that can add a grotesque moment or two to the trick. Instead of "piercing" your ear with your thumb alone, you can add a pen or chopstick. (If you do use a chopstick, make sure it's ceramic or plastic, not wooden, or you'll get splinters in your ear—I mean, unless you like that sort of thing.)

Start with the chopstick in your left hand. As you turn your left side to the viewers, place the chopstick underneath your thumb so that one of its ends is even with or just slightly past the tip of your thumb. Perform the other moves as already described, wrapping the flap of the ear and the lobe around your right thumb. When you turn to face the spectators, the chopstick will seem to be sticking through the hole in your ear next to your thumb.

But here's the kicker: using your left hand, reach under and behind your curled right hand. Most of the chopstick will be sticking out of the back side of your loose right fist, extending out well past the heel of your palm. With your left hand, grab that end of the chopstick. Still facing the audience and holding your ear firmly with your right hand, push the chopstick slowly forward. The more you grimace as you gradually and excruciatingly push the chopstick through the "hole," the greater the response you're likely to get. It's equally effective to simply shove the chopstick through in one motion. Grunt! If you do it this way, people may jump because it looks like you've forcefully rammed the chopstick from back to front. Let go of the chopstick with your left hand, reach around to the front of your ear and pull the chopstick the rest of the way "through" your ear. Set down the chopstick, and massage your ear to magically restore it to its original condition.

Blistered

Finally! A trick that can be performed as a real mystery. It's credited to magician Jack Tillar and first appeared in print in Volume 7 of *The Tarbell Course in Magic* (see Appendix B).

The method is so novel that it's almost irresistible not to tell your audience how it's done. But don't! It's too good!

Effect

You draw an outline of your left hand on a piece of paper. Someone touches a lit cigarette to one of the fingers on the picture. You immediately show a blister on the corresponding fingertip of your hand.

Preparation

None. You'll need a key, such as a standard house key, that has a small, round hole in its head, a piece of paper (approximately 8½"×11"), a pen, and a lit cigarette. Everything except the key can be borrowed when you perform this trick. Place the key in your right pants pocket.

Performance

This basic effect, in which a blister magically appears at the tip of one of your fingers, can be presented in many different ways, from simple gags to unsettling pieces clothed in overtones of the occult. I'm offering three basic versions of the trick, but once you've learned the method, you can experiment until you've developed a routine that works best with your particular style.

The fake blister shown with the key that produced it.

(Photo courtesy of Titus Photography.)

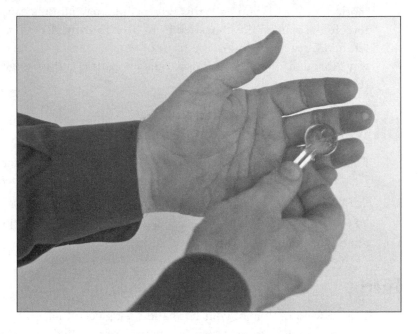

Version One

Do you believe in voodoo? Do you think voodoo dolls really work? I think I can prove they do.

Take out the piece of paper and set it on the table. Place your left hand palm down on the paper and, using the pen, draw an outline around your hand.

So far this looks like a piece of refrigerator art from a kindergarten class. But what's about to happen is something that you'll never see in any preschool.

Ask someone who has a lit cigarette to look at the drawing and think of one of the fingers or the thumb. Your volunteer is to really concentrate on that particular finger and, when the person feels the psychic urge, he or she is to touch the lit end of the cigarette to that finger on the drawing. (It's even more dramatic if you ask the person to lift the illustration and burn a small hole completely through the paper.)

While the person is doing all of this, here's what you're doing: Pick up the key in your right hand, and place both hands either under the table or behind your back. Holding the jagged end of the key in your right fingers, press the hole of the key firmly against the finger (or thumb) on your left hand that corresponds to the one the spectator is burning with the cigarette. Push the key as hard as you can, and hold it against your finger for a few seconds. This will create a very realistic-looking "blister" on your fingertip.

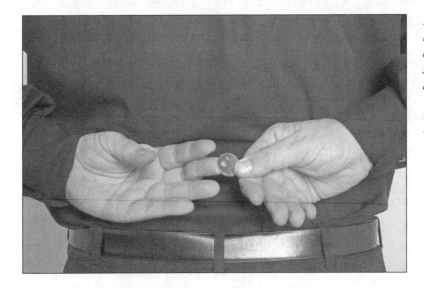

Behind your back, press the key against the finger that corresponds to the one your spectator is burning on the drawing.

(Photo courtesy of Titus Photography.)

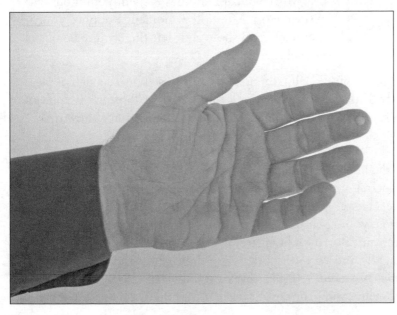

The keyhole creates a very realistic-looking blister.

(Photo courtesy of Titus Photography.)

Then casually bring your hands back out in front of you, and, at some point, drop the finger-palmed key back in your pocket. At this point, the person should still be applying the cigarette to the drawing.

Yes, I'm feeling something. It's getting hot. It's almost like I can feel the cigarette ... Ow!

Pretend to feel a sharp pain at the end of your finger. Shake your hand, or kiss your fingertip. Look down at your left hand in disbelief, and then slowly turn it so that the spectator can see the blister on your finger—the same finger that he or she just burned on the "voodoo" drawing of your hand.

This may bring gasps or complete silence. Either one is great! It means that your audience hasn't just been fooled: they've been startled into a state of disbelief. This trick is so strong that many people believe they've seen an actual demonstration of voodoo.

Charms

Because you don't create the "blister" until after the spectator has chosen a finger, you might be tempted to have your left hand examined before the trick. Don't. This is overkill. At that point in the routine, no one should be thinking that something might happen to your actual hand, or they'll keep watching it.

Since you're on the subject of the supernatural, you might want to wrap up the trick with a bit of "psychic surgery." Tell the spectator that you're not worried, because the same people who indoctrinated you into voodoo also introduced you to the homeopathic healing used by shamans and native healers. Press the tip of your right thumb against the "blister." Stare at your "burned" fingertip while you gently rub the sore. Move your lips a bit as if silently mumbling a mystic charm. After a few moments, remove your right hand, and show your left fingertip. The blister is gone!

Because the "blister" is just a bit of skin temporarily compressed into a small circle, rubbing your fingertip will spread out and smooth the skin. The "blister" disappears on its own. There's no magic to this, of course, but the spectators don't know that.

Version Two

Here's another use for the blister principle if all the rigmarole of drawing pictures and talking about voodoo doesn't appeal to you—but pain does. Just before you're ready to perform, secretly create a blister on one of your fingertips. Hold that hand so that the blister is facing away from your spectator. Tell the person that you've trained yourself to be impervious to pain. Borrow a lit cigarette, and blow on the lit end so that it really starts to glow. Lightly and very, very briefly tap the cigarette against the fingertip that's already secretly "blistered." (If this leaves a small bit of ash on your finger, all the better.) Don't react in any way. Turn over your hand so that your spectator can see the blister mark. Even though you've clearly burned yourself, you seem to be have felt no pain.

Just a small warning here. If you momentarily touch the burning end of a cigarette to your finger, you're not likely to feel anything, and it won't cause any permanent harm. But don't be stupid: don't hold the cigarette against your fingertip for any length of time. This isn't a *real* test of endurance.

Version Three

Okay, for you pranksters out there, here are a few bits that use the "blister" method to make people think you've accidentally been burned. Borrow a lit cigarette from a friend, and take it with the hand in which you've already created a fake blister. Pretend that the person handed the cigarette to you backward and that you've burned yourself. Drop the cigarette, supposedly in pain. Look down at your finger, and then show the blister to your friend. Make the person feel guilty!

Here's another evil practical joke: when a server hands you your dinner plate, pretend that it's really hot. Show the waiter your blister! Before you let the server in on the gag, you'll get apologies, offers of free food, and promises that you won't have to leave a tip!

You don't want to be so cruel to someone else unless you can take the heat yourself, if you'll pardon the expression. If you're in a restaurant or café where there are lit candles on the tables, reach for something on the other side of your table and pretend to accidentally touch the candle flame. Yell "Ouch!" (That's your only acceptable four-letter word I'm allowed to suggest.) Show the big blister on your finger. Bear in mind, if this was one of those romantic restaurants and you were on a big date, you've probably really ruined the mood.

Nose Candy

Now you're going to learn a trick that actually comes from the street magicians of India. In the original version, the fakir would take a small bean and swallow it. Then, slowly, ever so slowly, the bean would emerge from the tear duct in the corner of one of his eyes.

You'll be happy to know that you'll be learning a slightly different version so that you don't have to actually stick a bean in your eye. (Yes, that's how they do it.) Instead, you'll be doing the trick in reverse, with the bean going into your eye (or in your ear or up your nose), and it will pop out of your mouth. Not only is this version of the trick easier to learn and perform, but far fewer hospital stays are required.

Effect

You place a dried bean or pea up your nose—or in your ear or under your eyelid—and it comes out of your mouth.

Preparation

None. You'll need two small Spanish peanuts. This is most effective if you have them in a small dish filled with mixed nuts. If you prefer, this trick could also be done with dried beans, lentils, peas, or Tic Tacs instead.

Performance

Reach into a dish of nuts with your right hand, and locate two small Spanish peanuts. Finger palm one of them in your right hand. Hold up the other peanut between your right thumb and forefinger to display it.

Charms

If you have difficulty finding two peanuts and palming one of them with a single hand, try using both hands to sort through the nuts. The action of two hands digging through the dish of nuts will make it easier to hide the relatively smaller motion of your right hand locating and palming one of the peanuts.

Have you ever laughed while you were drinking something, and the liquid squirts out your nose? Neat, isn't it? And you know how your ears get clogged up when you go up in an airplane, but you can pop them by blowing your nose or yawning? You ever wonder why that works? It's simple biology. Everything's connected in there with little tubes and stuff. Even the tear ducts are connected to the back of the throat. Well, I wonder what would happen if I tried to use one of those tiny tubes for a bit of magic. But be warned: this may be a little gross.

Toss the peanut into your mouth, secretly adding the one that's palmed in your right hand as well. Roll them around in your mouth, and in the process, use your tongue to stick one of them between your bottom front teeth and your lower lip. Let the other one lie on your tongue.

I just have to juice it up with a little lube.

Reach into your mouth with your right fingers, and remove the peanut that's on your tongue. Display it between your right thumb and forefinger.

Act as if you're putting the nut into your left hand, but perform the Standard Vanish pass (see Chapter 8), and secretly retain the peanut in your right hand.

Pretend to work the peanut up to your left fingertips, and then pinch your left thumb and fingers together as if you're holding the nut. Meanwhile, casually drop your right hand to your side; and at some point when no one is watching, drop the peanut onto the floor.

Now comes the hard part.

You are now going to pretend to stick the peanut into the tear duct in the corner of your eye. Say what? Well, you know where the tear duct is, right? There's one in the inner corner of each eye, where the eye meets the bridge of the nose. And you know how to put in a contact lens, right? (Even if you don't wear them, you've seen enough other people put in their lenses.) So, let's put all that together, and here goes:

With your right fingers, pull down the lower lid of your right eye, as if you were about to put in a contact lens. Bring your left fingers, which are pinched together supposedly holding the peanut, up to the tear duct of your right eye. Pretend to slowly and painfully push the nut into the corner of your eye. Remember, this should not be pleasant. If you were actually doing it, this would really hurt. Wince. Swear, if you must. (But don't overact.)

Blink your right eye once or twice. You can even feel around your eye with your fingertips as if to be sure the nut is gone. Hold both palms up to show your hands are empty. Then, with both forefingers, point to your lips.

Purse your lips and, using your tongue, slowly move the Spanish peanut that's still hidden in your mouth out to your lips. Finally, spit the peanut onto the floor, into your hand, or—if you really want a strong reaction—back into the dish of nuts on the table. (You didn't hear that last suggestion from me.) It appears that the peanut has gone into your eye, worked its way down through the tear duct, and come out of your mouth. An incredible journey!

This doesn't have to be an eyeball trick, of course. You have plenty of other head orifices to play with. Instead of sticking the nut into your tear duct, you could pretend to shove it up your nose or into your ear. But somehow they don't seem like they'd be quite as painful, so for the biggest response, go with the eye.

This next trick could be a perfect follow-up to "Nose Candy." But it also holds up all on its own. In fact, it will probably get the biggest single reaction of any stunt in this book.

Tricky Tidbits _____

In fact, you don't have to stick with your face. In another trick made famous by Indian swamis, the street magician would swallow a bit of thread and then pull it out of his belly button. You could do the same trick using a peanut, again in reverse. After you've performed the pass, lift your shirt and pretend to press the nut into your navel. Squirm a bit as if you're working the peanut into your body, up your throat, and, finally, out of your mouth.

Eyescream

This amazing gag was invented by that crazy genius of a comedy magician, Mac King, who kindly allowed me to share it with you. It first appeared in his book (co-written with Mark Levy), *Tricks with Your Head*. Penn & Teller also featured it in their outrageous book *How to Play with Your Food*, which contains its own share of zany mealtime stunts. (See Appendix B for details on both books.) "Eyescream" should be in the arsenal of every street magician, but use it sparingly. Once seen, this trick is never forgotten.

Effect

While trying to get a grain of dust out of your eye, you accidentally poke a fork into your eyeball, spilling the gooey cream over yourself and the spectators.

Preparation

You'll need a fork as well as a little container of dairy creamer like the ones you'll find in coffee shops and fast-food restaurants. (I use the word "dairy" very loosely, because any similarity between what's in those little cups and a dairy product is completely accidental.)

Performance

Sometime before you're actually ready to do the trick, you have to palm one of those creamer containers and sneak it into your lap. You can do this when you're fiddling with all the things on the table—magicians do this all the time while they're trying to decide what they might want to use in a trick—or go to the bathroom and cop one as you pass an empty table.

When you're about to perform, reach into your lap and finger palm the creamer in your left hand. Hold it so that the top of the creamer is pointed downward toward your little finger.

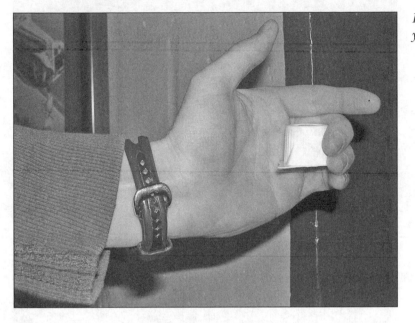

Palm the coffee creamer in your left hand.

Casually pick up a fork with your right hand and lean across the table toward your victim.

My eye is really itching. Do you see anything in my eye?

Now comes the part that you should never—*ever*—otherwise do in real life: point the fork toward your face, rest the tines on your left cheek just below your left eye, and use them to pull the skin downward to reveal the bottom of your eyeball.

Immediately place your left hand above your left eye, as if you're shielding your eye from the sun. Remember, the coffee creamer is still palmed in that hand, with the foil top facing down toward the tabletop. Then, slowly jab the tines of the fork into the top of the container. This won't take much pressure, just enough to punch through the foil.

When the top of the creamer pops open, you'll hear it. And, trust me, you'll really see it! In fact, if you squeeze the container a bit as it bursts open, the white liquid will literally gush out from under your hand onto the table and quite possibly onto you and your spectator as well. Gross me out!

Pull down the skin beneath your left eye with the tines of the fork.

Shield your left eye with your left hand.

Gently poke the tines of the fork into the top of the creamer.

Your eyeball seems to explode as the white liquid shoots out.

Anyone watching will assume you've poked out your eyeball and will jump and scream at the sight. How *you* react is up to you. You could act surprised, puzzled, or you could register nothing at all. I generally drop the fork, grab a napkin to cover my eye, and scream!

If you just want to play this for laughs, you can show your friends the coffee creamer. But I prefer to play it for real. If you do, too, as you close your left eye, lower your left hand and drop the empty container on the floor. If you're seated, you could ditch it on your lap, but remember, the container will probably still be leaking liquid. Rub your eye or dab it with a cloth, blink a few times, and then open your eye again. Good as new!

Curses

This shouldn't have to be said, but if you're going to perform this trick, be very, very careful when you have the tines of the fork anywhere near your eye. You don't want to have an accident. No trick, not even this one, is worth going blind over.

Well, that's it for the old blood and guts. But don't worry. There's lots more magic that can be performed with everyday objects that are lying around your house, dance clubs, and your favorite restaurants just begging to be used in your street magic.

The Least You Need to Know

- The finger palm enables you to conceal small objects in a loosely closed fist.

- The Bobo Switch is a useful sleight that enables you to exchange one small hand object for another.

- Much of street magic, especially tricks in which you're supposedly experiencing pain, depends upon shock value. Play them for real.

- As tempting as it is to reveal the secrets of some gags and stunts, remember that if you do, you reduce them from magic to mere jokes.

- No trick, no matter how cool, is worth getting hurt for.

Pimp This Trick

In This Chapter

- Amazing magic with everyday objects
- Using your lap to make stuff disappear
- How to direct people's attention away from your secret moves
- Classic tricks updated for street magic

If you were a real magician, you could do magic with any thing, any time, any place. In a snap, you could transform your life and the lives of those around you from the mundane to the magical.

That's why it's so important that you learn magic with ordinary, everyday objects. But to make them remarkable, we're gonna pimp them up so that they do sorcery at your fingertips. The magic is so unexpected that it makes the ordinary extraordinary.

The Jumping Rubber Band

This is one of those oddities of magic that seems to have been around forever, but we actually know who made it up. It was invented by a British magician named Stanley Collins, and he first published it in a magazine called *The Magician Monthly* in December 1911.

The reason it's still being performed is that, despite the ordinariness—is that word?—of its props (a couple of rubber bands), the trick is a real fooler and can be done without any set-up. The best part is that after you're long gone, people will still be unsuccessfully trying to do it for themselves. The memory of your magic lingers long after you've moved on.

Effect

You place a rubber band around two of the fingers on your right hand, and they instantly jump to encircle the other two fingers. You do it again under test conditions: you wind a second band around your fingertips, but the acrobatic rubber band still jumps across.

Preparation

None. All you need is one or two rubber bands.

Performance

Place a rubber band around the base of the first and second fingers of your right hand. Show both sides of your right hand to your spectator to prove that the band really is encircling your fingers.

I was watching an old Star Trek *episode the other day, and I think the thing that fascinated me most about the series was the Teleporter. Beam me up, Scotty. Wouldn't it be great if we could really do that? I mean, just zap things from one place to another. You know: Darn, I forgot my iPod. Zap. Here it is. I left that report at home. Zap. I won't flunk that class after all. Uh, oh. Here comes that really skanky girl (or guy). Zap. I'm outta here. Well, I'm testing the beta version of a handheld teleportation device right now. Wanna see?*

Hold your right hand so that the back of your hand is facing the audience. With your left thumb and forefinger, pinch the rubber band on the palm side of your right hand and stretch it away from your palm. Do this under the guise of showing how stretchy the rubber band is.

Close your right hand into a fist, but, as you do, secretly relax the band so that it stretches across all four fingertips of your right hand. The spectators see the part of the rubber band at the base of your forefinger and middle finger, but they shouldn't see the section of the band stretched over your fingertips. Open your right hand quickly, and the rubber band seems to jump over to surround your third and fourth fingers.

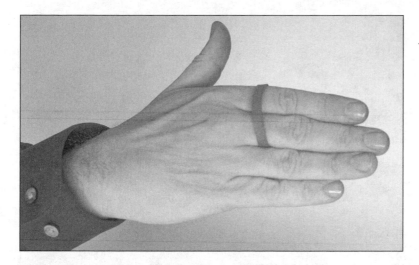

Place a rubber band around your first and middle fingers and slide it all the way down to the base of your fingers, audience view.

(Photo courtesy of Titus Photography.)

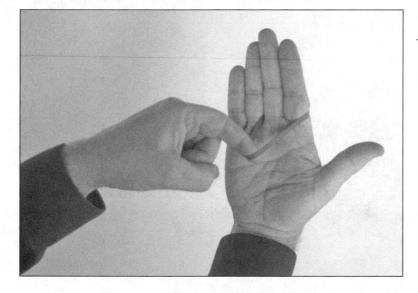

Stretch the rubber band away from your palm.

(Photo courtesy of Titus Photography.)

The rubber band stretched
around your first and middle
fingers, audience view.

(Photo courtesy of Titus
Photography.)

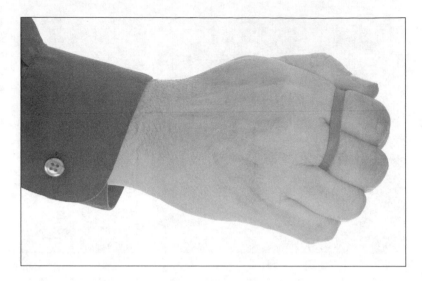

The rubber band is secretly
stretched across the tips of all
four fingers, your view.

(Photo courtesy of Titus
Photography.)

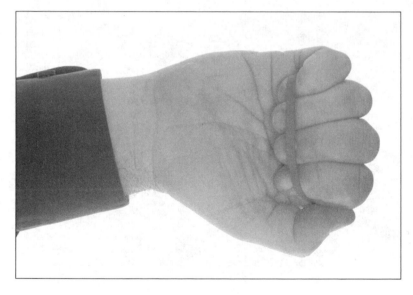

To repeat the trick, add this small variation first published by Harlan Tarbell in
Volume 1 of *The Tarbell Course in Magic* (see Appendix B). Start with one rubber band
encircling the base of the first and second fingers of your right hand, just like before.
Place a second rubber band around your right fingertip. Give the band a half twist,
and then stretch it around the tip of your middle finger. Follow this with another half
twist, and stretch the band over the tip of your ring finger. Give the rubber band a

final half twist, and wrap the rest of the rubber band around the tip of your little finger. Show both sides of your right hand, demonstrating how this "web" at the end of
your fingers traps the first rubber band in place, making it impossible for the lower
band to escape or jump over to the other fingers.

*Some people think that I somehow slip the rubber bands off the ends of these fingers and slide
them onto the others, too fast for the eye to see. I'll prove that's not what I'm doing.*

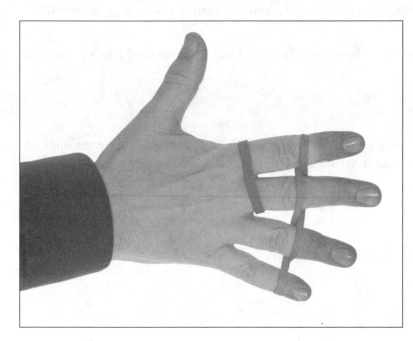

*Twist a second rubber band
around the ends of your right
fingers to "trap" the first
rubber band in place around
the base of your first and second fingers.*

*(Photo courtesy of Titus
Photography.)*

Just like before, secretly stretch the lower rubber band around the fingertips of your
right fist. Open your right hand. The lower rubber band magically jumps across to
your ring and middle fingers, even though it looks like the second, twisted rubber
band should have prevented it. Remove both rubber bands from your hands and drop
them onto the table or hand them to a spectator. You can stay to watch them try to do
the trick, but I think it's more fun to just walk away as they feverishly try to duplicate it.

The Great Escape

Who was the most famous magician of all time? Well, if you went back far enough,
you'd have to say Merlin, because of all those Olde English myths and hundreds
of books on Arthurian lore. If you're Gen X or just a bit older—would that be

Gen W?—your first thought might be David Copperfield. If you're under 21, or even 31, you probably said David Blaine or Criss Angel, because they're the guys on TV right now.

But to nonmagicians and people who know very little about magic, the answer is Harry Houdini. His posters advertised that "Nothing on Earth Can Hold Houdini a Prisoner." And it was true. Because Houdini could escape from anything, no matter how impossible the challenge, his feats gave him mythical status even in his own lifetime.

You're about to follow in the footsteps of Houdini, using a borrowed ring to represent the King of Escapes.

Effect

You thread a finger ring onto a string, hold the ring in your fist, and wrap the ends of the cord around your hand to secure everything in place. Nevertheless, the ring disappears!

Preparation

None, but you'll need a length of cord, such as a shoelace, about 2 feet long, and a borrowed finger ring.

Performance

Borrow a finger ring. Bring out the cord, which can be examined. If you remove one of your shoelaces in front of your spectators to do this trick, you're already proving it's "normal."

I'd like to perform one of Harry Houdini's greatest stunts. Since Houdini isn't available, we need a stunt double. For the purposes of the illusion, your ring will represent the legendary magician, and this shoelace will represent the chains and handcuffs that were used to lock him up. I call this trick "The Great Escape."

Thread the ring onto the string. Hold out your left hand, palm up, and set the ring on your hand at the base of your middle and ring fingers. Drape one end of the cord over the little-finger side of your hand; the other end drapes over your hand between your forefinger and thumb.

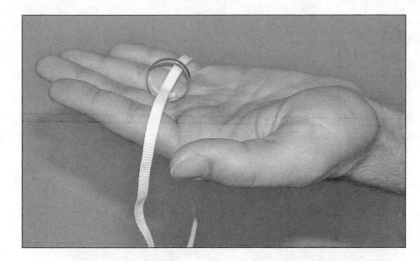

Set the threaded ring on your left palm between your middle and ring fingers, with the ends of the cord draping over the sides of your hand.

Close your left hand into a loose fist, and turn it palm down. As you do, allow the ring to drop to the base of your little finger. In fact, it should wind up as close as possible to the side of your fist without actually dropping out of your hand. (Let gravity and the weight of the ring do the work for you.) Hold your hand well below eye level so that no one watching sees the ring peeking out of the end of your hand.

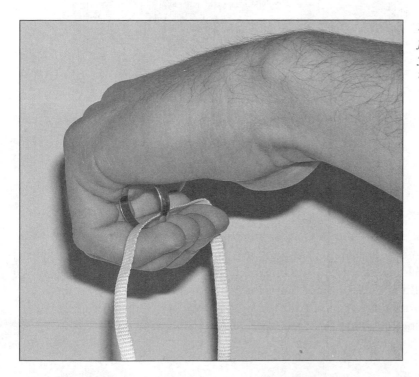

Hold the ring at the little-finger end of your fist so that you're just barely holding on to it, exposed view.

With your right hand, pick up the end of the cord coming out of the thumb side of your left fist. Lift it up and over the fist so that the cord drapes across the back of your hand, with its end of the cord hanging off the little-finger side.

Here comes the "secret move": cross your right hand over the top of your left fist, and curl your right fingers under your left hand. Release pressure on the finger ring and let it slide out of the end of your fist and onto your left fingers. Don't worry: the back of your right fingers will completely shield this from your spectators' view. (Again, the ring drops by gravity. The weight of the ring lets it fall into your right hand.)

Allow the ring to slip out of your left fist and onto your right fingers, exposed view.

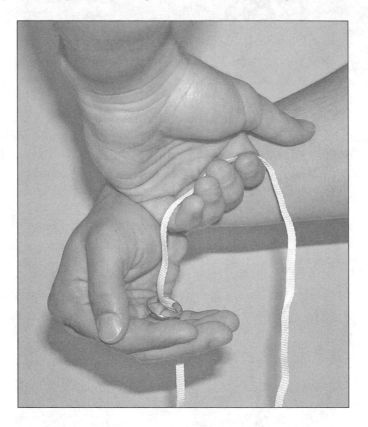

Close your right fingers a bit more tightly around the ring, just enough so that it doesn't fall out of your right hand. However, don't clutch the ring or close your hand into a fist: this would look suspicious and telegraph to the audience that your right hand is doing something sneaky. Slide your right hand to the end of the cord that's sticking out of the little-finger end of your left fist. As you do, your right fingers should carry along the ring that's threaded on the string.

When you get to the end of the cord, let the ring slip completely off the rope as your right thumb and forefinger grab the end of the cord. Bring this end of the string up and across the back of your left fist, completing a big "X" with the two ends of the cord crossing on the back of your left hand. The ring is still in your right hand, hidden in a finger-palm position.

Extend your left hand toward a spectator and ask him or her to place a finger on the "X" or even tie the two cords into a knot so that the ring can't escape. Then, casually reach into your pocket, claiming that you're going to get an "invisible key" or lock pick. While your hand is in your pocket, leave the ring there.

Houdini is locked in chains inside the jail. I'm going to use this invisible lock pick to help Houdini make his escape. I merely wave the key over his jail cell, and look …

Turn your left hand palm up. Open your hand to show that the ring is gone!

The ring is gone!

(Photo courtesy of Titus Photography.)

The trick *could* end right there, but chances are that the spectator will want the ring back. Once the volunteer sees that both of your hands are empty, you could simply reach into your pocket, pull out the ring, and admit, "I just sneaked it away. My hands are that quick. But be careful. That's how pickpockets get your wallet." This, however, is probably the weakest possible ending, because the audience may remember that your hand was in your pocket just a moment earlier.

Instead, you may want to keep the ring in your right hand instead of pocketing it. After the ring "escapes" from the string, you can immediately stick your right fingers into some nearby container—say an envelope, a sugar bowl, or a flowerpot, even a cup of coffee. Once your fingers are out of sight, let the ring drop to your fingertips. Then pull out your hand holding the ring, having magically "discovered" it in the new location.

Before I reproduce the ring, I personally prefer to show my hands empty, then do this clever ruse: first, I pat down my body with both hands, as if I'm feeling for the ring in one of my pockets. Then I actually reach into my right pants pocket and palm the ring at the same time as I stick my left hand into my shirt pocket. I first pull my right hand out of my pocket, letting it drop naturally to my side. Then I pull my left hand out of my shirt pocket and casually look down at my empty left palm. Nada. To the audience, it looks like I've casually checked all of my pockets for the ring but came up empty. I then "discover" the ring in some impossible place.

Finally, here's a popular ending you can do if you're performing for more than one person. You'll need to have a pen or pencil in your right pocket before the trick begins. Perform the trick up to the point that you cross the strands over the back of your left hand. (Remember, the ring is finger palmed in your right hand.) Ask one spectator to hold on to the two ends of the cord. Reach into your pants pocket with your right hand, and, as you pick up the pen, thread the ring onto it. Bring out the pen and hold it in your loosely closed right hand so that some of the pen sticks out of each side of your fist. Wave the pen over your left fist as if it were a magic wand. Ask a second spectator to hold the two ends of the pen.

Ask the first spectator to uncross the strands from the back of your hand, and hold the two ends so that the cord is vertical. (You'll have to give your fist a quarter turn so that your thumb and forefinger are pointing upward as your volunteer does this.) Tell both spectators to hold tightly. Pull your left fist back, stretching the cord as if you were drawing a bowstring. Aim your left hand toward your right hand, and then open your left hand. The cord will snap taut. Just an instant later, remove your right hand from the pen, spinning the ring around the pen as you do. It will look as if you have slingshot the ring from the rope onto the pen.

Go Fly a Kite

This tiny trick performed with common kite string actually has an unusual past, because two early versions of it were invented about 100 years ago by Harry Kellar and Karl Germain—guys who were known for their huge David Copperfield-size stage shows rather than for their close-up magic. Both of these illusionists went on to their Great Reward a long time ago, and many of the tricks they created haven't been performed since. But, like the Energizer Bunny, this tiny trick just keeps on going and going and going.

Tricky Tidbits

Among Harry Kellar's many claims to fame, in 1904 he introduced "The Levitation of the Princess Karnac," the stereotypical version of floating a lady in midair. Karl Germain suddenly quit magic in his 30s after a successful early career and became a lawyer. Imagine that! Within a few years of changing professions, Germain went totally blind. There's probably no connection; I'm just sayin'.

Effect

Two foot-long pieces of kite string merge into one in a spectator's hand.

Preparation

You'll need a piece of kite string or similar cord, which is actually composed of several smaller strands twisted together. Preferably, the piece should be around 2 feet long. Pinch the center of the string and separate about a 1-inch portion of the string into two separate sections, pulling some of the strands to the left and some to the right.

Twist each section of strands separately until they look like the ends of the string. Then rearrange the entire string so that it looks like you have two separate pieces side-by-side. Hold the "two" strings between your left thumb and forefinger: the two new "ends" should stick up above your thumb and finger. Your thumb and finger pinch the spot where the two strings cross (the actual center of the long string), and the real ends of the string dangle down below your thumb and finger.

Performance

Squeezing the string between your left thumb and forefinger, show your spectator that you have "two" pieces of string. (If you're very brave, and you've done an excellent job of configuring the gimmicked string, you can briefly display the "two" strings on your left palm.)

To prepare, separate a 1- to 2-inch length of the string into two sections.

(Photo courtesy of Titus Photography.)

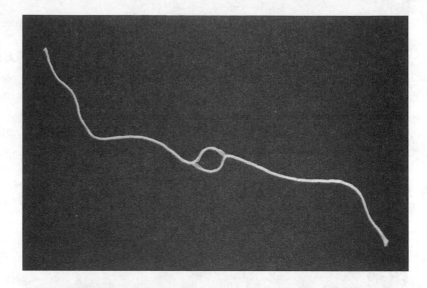

Twist the two sections from the middle of the string separately so that they look like the ends of the string.

(Photo courtesy of Titus Photography.)

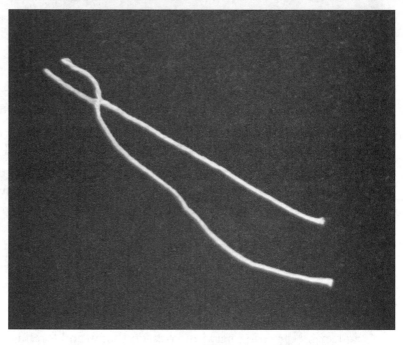

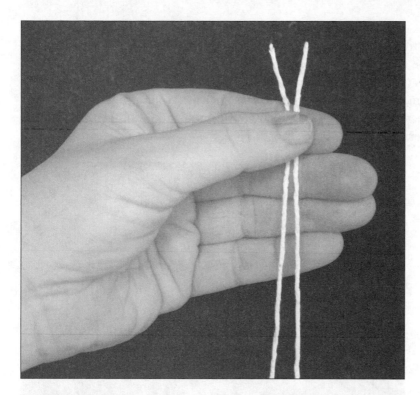

Hold the reconfigured cord so that it looks like two separate pieces of kite string by pinching it between your left thumb and forefinger.

(Photo courtesy of Titus Photography.)

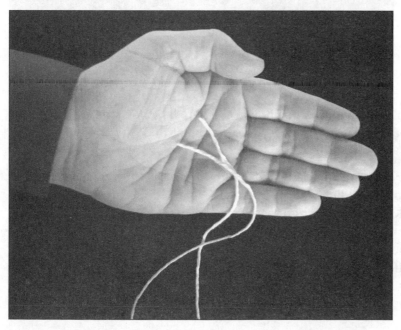

The gimmicked string can briefly be displayed on your open palm.

(Photo courtesy of Titus Photography.)

Hold the two strings over your spectator's open palm. Spread what appear to be the bottom ends of the "two" strings. Drape one end over the thumb side of the spectator's palm, and drape the other end over the little-finger side of her palm. Lay the top "ends" of the strings (actually the center of the gimmicked cord) onto the middle of your volunteer's palm, and ask the spectator to close her fist around them. Make sure that you keep the secret twist pinched between your thumb and forefinger until the person's fingers cover the "ends" of the string.

Lay the upper "ends" of the string on your spectator's open palm.

Rotate the spectator's hand so that it is palm down. There'll be one string sticking out of each side of the spectator's fist. The spectator thinks that these are two separate pieces of string.

Pick up one of the strings with your left hand and the "other" with your right hand. Pull the string that you're holding with your left hand a few inches; then pull the string that you're holding with your right hand a few inches. Continue this motion, pulling the string back and forth. Inside the spectator's fist, the string is secretly reassembling itself. To the spectator, it feels as if the two separate pieces of string are melding together in her hand. Finally, pull the string all the way through and out one end of the spectator's fist. The two strings have joined into one!

Pull the "strings" back and forth through the spectator's fist.

The string is restored!

Everything you needed for the tricks so far in this chapter have been pretty easy to find. Likewise, the next few tricks are perfect to perform in a restaurant or bar, because all the stuff you need is already on the table or nearby.

Trapdoor Trickery

This impromptu piece can be a real killer if you perform it as a throwaway at dinner. The penetration of the cloth is so convincing that onlookers swear you must have cut a slit in it.

If you're not comfortable playing with sharp objects, instead of a knife you can use some other piece of silverware, a pen, a pencil, or even a soda straw. I often perform it with my pocket comb.

Effect

You push a knife through the center of a napkin, claiming to use an invisible trapdoor. The cloth is then shown to be unharmed.

Preparation

None. You'll need a knife and a cloth napkin or handkerchief.

Performance

Pick up a cloth napkin (or pocket handkerchief) and show it to your spectators. They can examine it closely if they want to.

It's hard to believe, but there's a trapdoor in the middle of this napkin. Can you see it? No? But it's really there. Let me prove it.

Form your left hand into a loose fist and hold it so that your thumb and forefinger are uppermost. Cover your fist with a napkin so that its center is directly over the top of your fist.

Pick up a knife with your right hand. Gently poke the knife into the center of the napkin so that it pushes the cloth into your left fist between your thumb and forefinger, making a depression or well about an inch or two deep. (If you want to make sure that you don't actually cut through the napkin, use the handle end of the knife.) As you poke the knife downward, you can tilt your left hand toward the audience if you want to, so they can see that you're actually making the indentation.

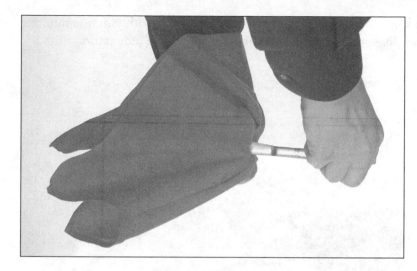

Using the knife, make a depression in the napkin that's covering your fist.

(Photo courtesy of Titus Photography.)

Turn your wrist so that the back of your hand (still under the napkin) is toward the audience. Under cover of the hanky, open your hand a bit so that there's space between your thumb and fingers, making your hand into a sort of "C" shape.

Open your fist into a "C" formation under cover of the napkin, exposed view.

(Photo courtesy of Titus Photography.)

Using the knife, make one or two more short pokes into the depression in the napkin. As the knife approaches your hand for one last poke, however, instead of making a downward thrust, push the center of the knife blade straight in against the side of the handkerchief between your left thumb and fingers. Continue pushing the knife into the open "C" formed by your left hand under the napkin until the knife butts the cloth up against your left palm. Immediately close your left fingers back into a tight fist, surrounding the knife and holding it in place. Performed smoothly in one motion, this should simply look like you're making one final poke into the indentation in the napkin.

The knife, seen here just before your fingers completely encircle it, exposed view.

(Photo courtesy of Titus Photography.)

Slowly push down on the knife. From the audience's angle, it looks like the knife is penetrating the middle of the handkerchief, but it's actually traveling through the secret "tunnel" you just created in your fist. Grasp the knife as it comes out the bottom of your fist, and set it aside. If you prefer, you can shove the knife through with one quick thrust, and you can also allow the knife to drop through to the floor or clang onto the tabletop. Whisk the napkin off your hand, spread the cloth out, and point to its center to show that there's no rip or hole.

The knife went right through the trapdoor. And once the trapdoor has slammed shut, the napkin is restored!

Salt of the Earth

In magical jargon, this trick as well as the previous one belong to the same category of effects: it's a "penetration"—where one object seems to go through another without causing harm to either.

In this routine, not only will you learn a seemingly spur-of-the-moment trick that will serve you for years to come, but you'll also find out about the fine art of lapping—a magical method used to make things disappear. You'll also be introduced to the concept of misdirection, in which you get the audience to look where you want them to look so that you can get away with the secret dirty work necessary to do the trick.

Effect

You say that you're going to make a coin penetrate through the top of a table. To hide the "secret move," you cover the coin with a salt shaker, and then cover the shaker with a napkin. You slap down on the napkin, and it crushes flat to the table. You've tricked them: the salt shaker, rather than the coin, has gone through the table.

Preparation

None, but you'll need a coin, a salt shaker, and a paper napkin large enough to cover the shaker. Needless to say, this trick should only be performed if there's already a salt shaker nearby. If you bring one out of your pocket, even if the salt shaker is ungimmicked, the trick won't have much impact.

Performance

Do you think it's possible to have two things occupy the same space at the same time? Of course not. But perhaps—and I don't what to get too technical here—perhaps on the atomic level, two objects can actually pass around or through each other. Isn't that how radio waves get through solid walls into a room when there aren't any windows? They don't go around the building and come in the back door. Somehow the atoms pass around each other but appear to be going through one another. Heavy, huh? Let me try an experiment to see if I can duplicate the phenomenon.

Toss a coin, let's say a quarter, onto the table.

I'm going to try to push this quarter right through the top of the table. Of course, now I've just broken one of the first rules of magic: never tell the audience in advance what you're going to do. Why? Because now you know what to look for, and it makes my job twice as difficult. So I have to hide the "secret move."

Cover the coin with a paper napkin.

Are you able to see the coin through the paper? You wouldn't tell me even if you could, would you? I'm going to make it impossible for you to see. But first, let's check to see if the coin's still on top of the table.

Lift the napkin with your right hand so that they can see the coin. Pull your right hand back toward the table's edge, supposedly to give the spectators a full view. In actuality, you're just setting this up as a natural action for when you have to do it later on in the trick.

Let's cover the coin with something that's even harder to see through.

Pretend to notice the salt shaker for the first time. Cover the coin with the salt shaker. (If there's no salt shaker on your table but you know there's one on a table nearby or at the bar, don't go for the shaker immediately. Look around, pretending that you're trying to find something that would be appropriate to use. Then decide on the salt shaker and ask someone to pass it to you. By letting the spectator hand you the salt shaker, you don't have to ask them to examine it to prove that it's normal.)

How about—the salt shaker? I know you can't see through that. *But, just to make sure, I'll cover it with the napkin as well.*

Place the napkin on top of the salt shaker, and press the napkin down so that the paper molds itself to the shape of the shaker. The napkin forms a sort of shell as it covers the salt shaker. Wrap your right fingers and thumb around the napkin-covered salt shaker. (If a single napkin doesn't completely cover the salt shaker, feel free to add more.)

Now, before I make it go through the table, does anyone remember what kind of coin it is? A quarter? I think I fooled you already.

Pick up the salt shaker, still covered by the napkin. As you look down at the coin, nonchalantly move your right hand back toward the edge of the table.

No, you're right. It's still a quarter. Here, let me bring the quarter real close to you.

The Magic Word

Lapping is a technique used by a seated magician to secretly drop something into the lap to dispose of it, usually to make it disappear. The magician is said to lap the object.

With your left forefinger, push the quarter across the table toward your spectator. As you do, bring your right hand back far enough to clear the edge of the table. Relax your pressure on the napkin, and let the salt shaker drop into your lap. (Magicians call this method of using your lap to get rid of an object *lapping*.) Even after the salt shaker has fallen out, the napkin will keep its shape.

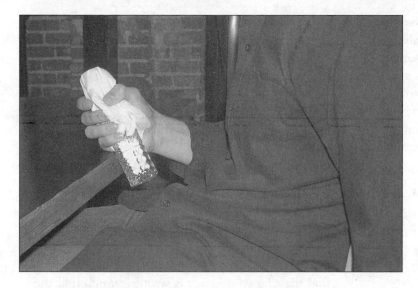

Release pressure on the napkin to drop the salt shaker into your lap.

Here are three things to keep in mind as you release the salt shaker into your lap:

◆ Keep your right hand and the napkin level with the edge of the table as you let the shaker fall out. If your hand goes underneath or drops below the edge of the table, the audience will be suspicious.

◆ You'll give away the trick if you shake the napkin to make the salt shaker fall out. Let gravity do the work.

◆ Make sure you continue to hold the napkin as if it contains the salt shaker even after it's dropped out. If you squeeze the napkin too soon, even a little, they'll realize the shaker is gone.

Extend your right hand to cover the coin with the napkin, which is still shaped as if it contains the salt shaker. Pause a few moments. Then lift your right hand, and immediately slap it down, crushing the napkin flat against the table. Pick up the napkin, and tear it into shreds.

I'm sorry. The coin hasn't gone through the table. That's too easy. It's the salt shaker!

Reach into your lap and pick up the salt shaker. Continue to extend your arm under the table so that it's directly underneath the spot where the shaker supposedly went through. Tap the salt shaker against the bottom of the table. Then bring it out from under the table, and set it in front of the spectator. This will enhance the illusion that the salt shaker penetrated the center of the table, far away from its edge.

Some magicians like to have the spectator share in the experience of crushing the napkin. The routine is the same, almost up to the moment you squash the napkin. After you lap the salt shaker, set the napkin shell over the coin. As you hold the napkin with your right hand, ask your spectator to gently place her hand on top of the salt shaker. Use your left hand to help move her hand into position, making sure that the person doesn't try to grab or push down on the napkin. After the spectator's hand is in place, rest your left hand on top of it. Pause just a second, and then push down hard with your left hand as you move your right hand out of the way. To the spectator, it will feel as if her hand pushed the salt shaker through the table, and she will swear that she actually felt the shaker up until the last second!

The Magic Word _____

Misdirection is a diversionary technique used to direct the audience, through word, look, or action, to focus their attention where the magician wants them to so that he or she can perform a sleight or other secret action.

Ideally, your spectators should be seated across from you at the table when you perform this trick. But after you've been performing it for a while, you'll find that the *misdirection* is strong enough that the audience can almost be surrounding you. In the case of this trick, you misdirect the audience by concentrating their attention on the coin instead of the salt shaker.

Because the success of this trick depends upon your ability to lap an object, here are a few suggestions on how to make your lapping technique easier and more deceptive:

◆ To prevent things from slipping and falling between your legs, sit with both feet flat on the floor and the knees pressed together.

◆ If there's a space between your thighs, cover your lap with a handkerchief or cloth napkin.

◆ Never look down into your lap when dropping or retrieving objects. The audience's eyes will follow yours, and it'll give away the secret.

The Gypsy Switch

A lot of people ask, "What's the big deal about being a magician? Sure, you can do card tricks. But can you do anything practical?" Well, that's quite a challenge. You may not be able to pick the winning lottery numbers, but you can change, say, a stick of chewing gum into a dollar bill. Is that practical enough for you?

Although I'm explaining this trick with a stick of chewing gum, you could just as easily change a blank piece of paper into a dollar bill, or you could change denominations from a one to a twenty. Known as the "Gypsy Switch," this is a practical move for a street magician to switch any two items, as long as the object can be palmed in your hand.

Effect

You cover a stick of chewing gum with a napkin or handkerchief. When you uncover it, it has changed into a dollar bill.

Preparation

Fold a dollar bill in half widthwise (so that the crease goes down the middle of Washington's face.) Fold it in half again along its width, and again. This will give you a folded bill that is almost exactly the same shape and size as a stick of chewing gum. Place the folded bill in your right pocket or where you can easily get to it.

Performance

While you're introducing the trick, casually reach into your pocket and palm the folded bill in your right hand. One of the bill's narrow ends should be pressed against the inside of your right middle and ring fingers, somewhere around the knuckle joint, and the other end should push up against the heel or mound at the base of your hand. If you slightly curl your fingers, the bill will stay pressed against your palm.

With your left hand, pick up a cloth napkin or a handkerchief. Place the napkin over your right hand, and, as soon as it's out of spectators' view, open it flat, palm up. Spread the napkin evenly over your hand so that it's centered over your palm.

Ask to borrow a stick of chewing gum. Lay it on the center of the napkin, directly on top of folded dollar bill. The two should be lined up as close to one another as possible, separated only by the napkin.

Hold your left hand over the napkin. Press your left thumb onto the stick of chewing gum. Wrap your left fingers around the end of your right fingers. Slide your right hand out from under the napkin, but as you do, pinch your left fingers against the napkin, holding the dollar bill in place. Lift your left hand, with the back of the fingers toward the audience.

Lay the napkin on top of your right hand, hiding the dollar bill, exposed view.

(Photo courtesy of Titus Photography.)

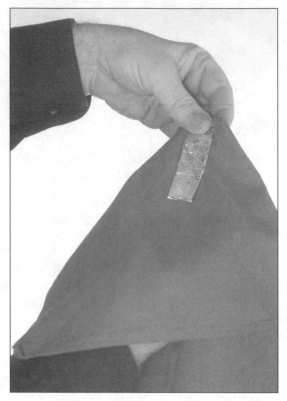

Pinch the dollar bill between the folds of the napkin as you lift it. Your left thumb presses the gum against the outside of the napkin, your view.

(Photo courtesy of Titus Photography.)

In the same continuous action, turn the whole bundle over, and lay the napkin on top of your right hand. The stick of chewing gum goes into the same position that the dollar bill was only moments before.

Wrap your left hand around the corners of the napkin, and lift the napkin away from your right hand. As you do, turn the back of your right hand toward the audience so that they don't see the stick of gum held in your hand.

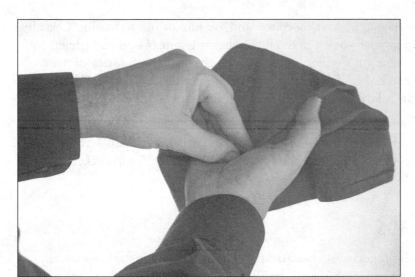

Lay the napkin back onto your right hand, so that the chewing gum is in the same position that the dollar was earlier.

(Photo courtesy of Titus Photography.)

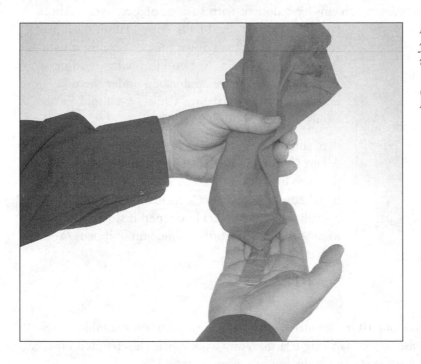

Lift the napkin away from your right hand, exposed view.

(Photo courtesy of Titus Photography.)

(By lifting the napkin away from your right hand, the spectator's eyes will follow the napkin. If you removed your right hand out from under the cloth, all eyes would follow your right hand, which is secretly palming the stick of gum.)

Hand the ends of the napkin to your spectator, and ask him or her to hold it. Casually place your right hand in your pocket to ditch the chewing gum. Or, if you prefer, reach into your pocket for your wallet and, while it is there, leave the stick of gum behind. Take out your ATM or debit card and wave it over the napkin. Say that you'd like to make a deposit. Ask the spectator to open up the napkin. The chewing gum has changed into a dollar bill!

I don't know about you, but learning all this magic has made me thirsty. Grab a Coke or a brewsky—or five—and you'll be ready for this next bit of tabletop trickery. And while you're at it, hold on to the bottle caps.

The Conjuring Caps

The trick in which four objects widely separated on a table come together—usually with no covering other than your hands—has been performed longer than anyone can remember. Over the years, magicians have done it with various objects such as dice, coins, corks, and small balls. Max Malini, born in Austria in 1873, was known for performing it with sugar cubes. In 1975, S. Leo Horowitz's version of the Malini routine was published under the now politically incorrect name "Chink-A-Chink" in the Louis Tannen book *Stars of Magic*.

> **Tricky Tidbits**
>
> This is a perfect trick for a bar or party where there'll be plenty of drinks served. Sure, you *can* use soda bottle caps. But if you're using the caps from bottles of beer that the people have just finished, you can always joke, "The more you drink, the better the magic will look. In fact, the more you drink, the better *I* will look."

A twentieth-century magician from New York, Albert Goshman, is credited with being the first to perform it with bottle caps. To introduce the trick, he whetted the audience's curiosity by bringing out a small wooden chest. He opened it slowly, dumped four bottle caps onto the table, and quipped, "You expected rubies?"

Effect

Four bottle caps, set about 10 inches apart in a square formation on the table, magically assemble into one corner. (In magic jargon, any trick in which separated objects come together in one place is generically known as an *assembly*.)

Preparation

You'll need five identical bottle caps, although the audience never sees more than four of them at any one time. You'll also need to be able to lap (which you just learned in an earlier trick, "Salt of the Earth.")

And before we get into the nuts and bolts of this trick, you'll have to be able to bust a move (okay, perform a sleight) known as the "classic palm." Now, I discussed palming in the last chapter, but this type of palm is a bit different. You'll actually be concealing the object in the middle of your palm, not curled in your fingers.

It'll be easiest to learn if you try the move first with a coin. If possible, use a half-dollar; otherwise, a quarter will do. Hold out your right hand, palm up. Place the coin in the center of your palm. Now *very* slightly cup your hand, flexing (or raising) your thumb and little finger. Notice how the coin is squeezed between the fleshy pads at the base of your thumb and your little finger? Want to see how well the coin stays in place? Move your hand around a little. Shake it. The coin stays put! And as long as you're not clutching your hand into a claw, the way you're holding your hand will look perfectly natural to an audience. This sleight is the classic palm.

Now, every hand is different, so don't give up if the coin falls out of your hand the first few times you try it. The coin doesn't have to be palmed in the exact center of your hand. In fact, I find that a coin stays in place better in my hand if I keep it about an inch closer to my wrist. You'll have to experiment to see where you can get the best grip.

Now that you know how to classic palm a coin, this trick will be a snap when you palm bottle caps. Try it! Set a bottle cap on the table with its ridges pointed upward. Lay your empty right hand palm down, onto the cap, so that the bottle cap is some-where near the center of your palm. Press down lightly on the cap. Notice how it digs into your palm?

Now, flex your thumb and little finger as you did when you practiced palming the coin. Lift your hand. The cap clings to your right hand in a classic palm position. This is the manner in which you'll be palming the bottle caps throughout this entire routine.

At the start of the trick, you'll need to have one cap secretly palmed in your right hand. Alternately, the five caps could be in your pocket, and when you reach in to bring them out, palm one of the caps and drop the other four onto the table.

A bottle cap in classic palm position, exposed view.

Performance

Lay four identical bottle caps, ridges up, in a square shape on the table in front of you, so that there's one cap at each corner of an invisible square. For the purpose of explanation, I'll call the two corners closest to you near the edge of the table, from your point of view, the Inner Left (IL) and the Inner Right (IR). The others will be the Outer Left (OL) and Outer Right (OR).

Set one bottle cap in each of the four corners in a square layout on the table. A fifth cap is classic palmed in your right hand, exposed view.

Set your left hand on any of the caps and your right hand (which still has a fifth cap palmed in it) on top of any of the others. Switch your hands to cover any two other caps. Don't drop or pick up any of the caps at this point. This byplay is just to accustom the audience to how you'll be covering the caps when you perform the trick.

Sequence One

Gently cover the IR cap with your right hand and the IL cap with your left hand. As you do, relax your grip on the palmed cap in your right hand, and let it drop next to the cap already at the IR position. At the same time, press your left hand down against the bottle cap in the IL position, and palm the cap. This should take just an instant. It shouldn't be obvious that you're pressing down on the bottle caps. Ideally, it should look as if the hands are only hovering over the caps and not actually touching them.

With your hands at their respective corners, wiggle your fingers, as if you were making some kind of magical gesture. Look from your right hand to your left hand as if you were seeing an invisible transfer taking place.

Lift both of your hands and draw them back to the edge of the table. Rest your fingertips on the tabletop, and let your palms extend back over the edge of the table. (By doing this action now, it'll look natural when you need to do it later to get rid of the extra cap.) To the spectator, it looks like the cap from the inner left corner of the square has joined the cap at the inner right corner.

Sequence Two

After only the briefest of pauses, cover the two caps at the IR corner with your right hand as you cover the cap at the OL corner with your left hand. Press down lightly on the bottle caps. Classic palm one of the caps at the IR corner in your right hand as you drop the cap palmed in your left hand, adding it to the one already at the OL position. Bring your hands back to the edge of the table, just like before. It appears that one of the bottle caps from the IR corner has joined the cap at the OL corner.

Sequence Three

With your left hand, cover the cap at the IR corner. Cover the bottle cap at the OL corner with your right hand. Be careful that you don't actually cross your arms, which would be needlessly confusing—and, if not confusing, certainly suspicious-looking. Classic palm the bottle cap at the IR corner in your left hand as you drop the cap in your right hand next to the two bottle caps already at the OL corner. Once again, bring your hands back to the edge of the table so that the audience can plainly see that the third bottle cap has jumped.

Sequence Four

Okay, so you're probably ahead of me. Cover the three caps at the OL corner with your left hand as you cover the cap at the OR corner with your right hand. Press down lightly on the bottle caps. Palm the cap at your OR with your right hand as you drop the palmed cap in your left hand next to the other three at the OL corner. Wiggle your fingers. Bring your hands back to the edge of the table to reveal that the fourth bottle cap has joined the other three at the OL corner of the imaginary square on the table.

As the spectator is gawking at the assembly of the four caps, relax your pressure on the bottle cap that's classic palmed in your right hand. Let the cap fall into your lap. Then casually turn both of your hands palm up to show that both hands are empty and that there are no extra bottle caps. (Don't make any mention of this; just let them decide it for themselves.)

While I'm performing this final sequence I sometimes say, "The last one is the most difficult, so I'll do it a little different." Why? Well, it's a common phrase that magicians use in the last phase of tricks that have recurring sequences—whether or not they're really planning to perform any kind of a variation. Sometimes it's said light-heartedly just to break up the repetitive nature of the sequences. But, in point of fact, the last sequence often *is* the hardest because you've broken the magician's rule of never repeating a trick. After the first time through, the audience knows what to look for, so every time you repeat the moves, it gives them one more chance to catch you.

The other thing that makes the end of this trick "harder" is that you have to get rid of the extra cap. Fortunately, everyone will be looking to see if the fourth cap has arrived, so lapping the extra cap shouldn't be too difficult. But your skills at misdirection will be severely tested if people are "burning your hand"—technical magician and gambler jargon meaning the spectators are looking so intently that they're "burning your hands" with their eyes. Once you've practiced and performed this trick a couple of hundred times, however, you'll no doubt be so perfectly proficient with palming and lapping that there won't be any problem.

Once you've learned this routine, feel free to play around with it. You certainly don't have to make the bottle caps jump in the order that I've described. (Horowitz and Goshman had theirs jump in completely different directions.) You may come up with your own sequences that make more sense or feel more comfortable for you to perform.

I usually perform this as a straightforward presentation of pure sleight-of-hand. I don't use any special patter or story while I'm putting the bottle caps through their paces.

When Goshman performed this trick, he did it to music. If you're at a party, you might try timing the trick to whatever's playing. But if you can come up with some story about why four people might congregate together, why not go for it? The bottle caps could represent …

◆ Meeting at the mall

◆ Speed dating

◆ Forwarding text messages or e-mails

◆ Hooking up with friends

◆ A track star jumping hurdles

◆ Playing "follow the leader"

◆ Running chores around town

◆ Terrorists moving between safe houses

◆ Unwanted presents being re-gifted

Up Yours

Before we wrap up this chapter, here are three more tricks with common objects that'll require you to use everything you've learned so far: misdirection, lapping, and your acting ability. In addition, you'll be given a totally new weapon—sleeving—to add to your arsenal as a street magician.

Effect

You scoop up a spoon from the table, twist it, and then make it completely disappear.

Preparation

None.

Performance

Place a spoon on the table directly in front of you, parallel and close to the edge of the table. It doesn't matter which way the bowl and handle are pointed.

Open both hands flat. Reach over and set the little-finger sides of both hands on the table in front of the spoon, overlapping the fingertips so that the spoon's completely shielded from the spectator's eyes.

Place your upright hands like a curtain in front of the spoon to hide it from the spectator's sight, your view.

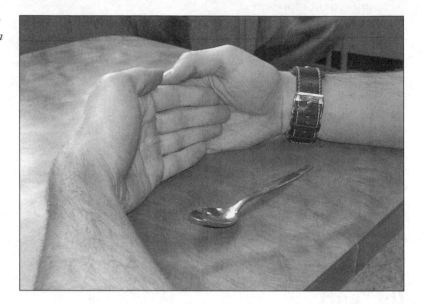

You'll now perform a series of moves in one continuous action. Keeping both hands together, move them to the edge of the table, dragging the spoon along. As you continue to pull your hands toward your body and past the edge of the table, let the spoon fall into your lap. Then curl your fingers, closing your hands into fists. Tilt both hands together so that the sides of your thumbs and forefingers meet. When you've finished, you'll be holding both hands in front of you in closed fists, side by side. This whole sequence should look like you've scooped up the spoon and are holding it in your closed fists.

Swivel your right hand forward, away from your body at the same time as you tilt your left wrist upward toward yourself. Then revolve both hands in the opposite directions. This should look like you're trying to twist and bend the spoon. Suddenly stop rotating your hands. Open both hands and give them one quick, loud clap. The spoon has disappeared!

Hold your two fists side by side as if your fingers were curled around the spoon. By revolving the hands in opposite directions, it will look like the spoon is being twisted out of shape.

Up the Sleeve

Almost anytime you make something disappear, no matter how big it is, someone says (or is thinking), "It's up your sleeve." Well, in this case, they'd actually be right. You're going to learn a very simple way to make an object disappear by shooting it up your sleeve. Now, there are many techniques for *sleeving*, most of which take years to master, but this one will work the first or second time you try it, guaranteed.

The Magic Word

Sleeving is a general jargon term for using the sleeves of a jacket, shirt, or blouse to conceal items to make them disappear or appear. By quickly shooting an object up the sleeve, it can be made to vanish. On the other hand, by having something hidden up the sleeve and lowering the arm, the object can secretly drop into the hand to be produced later.

Effect

As you pass a spoon across the table, it vanishes at your fingertips.

Preparation

None, except that you must be wearing a long-sleeved shirt, blouse, or jacket. The cuff should be loose fitting at the wrist, but not obviously so. (Although some magicians who do a lot of sleeving have their shirts or jackets specially tailored to flare the cuffs to make it easier, that's not necessary for this rudimentary trick, or, indeed, for most sleeve work.)

Performance

Sit down at a table opposite your spectator. Move one of the spoons on the table so that it's directly in front of your right arm, perpendicular to the edge of the table. Hold your right hand about an inch above the spoon. The pad of your middle fingertip should be right over the tip of the bowl.

Press down with your middle finger. This tilts the handle upward, off the table. With a quick, sudden snap, curl your middle finger into your palm. This will push the spoon backward, shooting it up your sleeve.

Your middle finger presses down on the bowl, pivoting the handle upward, exposed view.

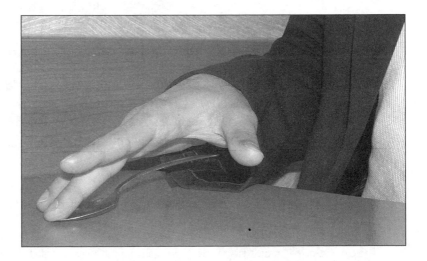

As soon as you feel that the spoon has made it safely up your sleeve, lift your right hand off the table. As you do so, lightly curl your fingers together to make it look like you're holding the spoon. Believe it or not, unless you call attention to the fact, the audience won't immediately notice that the spoon is already gone. Make a quick, upward tossing motion with your hand as if you were throwing the spoon into the air. As you do, look upward. The audience will follow with their eyes. The spoon will seem to vanish in midair.

Charms

Here's another way to make the spoon vanish: pretend to lift the spoon from the table as already described, but move your hand to your cup of coffee. Start to stir your drink, but then suddenly notice that you can't: the spoon has disappeared from your fingertips!

Later, to retrieve the spoon, let your hands drop into your lap and allow the spoon to fall out of your sleeve by gravity. You can then either pocket it, casually add it back onto the table when attention is elsewhere, or, if the room is carpeted, drop it on the floor. (If you don't take the spoon out of your sleeve, either you'll be taking it home with you or, worse, forget that it's there and accidentally have it fall out at an embarrassing moment.)

Here's an alternate ending to the trick, which also clears up the problem of getting the spoon out of your sleeve. You can make the spoon reappear! After it's vanished and you've shown both of your hands empty, stand up. Look down on the floor as if searching for the spoon. As you do, lower your arms to your sides, and curl your right fingers. The spoon will drop into your right hand. Clutch the spoon at your fingertips. Look up, and turn your head slightly to the left. Pretend to see something floating invisibly in the air about eye level. Thrust out your right arm, and show the spoon held at your fingertips. Because the spectator's eyes can't focus on the spoon until your arm stops, the spoon will seem to appear at your fingertips at that very instant.

The Vanishing Dagger

Here's a trick that you can play for thrills or laughs. It involves a knife, so it suggests a bit of urban danger and adventure. There's a suggestion of piracy, so it has a bit of street swagger. But most of all, it involves a real mystery. How does the dagger disappear?

Effect

You hold a knife clenched between your teeth. You cover it briefly with your hands and then, depending upon which presentation you want to perform, it either vanishes or you swallow it!

Preparation

First, you'll need a lightweight steak knife. Blunt and round the tip. Smooth down the blade so it's very, very dull. Let me repeat that again. You need a dulled and blunted knife. Its point should not be able to cut you. Its blade should be so dull that it cannot possibly pierce your skin. Got that?

You also have to make a *pull*, which is a gimmick used to make stuff secretly vanish. (Yes, some tricks actually are done that way!) On a pull, a piece of elastic is stretched from a hook-up (either up a sleeve or to the inside of your jacket) to the object that you're going to vanish.

> **The Magic Word** _____
>
> A **pull** is a secret gimmick used to vanish objects up your sleeve or into your jacket. One end of an elastic band is usually affixed to your upper arm, runs down your sleeve and is attached to the item you're going to make disappear. Rather than being hooked directly to the object, the end of the pull could be a receptacle of some sort into which the article to be vanished is stuffed or a clip to which the item can be attached. A release of the taut elastic "pulls" the object up your sleeve and out of sight. The pull could also be attached to your belt or the inside of a jacket to make things vanish inside your coat.

To make the pull for this trick, tie one end of a strong, black sewing elastic cord, or a very thick rubber band to a heavy-duty safety pin. The other end of the cord should be affixed to the end of the handle of the knife. How you attach it will depend upon your particular knife. You might have to wrap the cord around the handle several times before tying it off. If there's a hole in the end of the wooden handle, you could thread the cord through the hole and tie it up that way. The safety-pin end of the pull should be attached to your shirt or inner coat sleeve somewhere above the right elbow. When you let the knife dangle loosely along your arm, the tip of the very dull, very blunt knife should be about 2"×3" above your shirt cuff. Put on your jacket so that the knife is up your right coat sleeve, and you're armed and dangerous.

Performance

Just before you're ready to perform the trick, use your left hand to secretly pull the knife out of your sleeve and into your right hand. Turn slightly to your left so that the people watching are to your right side, just enough to conceal the elastic band coming out of your sleeve. Hold the handle of the knife at your right fingertips. Place the blade of the knife in your teeth in traditional pirate style. Keep your right thumb and forefinger pinched on the knife to prevent it from shooting up your sleeve. Otherwise, your right hand can be held fairly open. Strike your best Jack Sparrow pose.

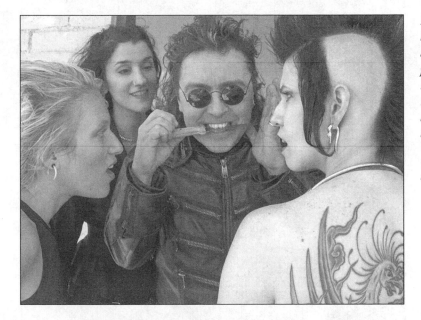

Hold the blade of the knife between your teeth in traditional pirate style. (In this posed shot, the elastic band has been removed. Normally, the right hand would be tilted downward more to hide the cord.)

(Photo by Paul Draper. Photo courtesy of Jeff McBride.)

Open your left hand flat and rest your palm against the rounded tip of the knife. Slightly curl your right hand, allowing the end of the handle to nestle down into your right palm. Bend the fingers of both hands at your knuckles, so that the backs of your fingers hide the knife from the spectators' view.

Slightly extend both arms forward away from your body. As you do, release the end of the knife handle from your palms and allow the elastic band to pull the knife up your sleeve. (The larger motion of your arms will cover any small movement at your cuff line as the knife zips past.)

Bring your fingers together in front of the knife, shielding it from the spectators' sight, exposed view.

(Photo by Paul Draper. Photo courtesy of Jeff McBride.)

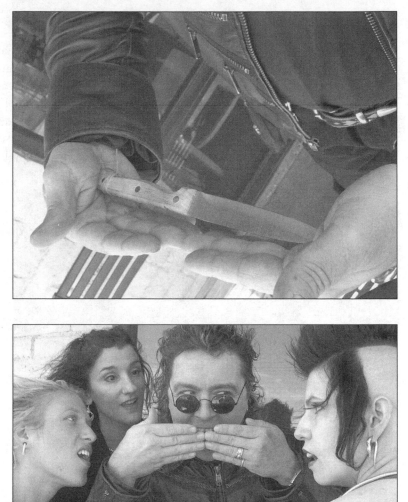

From the audience's point of view, you've merely brought your hands up to momentarily conceal the knife.

(Photo by Paul Draper. Photo courtesy of Jeff McBride.)

The success of the trick now depends upon your acting skill. The knife is already gone, but the spectators don't know that. If you simply want to make the knife disappear, separate your hands slowly and show both sides. The knife is nowhere to be seen. (You might want to keep your teeth clenched to reinforce the idea that the knife disappeared while it was still being held in your mouth.) Or you can toss both hands up into the air as you separate them. Follow the imaginary upward flight of the knife with your eyes. The audience will look up as well. When your eyes drop and meet theirs, just shrug. It's gone.

The knife is gone!

(Photo by Paul Draper. Photo courtesy of Jeff McBride.)

But here's an interesting and somewhat gruesome twist for a finish. Instead of tossing the hands upward, keep the fingertips of both hands pressed together. Raise your left hand a bit higher as you place the heel of your right hand against your open lips. Move both hands downward together, in a gesture that suggests you're shoving the knife down your throat. Swallow. Gulp. [Insert spectators' screams here.]

Well, that's about it for this section of the book. We've gone from playing cards to fire and pain, and then ended up with making the everyday unbelievable. So, now: do you like to get frightened? In the next few chapters, we'll deal with the Undead, the paranormal, and the unknowable.

The Least You Need to Know

◆ Some of the magic performed with ordinary objects is the most amazing because people know what the stuff can and can't do.

◆ Many of the tricks performed by today's street performers are classics dating back to legendary masters of the art.

◆ When performing while sitting down, magicians can get rid of gimmicks and make things vanish simply by dropping them into their laps.

◆ Magicians regularly use misdirection—the art of getting people to look where you want them to—to draw the audience's attention away from their secret moves.

Part 4

Things That Go Bump in the Night

Most people's worst nightmare when they hear a magician's going to perform is a geek in an ill-fitting tuxedo, telling corny jokes and doing tricks that make him or her look stupid.

Well, forget about all that. The tricks in this part are designed to blow those birthday party clowns out of the water. Think bizarre and eerie. Think communication with ghosts and poltergeists. Think tribal sorcerers, mind over matter, and hypnosis. Think Things That Go Bump in the Night.

These are the themes you'll be exploring in dozens of tricks that take you into strange, odd, and curious territory. You'll take on the spoon-bending and telekinetic powers made famous by psychics such as Uri Geller. I'll also reveal the tricks used by shamans to seem to be able to control the forces of nature and the workings of the human mind and body.

Turn the page, if you dare.

11

The Undead

In This Chapter

◆ Making contact with the Great Beyond

◆ "Living or dead" tests

◆ The center tear: a classic mind-reading trick

◆ Spinning keys and tiny hands

In ancient times, every wizard, sorcerer, enchantress, oracle, or shaman claimed to be in touch with the Spirit World. It was part of the job description. Why should the street magician of today be any different? Magicians, like the mediums of old, often perform tricks that suggest they can communicate with the dead. If you play your cards right, the phantoms will seem to do your bidding.

What do the tricks in this chapter have in common? In all of them, the street magicians apparently aren't doing the trick. Ghosts are. The magicians are just conduits for the paranormal activity. All of the phenomena—whether it's talking to the Great Beyond or a key spinning in your palm—are being carried out by the phantoms and poltergeists themselves.

The Ghost Whisperer

"Do you think that's it possible to communicate with the Dead?" What a perfect question for a street magician to ask to start out a trick. Because of its paranormal overtones, the *living or dead test* you're about to learn is another classic theme in bizarre magick.

The Magic Word _____

A **living or dead test** is a psychic demonstration in which the medium, "sensitive," or mentalist is able to identify which people are, well, living and which are dead just by hearing or reading their names (or other identifying properties).

This trick has real theatrical possibilities, because you can make the presentation as straightforward or as spooky as you want. And it can also be performed for one person or for a large group. By the time you're finished, your audience may believe you can actually (to paraphrase the movie *The Sixth Sense*) "see dead people—all the time."

Effect

Your spectator is given several pieces of paper. He or she writes the name of a different living person on all but one of them. On that last piece, the spectator writes the name of someone who's dead. The papers are freely mixed. Nevertheless, just by running your fingers over the names, you're able to tell which person is no longer among us—except in Spirit.

Preparation

None. All you need is a sheet of paper and something to write with.

Performance

Explain that you've discovered you have a unique ability: you can talk to ghosts. Just by reading a person's name, you can tell whether that person is living or dead. And you can prove it.

Take a rectangular piece of paper and rip it in half lengthwise, from top to bottom. Set one of the strips on top of the other and, holding them together, rip them twice, giving you six rectangular pieces of paper of roughly equal size.

There's a subtle difference in the pieces. Four of the pieces (the four corners of the original paper) have two straight edges and two jagged edges. The other two pieces (which were located in the middle of the original paper) have one straight edge and *three* ripped edges. The spectators will never notice that they're not the same if you don't call any particular attention to them. However, it's a simple matter for you to tell them apart. Mentally keep track of the pieces with three jagged edges. This method, utilizing the rough edges principle, is attributed to American magician Henry Hardin.

In just a second I'm going to ask you to write down the names of several people who are very special to you in some way. But to make this as fair as possible, I want it to be the names of people who I don't know. They don't have to be on your Top Eight or your Fave Five. But they could be friends, family members, someone from work, from school. Anyone. The only thing that's absolutely essential is this: they must still be with us. They must be living.

Pick up one of the pieces of paper that has three jagged edges. This has to be done nonchalantly, so it can't be obvious that you're sorting through them. It has to look as if you could have used any of the pieces of paper. Write the name of someone you know in large letters across the paper, show it to the audience, roll the paper into a loose ball, and drop it on the table.

Now, when you think of someone's name, I want you to write it down like this and roll the paper into a ball. I'll turn my head while you're writing, so let me know when you've rolled up the paper and set it on the table.

Discard your ball of paper, either by placing it in your pocket or dropping it on the floor. Pick up the remaining pieces of paper and casually stack them so that the only remaining piece that has three jagged edges is on the bottom of the pile. Hand the top paper to your spectator. Turn your head as your spectator writes the first name.

When your volunteer has finished with one piece of paper, hand the person another, until you only have one left, and there are four balled-up pieces of paper on the table.

For this last strip, I want you to do something a little different. How can I put this? I want this person to no longer be with us. I want you to think of a person who is dead. But, again, I need this to be someone who was very important to you when he or she was alive. And, again, I can't know that the person has already crossed over.

Hand your spectator the last piece of paper, the one that has three jagged edges. Turn your head as the name of the deceased person is written. When that paper, too, has been balled up and placed on the table, you can turn to face your audience. Ask the person to pick up the five paper balls and mix them so that neither of you knows which is which. Have the spectator set them all back on the table.

Now comes the spooky part. Pick up one of the balls, unfold it, and lay it out in front of you. Read the name silently, or murmur it quietly to yourself. Or you could simply run your fingertips across the name written on the paper strip. This is done in a completely serious manner. Do this for all five names. Don't rush. Take your time. To build the suspense, you may want to go back and check one or two of the strips a second time.

Finally, pause over one of the strips. (This is, of course, the rectangle that has three torn edges—the piece that you know contains the name of the dead person.) Pretend to be picking up some sort of vibration or silent communication from the Beyond. Perhaps close your eyes, or arch an eyebrow. Finally, hold out the strip and read the name on it. Announce, correctly, that this is the person who is on the Other Side.

The name of the dead person is written on one of the sections of the paper that has three jagged edges (marked here for illustration purposes with an X).

(Photo courtesy of Titus Photography.)

If you're performing this for a group, you can have five different people each write down a name on one of the pieces of paper. Just make sure that you instruct the person who receives the piece with three jagged edges to write down the name of someone who has already passed over; the other four write down the names of people who are still among us.

If you play this trick straight rather than for laughs, you have the possibility of sending a real shiver up the spines of your spectators.

The Pentagram of Doom

This is a classic mind-reading trick that's been in use by magicians since at least the 1920s. For reasons that will become obvious, it's known as a *center tear*. The method may even have been used by fake mediums to obtain secret information about the dead during séances, but you don't have to be trying to contact ghosts to perform the trick. The fact that you seem to be able to read someone's mind will creep out the person just as much. Couple that with the use of a pentagram, and you have the perfect trick to show your Goth buds.

The Magic Word

The **center tear** is a technique by which you secretly obtain and see a word, message, or drawing that was previously written in the center of a folded piece of paper.

Effect

You show a small piece of paper containing a pentagram, the occult symbol of a five-pointed star within a circle that many associate with the Kabbalah and others with demon worship. Your spectator writes a word, question, or illustration in the center of the star and then folds the note into quarters. You hold the packet to your forehead, and then rip it up and burn the pieces. Even though you didn't open the packet or examine any of the torn pieces, you're able to determine the message that was written on the paper.

Preparation

All you'll need is a small, square piece of paper, a pen, an ashtray, and matches or a lighter. Any paper will do, but a piece of gray or yellowish parchment or textured paper will add a mystical touch to the proceedings.

You'll want to practice this trick once or twice just to see how it works. Take a piece of paper about 3" square. Write a small word in the exact center of the note. Fold the paper in half, then in half again, with the writing to the inside.

Notice that one of the corners of this folded packet has no open edges. Rip out a small semicircular piece of this corner. If you open up this section, you'll see that this is actually the center of the piece of paper, exactly where the message appears. This center piece is the one that you'll have to keep control of when you perform the trick.

When you rip along the dashed lines (shown here for illustration purposes only), you're actually tearing out the center of the paper.

(Photo courtesy of Titus Photography.)

Performance

Draw the largest circle possible on one side of the paper. Inside the circle, draw a large, five-pointed star, making a pentagram. Ask the volunteer to write her message inside the center of the star. This guarantees that the message will be positioned at the center of the piece of paper—also that the word or message will be short. Turn your head away while the person writes the message.

Do you believe that it might be possible to read another person's mind? You do? Oh, good: I love to work with the weirdos. (Or, You don't? Oh, good: I love to work with the skeptics.) Back in the Old Times, sorcerers used to stand inside a mystic circle or pentagram to conjure up the Devil. Others thought they stood inside the sigil, as these occult circles were called, in order to prevent the forces of Evil from reaching them. Either way, I'll try to be careful.

Have your spectator write a word inside the center of the pentagram, and then fold the paper into a small packet.

(Photo courtesy of Titus Photography.)

Also, although I don't make a big deal of it, when I ask the spectator to inscribe something on the paper, I use the word "print" instead of "write." She is more likely to print the word, which will then be much easier to read than cursive script.

I just want you to print a word, a short message, or a question, or perhaps make a simple drawing, inside the center of the pentagram. Something that means a great deal to you. The magic circle and pentagram will help you focus on your image. As soon as you're done, fold the paper in half, and in half again, so that I can't possibly see what you've written.

The spectator folds the paper into quarters, with the writing to the inside. Take back the folded paper. Hold it to your forehead, as if trying to read the words with your "mind's eye." Tear the packet into pieces, but, as you've practiced, be careful not to rip up the corner that contains the message.

Drop the pieces into an ashtray, but secretly retain the folded corner piece in your hand. The easiest way to do this is simply to curl your ring and little fingers around the paper, and close your hand into a loose fist.

Now all you have to do is open the folded paper, read the spectator's message to yourself, and then pretend to divine the billet's contents. ("Billet" is a word seldom heard today for a small letter or note. Magicians continue to use the word as jargon for any small piece of paper, usually one on which secret information is written for use in mind-reading demonstrations.) Some magicians open the paper just below the edge of the table where they're seated. I prefer just to turn my back to everyone watching, open the little piece of paper, and read it to myself.

Here's how I get away with it: after I have the center piece palmed and drop the other pieces into an ashtray, I ask the spectators to rip the bits of paper even smaller. As they do, I turn my body away, explaining that I don't want to even accidentally catch a glimpse of any part of the message that's been written.

With my back turned, I quickly open the paper I have hidden in my hand and read the contents. I then roll the paper into a small pellet and discreetly drop it on the floor or palm it to discard later. Then I turn around to face the audience.

Put the pieces in an ashtray and set them on fire. Needless to say, be very careful that you don't burn yourself or your volunteer. (Duh.) Stare into the flames. Then, with some struggle, divulge the word(s) or illustration, or answer the question that you secretly saw on the small corner of paper only moments before.

To make this revelation as mysterious as possible, don't simply blurt out the word. Pretend to see the word written in the flames. Make believe that you're having real difficulty. Ask everyone who saw the word to concentrate on it. You might "sense" just the first letter of the word, then the next letter, and then spell out or say the complete word. If you prefer, you could reveal the word or picture by drawing it on another piece of paper.

Tricky Tidbits

The center tear can also be used as an alternate method for a living or dead test. Have your spectator write the name of a deceased person in the pentagram, and say that as you stare at the flames, the individual's Spirit will reveal its identity to you. An amusing presentation might be to play up the satanic connotation of the pentagram by asking your spectator to write down the name of a dead person who they're pretty sure is already in Hell. You stare in the flames to divine the name of the damned soul.

It'll take several performances before you know exactly how far you can go with any of this without sounding hokey. But if you can make the audience believe that there was no way you could have seen the words or drawings they wrote, you have a real shocker.

Spinning in Your Grave

To some people, this spooky little trick looks like you're able to move objects with your mind. (Don't worry: we'll be covering that kind of thing in our next chapter.) But in this presentation, the trick has a Dark Side: it tells the story of a ghost trying to use your key to unlock the door of a haunted house. The mini-miracle is easy to carry around with you and not that difficult to perform. The hard part is convincing your audience that you're not just rolling the key over in your hand. Phantom fingers are turning it!

Effect

An old-fashioned door key from a haunted house turns over on your open palm.

Preparation

None, except that you'll have to find and carry with you one of those antique metal keys that has a round shaft. Although this type of key is often referred to as a "skeleton key," to a locksmith they're known as mortice keys.

There's no trick to the key itself. For best results, however, you want to find one that has a very large, heavy head or "handle" (the circular or oval end), especially in comparison to the "bit" (the end that goes into the lock.) The only problem is that such keys are no longer in general circulation. You'll have trouble finding one in a regular hardware store. Try an antique shop, a thrift store, or possibly a Goodwill or Salvation Army outlet. I found the one that I use in a secondhand store called "Used Treasures."

You might be asking, "If this kind of key is no longer an ordinary object, should a street magician be performing this trick?" In this case, yes. I think the unusual nature of the key is actually a benefit. The key is so strange that people are curious and like seeing and playing with it, which they can do to their heart's content because it's ungimmicked. Also, the patter about ghosts is just disturbing enough to work well for a street magician's character.

Performance

Do you believe in ghosts? Have you ever seen a ghost? Me neither. But I have been in a haunted house. How do I know it was haunted? Did I see anything? Or hear anything? No. But I could feel that there was, well, a presence.

When I growing up, I saw all the movies about people being haunted by ghosts. But you know what? Ghosts don't haunt people. They haunt places. They return to where they were happy or where something important happened in their lives or where they felt at home … or where they died. This is the key to that house I visited. And I think, just like the house it comes from, it's haunted.

Lay the key widthwise across your open palm, just under the fleshy mounds at the base of your fingers. The entire shaft of the key should rest on your palm except for the key's handle, which should lie flat, parallel to the floor, and just overhang your hand at the base of your little finger. The bit should lie flat on your palm, and the cut edges should be pointing toward your wrist.

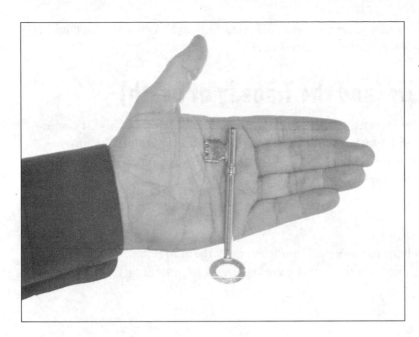

Lay the skeleton key on your palm at the base of your fingers with the handle over-hanging the little-finger side of your hand.

(Photo courtesy of Titus Photography.)

Now comes the only "move": ever so slightly tilt your hand so that the fingers slant a bit more toward the floor. The movement of your hand must be absolutely impercep-tible. I cannot stress this enough, because you're actually doing what most people will suspect. If the audience sees you tilting your hand, the trick is over. If you have a well-balanced key of the proper weight, it will automatically begin to revolve on your hand.

Take your time with this. To quote the old cliché: slow and steady wins the race. In fact, you may find that once the bit is pointing upright, vertical, that the key starts to speed up. You can slow down the revolution by slightly tilting your hand a bit upward. Again, the minute change in the angle of your hand must be completely undetect-able. The key will still continue to turn, just more gradually. The more slowly the key moves and the longer it takes to completely roll over, the creepier the trick will look.

To convince your spectators that you're not moving your hand, you can ask someone to place his or her fingertips on top of yours. Instead of tilting your hand down, raise your wrist up.

You can perform this trick in silence, with everyone staring at the key. Or you can comment on the movement with such lines (and lies) as …

♦ *Notice that I'm holding my hand completely still.*

♦ *I can't believe it. The key is getting icy cold.*

♦ *Something—someone—is turning the key.*

Now, how about if we really scare the pants off your audience? What if they could *see* the ghostly hand that's turning the haunted key?

The Miracle of Life (and the Tragedy of Death)

This trick is a personal favorite of mine for so many reasons. It's shocking. It's unexpected. It's frightening. It's cute. And it's just so *different* than anything else anyone has ever seen a street magician do. It was invented by Canadian magician and attorney Bob Farmer. A tricky lawyer? What are the chances of that?

Effect

The magician shows both hands empty, and then cups them together. Slowly, a tiny hand crawls out from between them and waves to everyone watching.

Preparation

The teeny hand is really the plastic arm from a doll. When you perform the trick, you'll be wearing the arm on the end of your little finger, so that gives you an idea of the size of the doll arm that you'll need to find. It's probably best if you don't dismember one of your little sister's play toys, so look for doll parts at an arts and crafts store. Or, if you have to tear apart a full doll and don't want to splurge for retail at a toy store, you can probably pick up a used doll at a swap meet or yard sale. This may be the way to go, because you might have to cut up quite a few dolls until you find an arm that's just the right fit for your pinky finger.

Charms

If you're going to do this trick, be prepared to have people scream in your ear and jump around. It's that startling and just plain weird. It'll provide instant gratification for any of you who got into street magic so you could freak people out.

The shoulder end of the arm has to be an open tube so that it can be stuck on your finger like a thimble. The doll's arm doesn't have to fit completely over the tip of your little finger, but it has to fit snugly enough that it stays attached.

Because the size of everyone's hands is different, you'll also have to experiment with the length of the doll arm. Because only the doll's hand and forearm are going to be seen during the trick, you may want to cut off the arm closer to the elbow. This will give you a wider opening as well, perhaps making it easier to fit over the end of your finger. (In fact, some magicians prefer to attach the doll's arm to their middle finger rather than the pinky, which would certainly require a larger diameter opening to the doll arm.)

When you're ready to perform, stick the doll arm on the end of the little finger of your right hand. As long as you keep your hand in motion, it's unlikely that anyone will notice the plastic arm unless he or she really stares at your hands. To be safe, I always keep the fingers of my right hand slightly curled when I start this trick so that the doll's arm is against my palm and shielded from the spectators' view by the back of my hand.

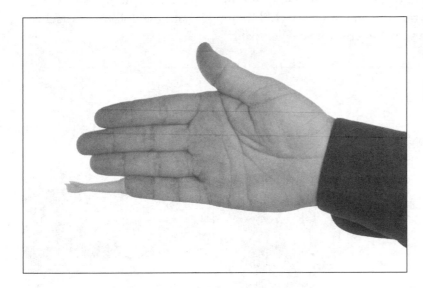

Wear the doll's arm on the end of your right little finger, exposed view.

(Photo courtesy of Titus Photography.)

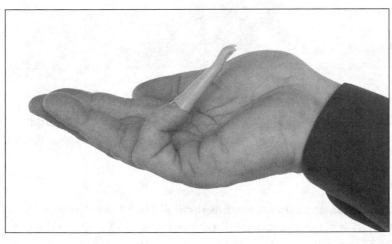

By slightly curling your fingers, you can keep the doll's arm from being seen, exposed view.

(Photo courtesy of Titus Photography.)

Performance

Did you ever see that TV show, The Addams Family? *My favorite character was always Thing, the hand that popped out of a black box. In the movie versions, you actually got to see the disembodied hand running around. Cool. I wonder if I could ask Thing to visit us tonight? But don't be scared.*

For this trick to be effective, you first have to show that your hands are empty. But you don't want to make a big deal out of it. Start with the fingers loosely curled on both of your hands. Open your left hand, and turn it palm up, above and slightly covering your right hand. Open your right hand, and turn it palm up as well. As you do, however, make sure that the end of your right little finger (and the doll's arm attached to it) is hidden from view underneath your left palm.

Your right little finger (and the doll's arm attached to it) are hidden underneath your left hand.

(Photo courtesy of Titus Photography.)

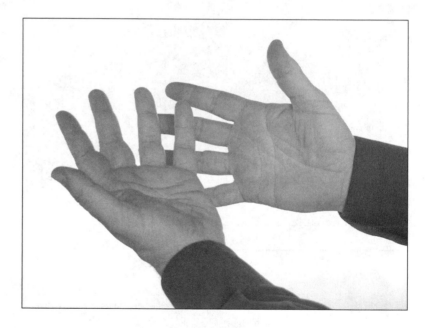

Turn your left hand palm down, covering your right fingertips. (Make sure that the doll's arm isn't seen when you do this.) Slightly bend the fingers of both your hands, and press your hands close together but keep an opening between your left thumb and forefinger.

And now, the mystery of life!

Slowly bend your right little finger so that it extends the doll's hand into the gap between your two hands. To say the spectators will be startled is mild. Wiggle the small hand back and forth. Is it waving? Or is it trying to claw its way out?

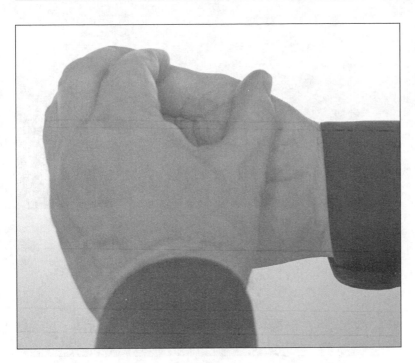

Cup your hands together, leaving a gap between them.

(Photo courtesy of Titus Photography.)

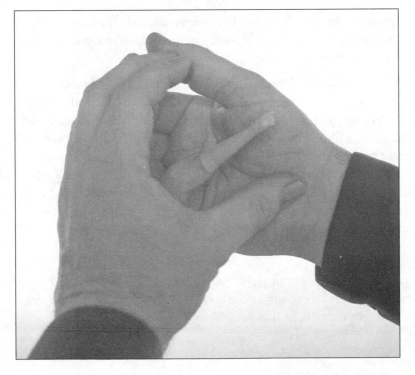

Bend your right little finger, extending the doll's arm into the opening between your hands, exposed view.

(Photo courtesy of Titus Photography.)

A tiny hand appears!

(Photo courtesy of Titus Photography.)

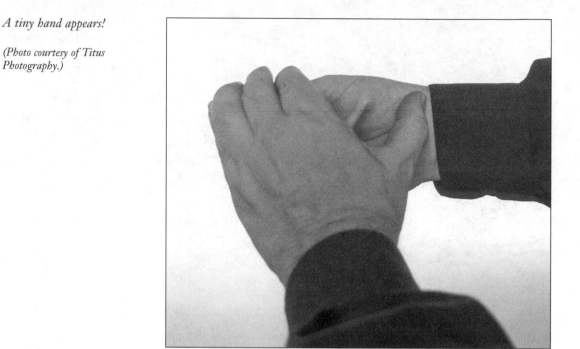

How long should you allow the hand to be seen? Five or ten seconds is plenty, because once your audience is past the initial shock, they'll only be interested in figuring out where the hand came from and how you're manipulating it.

So you have to make the Tiny Hand of Doom disappear. And that's easier to do than you might think. Turn so that your right side (or at least the back of your right hand) is toward the spectators. In one fluid motion, turn over both of your hands, open and separate them. Your left palm will be pointing upward and your right hand will be palm down with the right fingers still slightly curled. (From their angle, the spectators shouldn't be able to see the doll arm.) Without pausing, clap your hands together once—a single, good, strong clap, palm against palm. (You shouldn't clap so hard that the doll arm flies off your little finger, however.) By clapping your hands, you have "proven" that your hands are empty without having to say so.

... and the tragedy of death!

Drop your hands to your sides, curling your right fingers into a loose fist. I usually stick both hands in my pockets and then immediately withdraw them (leaving the doll arm behind, of course) with an expression that says, "Nope. It's not in my pockets, either."

The Least You Need to Know

◆ In ancient times, magicians claimed to be able to call up the Spirits of those who have passed over.

◆ "Living or dead tests" are tricks in which magicians or pseudo mind readers are able to identify whether people have moved on simply by hearing or reading their names.

◆ In order to gather secret information from spectators to pretend to read their minds, mentalists have used center tears since at least the 1920s.

Get Bent!

In This Chapter

- Telekinesis trickery
- The classic bending spoon
- Shape-shifting metals with nails and coins
- Psychokinesis prestidigitation with paper
- The spinning pen

There are invisible forces all around us. Some, like gravity and magnetism, we accept without question, even though we can't "see" them. So why is it so hard for some people to believe in a sixth sense—not just the ability to "read" minds, but also the capability of using the mind to exert control over our surroundings?

Bent Out of Shape

Few things that street magicians can do have a stronger impact on people than *telekinesis*—being able to make objects move or bend without touching them. Magic tricks with silverware, including bending and vanishing it, have been in the magicians' bag of tricks for centuries. But in the 1970s, Uri Geller, an Israeli psychic, added a layer of mysticism by claiming that

The Magic Word

Although **telekinesis** (or TK) is sometimes used synonymously with psychokinesis, it more specifically means the ability to make objects move by mind power. **Psychokinesis** (or PK) is the purported paranormal ability to influence matter or energy by power of the mind alone. (A good example would be bending a spoon without touching it.)

it was his mental power, not sleight-of-hand and misdirection, that was causing metal objects to bend. He inspired a generation of believers to try to bend spoons or keys.

And the phenomenon doesn't seem to be going away. My recent online search of "spoon-bending" turned up over a half-million hits. Some people have even started holding "spoon-bending parties," where folks sit around trying to bend their host's flatware by *psychokinesis*. But don't worry: you don't have to throw a big bash for your chance at success. Here are more than a half-dozen ways to convince your spectators that you can bend spoons, coins, or nails with your brain!

The word "telekinesis" was coined way back in 1890 by Alexander N. Aksakof, a German-Russian researcher of psychic phenomenon. It comes from two Greek root words meaning "spirit" and "movement," and originally the word only referred to objects that were supposedly being shifted around by ghosts, poltergeists, and other Spirits. The word "psychokinesis" was first used in 1914 by Henry Holt, an American author and publisher in his book *On the Cosmic Relations*. J.B. Rhine, one of the twentieth century's top ESP investigators, popularized this word, because it removed all connection to the Spirit World and concentrated on the possibilities of the human mind. Nevertheless, "telekinesis" remains in common use, and the words are often used interchangeably.

The Rubber Spoon

This quick sight gag takes no more than a few seconds to perform, and it isn't really magic. But it makes a fun and visual lead-in to any of the true "bending" tricks in this section. By showing that you can make something solid look like it's made of rubber with a simple optical illusion, it makes the actual trick even stronger when you do bend something for real.

This stunt is most often explained using a pencil. In fact, once you master the balance and timing necessary to do the trick, you'll be able to perform it with anything that has a similar shape, such as a pen, swizzle stick, or knife.

Effect

A solid spoon seems to turn to rubber.

Preparation

None.

Performance

Pinch a spoon about an inch from the end of its handle, very loosely between your right thumb and forefinger. The rest of your hand should remain open, with your palm toward the spectator. The spoon should be held horizontal, parallel to the table or floor, with its bowl pointing to your left. Raise and lower your hand straight up and down in a continuous motion, but only an inch or two in each direction on every wave. If all of this is done properly, the spoon will seem to wiggle as if it were made of rubber.

You'll want to experiment by holding the spoon at different points along its handle and by adjusting the tension of your grip in order to achieve the best possible illusion. Before long you'll get the feel for it, and the spoon really will look like it wobbles when you shake it.

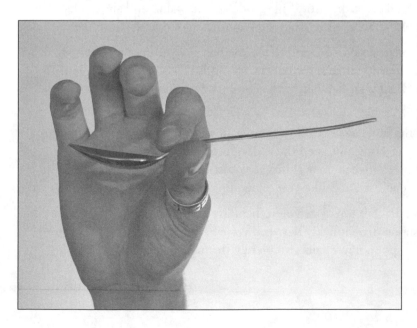

Pinch the spoon's handle between your right thumb and forefinger. Let the spoon wobble as you move your arm up and down to make the spoon look like it's made of rubber.

The Bending Spoon for Beginners

This is a classic that's in just about every book on close-up or tabletop magic. Perhaps because it was one of the first tricks they learned or because the method is so diabolically simple, magicians frequently perform this as a throwaway, treat it as a joke, or even expose how it's done. But performed properly, it still really fools people.

Effect

You bend the handle of a spoon, but it instantly restores itself to its original shape.

Preparation

None. Although I perform this with a teaspoon, you could also do the trick with a larger spoon or other utensil.

Performance

Pick up a spoon with your right hand, and display it to show that it's unbent. Lightly tap it against the table one or two times to prove that it's solid. Grasp the spoon in your right fist with the top side of the spoon resting on (and perpendicular to) the fingers. The bowl extends past the little-finger side of your hand and should face the spectators. The end of the handle must not stick out past your right forefinger.

Hold the spoon in a vertical position, and touch the bowl of the spoon to the table. Tilt your hand back toward yourself, so that the spoon is at a 45-degree angle with respect to the table. Clasp your hands together by covering your right fingers with your left fingers.

Press the bottom of the bowl against the tabletop. Slowly tilt your wrists and hands upward, away from your body, but keep the spoon in place. Let the handle of the spoon slowly slide down between your palms as you continue to tilt your wrists upward. To your audience, it looks like you're bending the spoon.

If you prefer, you can make it look like you're bending the spoon with a single, hard push by letting the spoon drop quickly between your hands. Either way, make sure that the handle of the spoon never falls completely through your palms to clunk against the table.

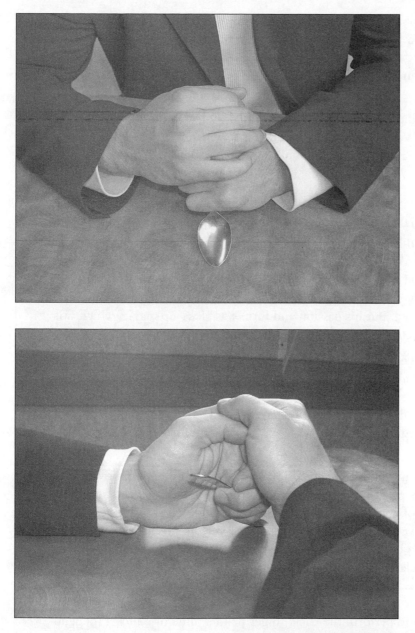

Your hands in position to bend the spoon, audience view.

Exposed view of the spoon "bending."

To restore the spoon, cover it with both hands as you lift it away from the table. Hold the spoon horizontal, parallel to the tabletop. Grasp the bowl of the spoon with your left fingers, and gently slide your right fingers along the length of the handle, all the way from the bowl to the other end. It will look like you've somehow straightened the spoon without any physical effort. Or, you can simply hold the spoon by the end of its handle and shake it a few times before dropping it on to the table with a clatter. (The audience will swear they actually saw it "unbend" as you waved it in the air.) Either way, the audience can see for themselves that the bent spoon has been magically restored.

A very deceptive addition to this trick was invented by David Derrick Vernon, the younger son of Dai Vernon, one of twentieth-century magic's greatest proponents of close-up magic. The routine was first published as "Nickleplated" in a magazine for magicians called *The Phoenix* (April 17, 1950, issue).

Dai Vernon (1894–1992) was one of the most important magicians of the twentieth century, and his influence on card magic in particular is incalculable. Born David Frederick Wingfield Verner in Ottawa, Ontario, Canada, Vernon first became interested in magic at the age of 8. After moving to New York in 1915, he spent his early years cutting silhouettes, and he had a brief career with a nightclub magic act. But his passion and forte was close-up magic, which was just becoming recognized as a separate, distinct genre of magic.

Over the years, Vernon became the confidante of magicians, card sharps, gamblers, and cheats alike. His emphasis was on making every hand movement natural, so that any "secret move" or sleight was indistinguishable from the normal action it mimicked. Never famous outside of the magic fraternity, Vernon was nevertheless recognized as "The Professor" for his performance skill and depth of knowledge.

In 1963, Vernon moved to Hollywood, California, where he became one of the leading members of The Magic Castle, a private club for magicians and their friends. Several of the tricks that Vernon invented, as well as those of others that he improved, have become classics. To this day, Vernon's routines for the Cups and Balls and the Linking Rings are considered "standards" and are still performed by magicians worldwide.

Before you're ready to perform the trick, finger palm a dime or a nickel (depending upon the size of the handle of the spoon you're going to use) in your right hand. Instead of holding the coin at the base of your ring and little fingers as you do with a regular finger palm, keep the coin near the base of the forefinger and middle finger.

As you curl your right fingers around the spoon, as first described, use your right thumb to slide the coin upward so that it just barely peeks above your forefinger.

The rounded edge of the coin looks like the end of the spoon's handle (which is actually hidden in your curled fingers).

Perform the trick exactly as it's been explained, but keep the coin visible throughout. This creates the powerful illusion that the handle of the spoon is almost folding over double.

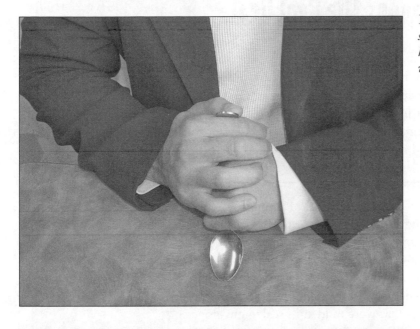

Your hands hold the bent spoon with the "end" of the handle showing, audience view.

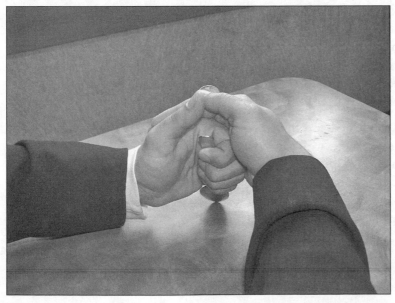

A coin substitutes for the end of the bent spoon's handle, exposed view.

When you "unbend" the spoon, use your right thumb to pull the coin back into a finger palm position. You have plenty of time to get rid of the coin while the audience is examining the spoon.

The Bending Spoon: The Real Deal

What I'm about to explain is the real work, even though it sounds too simple to fool anyone. So don't dismiss it before you've read the whole explanation. Unless you've seen this performed, it'll be hard to believe how powerful and convincing this trick can be. In fact, chances are, even after you read the explanation, you won't believe you can get away with it until you've tried it a few times. It depends completely on boldness and misdirection. It's probably the closest in effect to the type of spoon-bending that was popularized by Uri Geller.

Uri Geller was born in Tel Aviv in 1946. An internationally known psychic entertainer, he says that he first noticed his special powers at the age of 4. After serving in the Israeli Army and being wounded in the Six-Day War, he began work as a model and a nightclub performer. His fame dates back to the 1970s following a series of televised demonstrations in which he claimed paranormal abilities to bend spoons, force watches to stop, make broken watches start, and duplicate drawings that were hidden in sealed envelopes.

Geller has attracted many skeptics and critics over the years, most visibly American magician James Randi. Geller himself freely admits that magic could be used to perform some of his feats but that he's using telepathic and psychokinetic abilities to achieve them. He withdrew from the public arena in the 1980s, preferring to concentrate on private clients, occasional personal appearances, and writing. Geller currently resides in Berkshire, England.

Beginning in 2006, he hosted a reality television series in Israel called *The Successor*, in which contestants who wished to follow in Geller's footsteps vied to be designated his heir by reading minds, bending spoons, stopping their heartbeat (you'll learn that as "Tourniquet Trickery" in Chapter 13), and other paranormal stunts. Geller also performed on each episode. You can learn more from his website, www.uri-geller.com.

Effect

A spoon held at your fingertips visibly bends.

Preparation

None. You'll need at least two spoons, identical if possible. If you wish, you or a spectator can select the spoons out of a pile of flatware. For best results, you should use a lightweight spoon so that it can be bent without too much force.

Performance

This trick is perfect to perform for a group, because everyone can participate by grabbing a spoon and trying it along with you. You'll have all the misdirection in the world to make your move as people watch their own spoons to see if they bend.

It's always best to wait until someone else brings up spoon-bending before you perform it. Otherwise, it loses much of its mystique. You should confess that you've tried it and had a bit of success, and eventually you agree to attempt it. Of course, you *can* always introduce the subject yourself by claiming, "I just saw another one of those guys on TV last night who said he could bend spoons. Did anyone else catch it?"

Show two spoons. Nest them by laying one on top of the other to show that they're both unbent, with straight handles. Take one spoon in each hand. Close your hands into loose fists, with the handles hidden inside your curled fingers. In each hand, your thumb should be pressing against the "neck" of the spoon, pinching it between your thumb and forefinger, right where the bowl meets the handle. The backs of the bowls should be facing you; the spectator is looking into the bowls. This should all look very casual, not like you're deliberately holding the spoons in any specific way.

As you raise your right hand, drop your left hand on to the table directly in front of you. The tip of the inverted bowl of the spoon should rest against the tabletop. But, again, don't pay any attention to your left hand. Look at your right-hand spoon and say, "This will be our control."

Lean forward across the top of the table to give the spoon in your right hand to the spectator as you say, "Here. You hold on to it." As you do, press down on the spoon in your left hand. Because of the angle at which you're leaning, your body weight will bend the handle of the spoon at its neck. (You'll have to experiment, but generally the closer your left hand is to the edge of the table and the farther you have to lean, the easier it will be to bend the spoon.) Your body probably will hide this entire action from your spectator's view, but handing the other spoon to the spectator provides complete misdirection. If you're performing for more than one person, have everyone else grab a spoon to play along.

If you're not performing at a table, you can bend your spoon by dropping your left hand to your side. When you lean forward to hand the spectator the spoon in your right hand, simply bend the spoon in your left hand against the outside of your thigh.

Lean forward to hand your spectator one spoon while you secretly bend the other spoon, exposed view.

As you hand the spectator a spoon, simply bend the spoon against your leg.

As soon as your spectator has taken the spoon from your right hand, stand up straight. As you do, turn the spoon in your left hand over and revolve it 180 degrees so that the back of the bowl lies on your fingers and the neck of the spoon is between your left thumb and forefinger. Your left fingers help to shield the fact that the spoon is already bent, but it shouldn't look like you're trying to hide the spoon. Again, don't make a big deal about rearranging the spoon. From the audience's perspective, nothing sneaky has happened. Unless you've pressed the spoon into a U shape, they won't even notice the bend because they're not holding it close enough to their own spoons to compare.

Turn your left hand palm down. Ask your spectator to grip his spoon the same way. Hold your spoon so that its handle is horizontal, parallel to the tabletop or floor. Stroke the length of the handle of your spoon several times from the neck to the end of the handle, slowly and gently. Do it again, each time barely touching the metal. Tell the spectator to do the same with the spoon he is holding.

After a few strokes, using a slow but increasing pressure, pinch your thumb more tightly against your forefinger. This makes the bowl of the spoon pivot, tilting the handle of the spoon upward—which creates the illusion that the handle is bending. The small action of your thumb and the movement of the bowl are completely hidden by the back of your left fingers.

If you prefer, instead of pressing with your thumb, hold your thumb and forefinger still and slightly press down with your left middle, ring, and little fingers. Your thumb and forefinger will act as a pivot point, and the handle will tilt upward.

Look! It's starting to bend! Can everyone see it? Look at the handle!

Allow the handle to pivot upward as you gently stroke it.

After the handle has seemingly tilted to about a 45-degree angle, grab the spoon with your right hand. Show the spoon to the spectator, and drop it on the table. Take back the volunteer's "control" spoon and compare it to show how much yours has bent.

Charms

There are no exact right or wrong ways to hold the spoon throughout this trick. Practice various grips until you come up with ones that look natural but are easy for you to bend the spoon quickly and unobtrusively and, later, look convincing when you're supposedly doing the visible bending. The only thing that matters is that the audience is caught completely off-guard. In fact, you should pretend to be as surprised as anyone that the bending actually occurred.

You Bent It!

Here's another bending effect that depends 100 percent upon audacity. Again, you won't believe you can actually get away with it until you try it for real people. So don't pass it by, thinking, "Oh, that'll never fool anybody." You can and you will. The best part of this particular routine is that the bending seems to take place in someone else's hands, not yours!

Effect

A spoon bends in a spectator's hands.

Preparation

None.

Performance

Pick up two spoons and "nest" them to show that they're unbent and that their handles are at the same angle. Hand one of them to a spectator. Hold the spoon on its side, parallel to the floor, so that the bowl is to the left and its back is facing you. Cover the front of the bowl with your left fingers, and cover the front of the handle with your right fingers. Pinch the neck of the spoon between your forefingers and thumbs.

Check it out. Make sure that the spoon is nice and solid.

Look directly at the spectator as you're saying this. It should look and sound as if you're demonstrating to your spectator how she should examine the spoon. When you're sure that the person's eyes are meeting yours or are checking out her own spoon, give your spoon one quick, very small bend at its neck. This should be a miniscule bend, so small that it won't be noticed until the two spoons are held right next to each other to compare.

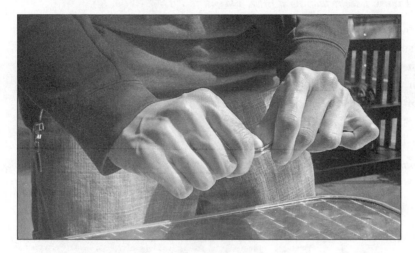

Holding the spoon horizontal but on its side, secretly give it one quick, small bend.

This is bold, I know. How can you get away with folding the spoon right in front of people while they're watching?

- ◆ Your boldface lie, asking them to check that their spoon is solid, completely disarms them.

- ◆ The openness with which you hold your spoon eliminates any suspicion.

- ◆ The bend is so small that it's indiscernible.

- ◆ They don't know what's going to happen.

As soon as you've made the bend, tap the spoon on your left palm or the table, as if to reinforce its solidity. Take back the spectator's spoon with one hand and hold yours in the other. Display them so that the spectator can see both spoons, but don't place them right next to each other. This is the end of the "examination" portion of the trick.

Hand the spectator the spoon that you just secretly bent. Place the other spoon in your left hand, with your thumb in the bowl and your fingers underneath the bowl, and then turn your left hand palm down. The handle should be horizontal, parallel to the floor. Ask the spectator to hold her spoon the same way. Stick out your right forefinger and gently stroke the handle of your spoon.

The spoons look okay, right? Here: hold yours the same way that I'm holding mine. Concentrate on the spoon. Stroke the handle and think, "Bend. Bend." Do you see anything moving? Is yours bending? Yes, I think I see it moving a little. Do you feel it?

Look down at your own spoon and admit defeat. Nothing has happened to yours. But then, check out the spectator's spoon. Say that it looks like hers might be bending—just a little. Hold out your spoon with your left hand, horizontal and bowl up. Take the spectator's spoon with your right hand. Turn it over, examining it on all sides. Then lay it on top of yours, nesting the bowls. There is a very small but very definite bend upward in her spoon. The bending has apparently taken place in your spectator's hands!

Be careful what you touch later. Especially your car keys! If they bend, you might not make it home tonight.

Nest the spoons to show that the handle of the spectator's spoon (on top) has bent upward.

This is another trick that can be done for a large group. By the time you've taken back the spectators' spoons, examined and redistributed them, no one but you will know who winds up with the spoon that you originally handled. That's the spectator whose spoon is magically going to bend.

The Breaking Point

Having the bowl break completely off a spoon is a natural follow-up to bending a spoon, but the trick also stands up well on its own. This is another great trick to do for a bunch of people at the same time. Everybody can be waving around spoons, trying to make them bend and break.

Effect

You show a spoon by the end of its handle, and, after a few shakes, the bowl falls off all on its own.

Preparation

This is one of the few routines in this book that the preparation may take longer than performing the trick itself. You can use one of the spoons at the event where you'll be performing, but bear in mind that you'll be destroying the spoon. The risk is up to you.

Rather than sneak away into the bathroom to prepare one of their spoons, I find it easier to bring one of my own that I've already gimmicked in advance, and then slip it on to the table before I'm ready to perform. If you're planning to make this a regular part of your bag of tricks, take a trip to a thrift store and buy a used set of the crappiest silverware you can find. The spoons will probably be perfect for this trick.

With all this in mind, here's how you gaff the spoon: bend the spoon in half at the neck, its weakest and thinnest point. Then bend it back as far as you can in the other direction. Do this back and forth, over and over. You'll start to feel the metal getting warm. (Be careful, because it could actually get quite hot and burn you.) You'll also start to realize that the spoon's getting easier for you to bend. That's because you've worn down the metal to the point that the neck is almost ready to snap. Slow down, and check the neck of the spoon each time before you fold it. Eventually you'll notice a little crack or fracture in the metal. Stop. The spoon is ready. And don't worry: no one else will notice the crack. It's only obvious and screams for attention to you.

To secretly prepare your spoon, start by folding it in half at its weakest point, the neck.

(Photo courtesy of Titus Photography.)

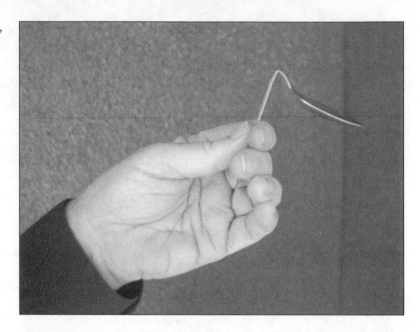

Bend the neck of the spoon in the opposite direction, and then continue folding it back and forth.

(Photo courtesy of Titus Photography.)

Continue to bend the spoon until a tiny stress fracture appears across the neck of the spoon, exposed view.

(Photo courtesy of Titus Photography.)

Performance

At some point before you're ready to perform—ideally even before you bring up the subject of spoon-bending—add your gimmicked spoon to the silverware sitting next to you on the table. (Unless you're OCD, don't worry that it doesn't match the rest of the place setting. Even good restaurants have to add in an odd piece of flatware from time to time to replace ones that have been lost or damaged. Just make sure to keep track of this gimmicked spoon so that you'll be able to recognize and separate it from the others later.) Ask everyone to pick up a spoon or a fork. Needless to say, make sure you pick up the spoon you prepared.

If you're at a bar or restaurant and no silverware is on the table, tip the server a five and ask to borrow a bunch of spoons and forks from the wait station. If you're at a private home, just have someone go into the kitchen and grab a bunch of flatware. (Here, tipping is optional.) Toss all of the spoons and forks onto the center of the table, and ask everybody to grab one. In all of the commotion, it should be an easy task for you to simply take yours out of your pocket.

Charms

Don't be upset if the first time (or several times) you try to prepare one of these spoons you give just one bend too many and the bowl falls off. It happens. Eventually you'll get the hang of knowing just when to stop before it's too late.

If you're really concerned that someone will catch you trying to sneak your own spoon on to the table, wait until you're sitting down and, first, only move it as far as your lap. When everyone's grabbing a spoon from the table, pick one up, let your hand fall naturally into your lap, switch the spoons, and bring the gimmicked one into view. Later, you'll have plenty of time to get rid of the regular spoon.

Ask everyone to pinch the neck of his or her spoon or fork between a thumb and forefinger and hold the silverware parallel to the floor. Have them wave their arms up and down, about an inch in each direction. Have them stroke the handles to try to induce some sort of bending or paranormal movement in the flatware. Ask, "Does anyone feel like their spoon or fork might be bending?" Don't be surprised if the power of suggestion has one or two people shouting out that they do.

Wait! I think I feel something. Will you two hold on to the ends of my spoon? Hold on tight. But give me just a little wiggle room.

Have the spectator hold on to the ends of your spoon as you pinch its fractured neck.

Have someone hold your spoon between his or her two hands, horizontal, parallel to the floor. One hand holds on to the end of the handle, and the other holds on to the bowl. (Of course, if you're performing for a group, two people can help, with one holding on to each end.) Hold your right hand over the spoon, and pinch the spot where it's secretly cracked between your right thumb and forefinger. Raise your hand straight up about an inch or two, then down 2 inches, then up, then down, over and over. Each time this will weaken the fracture a bit more, and before long, the spoon will break in half. No one will be more startled than the person holding the two ends of the spoon!

Busted!

After you've performed "The Breaking Point," don't get rid of the two pieces of the broken spoon. Oh, no. You can use them later to perform a gag that's simply intended to be funny but might just fool some of the spectators as well.

Effect

A spoon visibly bends and breaks in half at your fingertips.

Preparation

You'll need to separate the bowl from the handle at the neck of a spoon. Lay the two pieces next to each other, "reassembling" the spoon. Pinch the spot where the broken ends meet between your left thumb and forefinger, and pick up the two pieces together so that they look like they're still connected. Hold the pieces horizontal so that, to a spectator, it simply looks like you're holding a spoon by its neck between your left thumb and index finger.

Performance

Display the "spoon." Even though it's secretly already split in half, as long as you hold on to the pieces tightly, you can gently tap the bowl or handle on the table. Then hold the spoon horizontal, parallel to the table, with your middle, ring, and little fingers curled up into your palm.

Still pinching the neck of the spoon tightly, slowly release pressure. Keep the handle horizontal. The bowl will slowly droop, then wobble, and then finally fall with a clang to the table. You are left with only the handle in your left hand. The spectators may laugh, or, if you don't play the bit for comedy and put the two pieces away quickly, the spectators may be left with a bit of a mystery.

Oh, Fork!

At first glance, this trick will look very similar to "Busted!" which was little more than a sight gag. But here you take the same idea one step further and make it into a real trick, with a restoration of the spoon, to boot. It's taking your street magic powers to the max.

Effect

A spoon visibly bends until the bowl breaks off and clatters to the table. You restore the two pieces into a single piece of silverware. (As an alternate climax, in the process of fusing the pieces together, the spoon changes into a fork.)

Preparation

You'll need two thin, lightweight (that is to say, cheap) spoons that can be bent easily by hand. Take one of the spoons and break off the bowl at the neck by folding the neck back and forth repeatedly, as you did to prepare for "The Breaking Point" earlier in this chapter. For this trick you won't need the handle.

Fold the other spoon at its neck by bending it over your left forefinger until the bowl is at about a 90-degree angle to the handle. Set the inverted bowl of the spoon on your left fingers. Position the spoon so that the bend in its neck rests on the second bend of your left forefinger. Curl your left fingers up and around the back of the bowl, making your hand into a very loose fist. Lay the neck of the separate bowl on your left forefinger so that it meets the bend in the spoon. Cover this juncture with your left thumb, pressing both the bent spoon and the separate bowl against your left forefinger. This is the way in which you'll display the two pieces to make it look like you're holding a single, straight spoon.

It'll only take an instant to get into this position when you're ready to perform. If you don't want to carry a whole spoon with you, carry just the separate bowl. When you're seated, you can lower a spoon from the table into your lap. Bend it, add the separate bowl, and then bring the whole thing into view. No one will notice that the bowl doesn't exactly match the handle of the spoon that you took from the table.

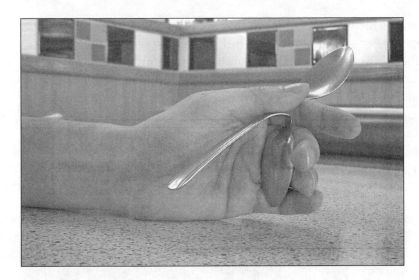

Set the neck of the separate spoon up against the bend of the whole spoon, and cover the junction with your left thumb, exposed view.

Performance

Show the "spoon" in position in your left hand. Yes, it *is* an awkward-looking way to hold a piece of silverware, but magicians do much stranger things. Because you're not using the spoon to eat, it won't seem all that unnatural: you're just holding it in this weird position so that the maximum number of people can see the spoon.

Pretend to concentrate on the spoon. Ask others to help you as you try to mentally bend the spoon. Gently release pressure with your left thumb so that the bowl begins to droop forward over the front of your curled left fingers. Do this as painstakingly slow as possible. Finally, let the bowl of the spoon fall from your left hand and drop to the tabletop. (Alternately, you could use your right fingers to "snap" the head off just before it falls free.)

Look stunned. You expected the spoon to bend but not to break! Now what? Keep your left hand in the position it's in (with the fingers curled around and hiding the bowl of the bent spoon and your thumb still in place at the second bend of your forefinger), but lower it so that the little-finger side of your loosely curled fist is lying against the table, just to the left of the severed bowl. Slightly curl the fingers of your right hand, and set the little-finger side of your right hand on the table directly in front of the separated bowl, hiding it from the spectators' view. Move your left hand to the right so that the fingers of the right hand partially overlap the back of the fingers of your right hand.

Now comes the "move," which is very similar to the one you used in "Up Yours" (see Chapter 10). Slide everything—your hands, the bowl, the bent spoon—toward you to the edge of the table. Continue moving both hands in a straight line toward your body. When you clear the edge of the table, the bowl will drop silently and unnoticed into your lap. As soon as you feel the bowl clear the tabletop, lift your hands, still pressed together, up to around eye level. As you raise your arms, slip your right fingers under the handle of the spoon, and bend it upward, making the spoon as straight as possible. Reveal the restored spoon. (This should all be performed in a flowing, continuous action. It's not "slide, drop, lift." Rather, it should look as if you're scooping up both pieces of a broken spoon from the table.)

Slide the bent spoon in your left hand and the separate bowl to the edge of the table, allowing the bowl to fall into your lap, your view.

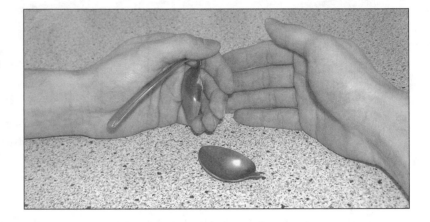

By the way, you can perform this trick standing. When you approach a spectator, you can already have the "spoon" in position, or pick up a spoon from the table and bend it behind your back while you're idly talking and add the bowl (that's been in your back pocket the whole time). Later, when the bowl falls off in the middle of the trick, let it drop on to the floor. Bend down and pretend to pick up the bowl, but just leave it there. As you stand back up, having pretended to retrieve the bowl, simply unbend the folded spoon. The larger motion of your standing upright covers this small action with your hands. Pretend to fuse the two pieces back together and drop the spoon on the table or hand it out for examination. While everyone is looking at the restored spoon, kick the bowl that's still on the floor under the table or across the room.

Once you get hooked on the audience's reaction to your being able to bend spoons and forks, you won't want to stop. Before you enter rehab, however, let's try to apply your newfound psychokinetic ability to a few things besides cutlery.

Double Whammy

Remember the expression "If they liked it once, they'll love it twice" and the old advertising slogan "Double your pleasure, double your fun"? Well, in this trick, instead of bending just one nail, you bend two of them at the same time. This novelty was created by hobbyist magician John Demotte during the height of Uri Geller-mania back in the 1970s.

Effect

You hold two nails at your left fingertips. First, both nails bend to 90-degree angles. Then, with a gentle squeeze, both nails fold completely in half and are dropped on to the table for examination. They are solid and cannot be unbent. The nails seem to have completely folded in half without any real visible effort by you.

Preparation

Obtain two nails that are approximately 3½ inches in length. Bend each nail exactly in half, into horseshoe shapes. The easiest way to do this is to hammer them over a vise.

Set the two nails on the table, as shown in the photo, so that the centers of the curved nails meet. Especially note that the head and point ends of the nails are reversed. Pick up the two nails and pinch them between the tips of your left thumb and forefinger. Once the spot where the two nails meet is hidden, it looks like you're holding two straight nails pointing in opposite directions. This is the secret grip you'll be using when you perform the trick.

Position the two bent nails as shown, so that the centers of the nails touch.

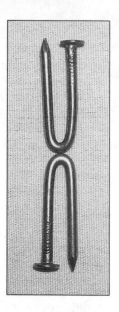

Before you're ready to begin, place the two nails in position, and then add a straight, unbent nail beside them so that you appear to be holding three regular nails pinched between your left thumb and forefinger. Pick up about 10 more straight nails in your right hand, and you're set to approach your audience.

Hold the two nails between your left thumb and forefinger, hiding the spot where the nails meet.

(Photo courtesy of Titus Photography.)

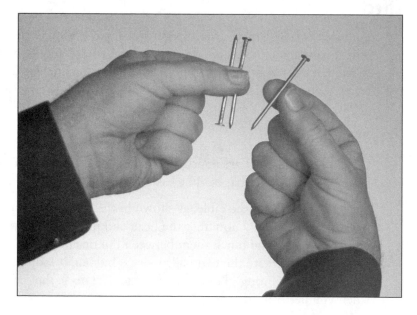

Performance

Drop the nails from your right hand on to the table. Ask your spectators to pick up one or more nails and try to bend them. It's important that they know the nails are solid and can't be bent by brute force. Tell them that everyone's going to have a chance to try to bend the nails by telekinesis.

(If you feel or think it looks a bit awkward walking up to a table with the gimmicked nails already in position, then here's an alternate handling: carry all of the nails in a small bag or, if you're careful not to rip your clothing, in a pocket. Reach into the bag or pocket, pull all but one of the straight nails, and toss them on to the table. Ask everyone to pick up a couple of nails and test them to make sure they can't be bent by hand. Then, while everyone is occupied, go back into the bag or your pocket, fish out the two bent nails and the remaining straight nail, and set them into position in your left hand as you remove them. It will simply look as if you've found a few more nails in the bottom of the bag and have decided to use those for your trick.)

Show the three nails in your left fingertips, holding them in a vertical position. Seemingly decide that you only need two nails for your demonstration. With your right hand, remove the straight, ungimmicked nail from between your thumb and forefinger, making sure that you don't accidentally expose the bends in the other two nails. Drop the solid, unbent nail on to the table. (This nail's only purpose is to help subtly convince the spectators that the other two nails in your left hand are also straight and solid.)

Hold your right thumb and forefinger about 4 inches apart. Gently press your right forefinger against the two ends of the upper U-shaped nail in your left hand. Likewise, press your right thumb against the two lower ends of the bent nails.

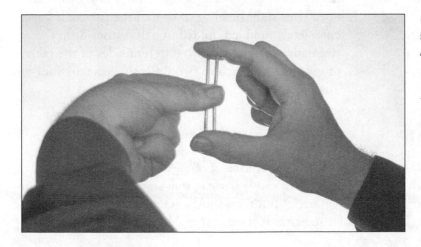

Contact the ends of the bent nails with your right thumb and forefinger.

(Photo courtesy of Titus Photography.)

Pull your right hand to the right, using your left thumb and forefinger as a pivot point. The nails both appear to bend.

(Photo courtesy of Titus Photography.)

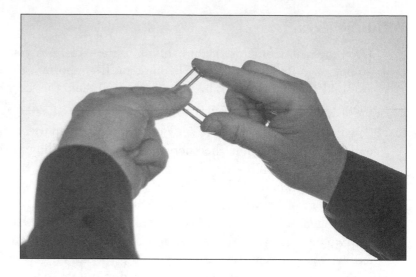

Continue to pinch the bent nails between your left thumb and forefinger. Very slowly, move your right hand to the right, pulling the ends of the nails along. The pads of your left thumb and forefinger act as a pivot point, and both nails will appear to bend. Keep moving your right hand to the right until it looks like the two nails, side by side, have bent to about a 90-degree angle. Pause to allow the effect to register to your audience.

Well, they couldn't be bent by hand before. But they feel a little warm now. Let's see if the metal has softened up a bit.

Curses _____

Don't allow one person to handle both nails at the same time or the spectator may discover the secret by accidentally holding the two bent nails in the correct position.

Wrap your right hand around both nails. Once your right hand is completely closed, remove your left hand, leaving the nails behind. Squeeze your right hand into a tight fist. Squeeze again. For the climax, open your right hand to show that the two nails have completely doubled, folded in half. Either drop the two nails separately at two different sides of the table, or give one nail each to two different spectators for examination.

The Folding Coin

This is actually a two-parter: two tricks for the price of one. As first, your spectators will think that it's just a joke. (In fact, it *is* a clever bar gag that stands on its own if you don't want to perform the follow-up trick.) But then things get all psychokinetic as a coin actually folds in half while the audience is staring at it. Mentally awesome!

Effect

What seems at first to be a rubber quarter is actual solid metal that folds into a 90-degree angle.

Preparation

You have to bend a quarter across its diameter at a 90-degree angle. The easiest way to do this is to wrap a piece of cloth or padding around the bottom half of a quarter, and clamp it into a vise. (The cloth prevents the coin from getting scratched from the ridges on the vise.) Then hammer the top half over the vise until it's at the angle you want. Because the back designs of quarters differ, bend the coin so the back side of the quarter is to the inside of the fold. Carry this coin with you in one of your pockets.

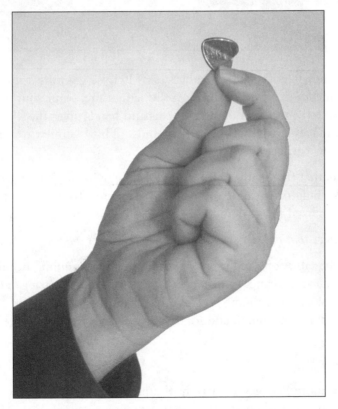

The bent quarter.

(Photo courtesy of Titus Photography.)

Performance

Borrow a quarter. Hold it loosely between the fingertips of both hands, horizontal and at eye level. The coin should be gripped along its edge, with your thumbs on the bottom of the quarter and the tips of your index and middle fingers on top.

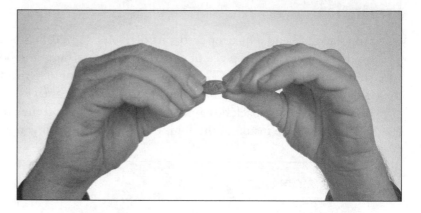

Hold the quarter at the fingertips of both hands. By moving the arms up and down at the same time as you flex your wrists, the coin appears to be made of rubber.

(Photo courtesy of Titus Photography.)

To make the quarter look like it's made of rubber, slowly raise your arms up and down a few times, about 3 inches in each direction. At the same time, bend your wrists up and down. Timed correctly, this motion of the arms and hands gives the illusion that the coin is rubbery and is bending between your hands. (This is similar to the illusion of "The Rubber Spoon" earlier this chapter.)

Some magicians think that the bending illusion is more convincing if they hold the coin vertical, with Washington's profile toward the spectators. To make the coin look rubbery, the arms are moved forward and back while the wrists bend in and out.

You know, you should have that quarter checked out. It looks like it's made of rubber.

Toss the quarter on the table, or hand it back. While they're examining it, finger palm the bent quarter in your right hand. Ask to look at the spectator's quarter one more time. Take it between your right thumb and forefinger and toss it into your left hand. Pick it back up with your right thumb and forefinger, and toss it into your left hand again.

No, it seems solid enough.

Pick up the coin once more between your right thumb and forefinger. Pretend to toss it into your left hand, but actually perform a Bobo Switch (as described in Chapter 9), tossing the bent coin into your left hand. Curl your left fingers just enough to shield the coin from the spectators' view as you finger palm the regular quarter in your right hand. (If you close your left hand into a fist at this point, it'll look suspicious. The spectators won't know *what* you've done, but they'll think you did *something*.)

Using just your left thumb, reposition the bent coin so that it's at your fingertips. With your thumb, slide half the coin into view, just up to where the fold begins. Hold the quarter horizontal, up at the spectators' eye level. Slowly push your thumb toward (and past) the ends of the fingers, sliding more and more of the coin into view. The quarter appears to be visibly bending in half in front of the spectators' eyes. When the quarter is fully exposed, drop it on the table or hand it back to the spectator.

If you haven't already done so, this would be a good time to casually drop the regular quarter into your pocket. Or, you could reach into your pocket, pretend to remove the quarter that you have finger palmed, and hand it to the spectator to replace the one that you just bent.

> **Charms**
>
> Unless I plan to repeat this trick the same evening, I let the spectator keep the folded quarter. It makes a unique souvenir. Plus, it'll help spread your reputation as a street magician when the spectator shows it to his or her friends and tells how you made it bend.

Paper Psychokinesis

Your demonstrations of telekinetic talent don't have to be limited to silverware, nails, and coins. They're very dramatic, because everyone knows that it takes a great deal of strength to make metal bend. But oftentimes, it's just as effective to simply make an inanimate object *move*. And here's the beauty: the items don't have to move very much. Sometimes less is more. A little movement might puzzle or even unnerve your spectators more than a whole lot of bending and twisting, because it seems less like a trick and more like real magic. Here are some final psychokinetic manifestations with everyday items to freak out your friends.

Rolling Papers

You're about to make a cigarette move under its own power. These are actually several versions of the same trick, but I've broken it down into three basic steps so that you can perform them either alone or back to back to build a longer routine. (Although cigarettes work best, these three tricks sometimes can be performed with rounded toothpicks, soda straws, or swizzle sticks.)

Sequence One

Lay a cigarette on the table in front of you, parallel to the edge of the table. Reach over the cigarette and, using your right forefinger, draw a straight line on the table-top leading away from the cigarette toward the other side of the table. Do this two or three times. (Perhaps you might rub your finger on your sleeve as if you were building up static electricity, the way you did in "Static Cling" and "The Levitating Lady" in Chapter 5. Alternately, some magicians pretend to pluck an invisible hair from their head, encircle the cigarette, and use that to "pull" the cigarette across the table.) On your last try, as you move your finger across the table, the cigarette will slowly follow it, rolling its way across the top of the table.

The secret? You're simply blowing on the cigarette. Of course, this can't be obvious. As you reach your arm across the cigarette, you'll naturally be looking down at the cigarette, supposedly watching for any telltale signs of movement. All it takes is a very, very small blow—little more than merely exhaling—to start the cigarette rolling.

Sequence Two

Many people will suspect this method—which is why they'll be confounded when the cigarette rolls back toward you. Surely you can't be sucking it in! You use your fore-finger to draw a line toward you (or wind an "invisible lasso" around the cigarette and pull it toward you), and the cigarette, indeed, rolls back across the table toward you.

There are two methods to achieve this. Unfortunately, the simplest requires a stooge, a secret helper who's in on the trick. Rehearse with someone in advance, and plant the person among the other spectators. Have her sit opposite you at the table. When you draw a line on the table from the cigarette to you, your confederate gently blows the cigarette toward you. She can even lower her head closer to the table to do this; it will simply look as if the person's trying to get a better view. The other spectators won't know the person is a secret assistant.

You can perform the same feat on your own, but the effect's not quite as striking. Plus, the cigarette has to start much closer to you on the table. But it does work. Place your left elbow on the table, near the edge. Rest the side of your forearm on the table so that it's at about a 45-degree angle with respect to the edge of the table. Place the cigarette on the table midway between your left arm and the edge of the table. In addition, the cigarette must be angled so that it's parallel to your forearm. You now go through the motions of trying to telekinetically pull the cigarette toward you. As you lower your head to watch the cigarette, gently blow against your forearm. The air, rebounding off your arm, will force the cigarette to roll toward you.

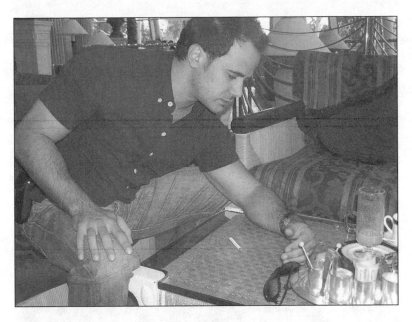

Wrap your left forearm around a cigarette, and blow on your arm to have the cigarette roll toward you.

Sequence Three

Here's one last telekinetic bit with cigarettes, and I'll make it brief. Set two cigarettes on the table about an inch apart, parallel to each other but perpendicular to the edge of the table. If you blow between the cigarettes, they will roll in opposite directions, away from each other. You can pretend to invisibly pull them as you did in the previous steps, or you may wish to make some other sort of magical gesture as they separate, such as drawing a circle in the air above them.

Timber!

Borrow a crisp dollar bill (or other piece of currency) and fold it in half, lengthwise. Partially unfold the bill so that it forms a long tent shape. Stand it up on its narrow edge so that the open end of the "V" is pointing toward you.

You're going to make the bill fall over, but without blowing on it. And to prove it, very openly cover your mouth with your left hand. Glare at the bill. Ball your right hand into a fist. Pull back your right arm as if you were about to pitch a baseball. Make a swooping gesture toward the dollar bill, but stop short, about a foot away from the bill, and open your hand with the fingers spread wide. Believe it or not, the air pressure moving from your hand will be strong enough to topple the bill. For some reason, the spectators don't suspect this method—perhaps because, by covering your mouth, you removed the method they most suspected. Besides, you weren't waving your hand, fanlike, at the bill. You were just making a magical gesture!

Set the folded bill on end, and make a sweeping gesture toward the open end.

You'll have to practice this several times to be able to make it work consistently with as small of a sweep as possible. Eventually, you'll find that you barely have to move your arm at all. You can gather up enough air pressure by simply thrusting your open hand forward just a few inches. This trick can be performed with any lightweight piece of paper that you can fold and stand up in a "V" shape. I've used index cards, business cards, and even those table tents that advertise "Daily Specials," appetizers, or desserts.

PK Pen

This is as close to looking like real magic as you can get. It is really, really something! Once you've gotten the trick down, believe me, you have a true miracle on your hands. It's a favorite of magician Jeff McBride, who offered it for this book.

Effect

You balance a standard plastic ballpoint pen on top of a soda or water bottle. You place your finger near the pen, and it starts to spin. Then you "empower" a spectator with telekinetic ability so that he or she can make it spin as well.

Preparation

None, except that you'll need a translucent plastic pen that will hold a static electric charge. As just one example, the Bic Ultra Round Stic Grip USA pen is perfect for this trick and is easy to find. You'll have to experiment with different brands and models in order to find the ones that work best for you.

Charms

If you want to make sure that the pen picks up a good static charge, here's a bit of prep you might want to do. Take a little piece of sheepskin or other wooly material and make an open-ended tube or sheath out of it to hold the pen. (If you're not into sewing, the quick and dirty way to make one is to encircle the pen with the material, and then wrap gaffer's tape around the cloth.) Keep the pen inside the tube, and put them both in your pocket. When you pull the pen out of your pocket (leaving the sheath behind), the pen will automatically be charged.

When you're ready to perform, you'll also need a bottle (preferably at least partially filled, just so it doesn't tip over during the performance) with a plastic cap. The trick works best if the bottle cap isn't perfectly flat but is somewhat convex.

Performance

Set the capped bottle upright on the table in front of you. Remove the pen from your pocket. (Leave the cap on the pen. The clip helps balance it later.) You now have to secretly charge the pen with static electricity. If you carry the pen and just pulled it out of its woolen casing, that part's already taken care of. Otherwise, the best way to surreptitiously charge the pen is simply to rub it on your pants legs or the edge of the tablecloth under the table. The larger the wool or high-cotton content, the greater the static charge will be.

Set the pen on the bottle cap. It must be balanced so that an equal length of both ends of the pen extends over the bottle cap. This will require practice to find the balancing point, where the pen just sort of teeter-totters as it rests on the cap. The problem here is that you have to set the pen down in a single motion. Once you've let go of the pen, you can't touch it again to adjust or realign it. If you do, it will lose its charge into your body.

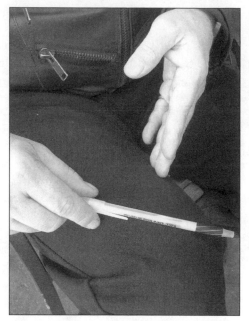

Charge the pen by secretly rubbing it on your pants leg, seen here, on the tablecloth, or a piece of wool-like fabric in your pocket.

(Photo by Paul Draper. Photo courtesy of Jeff McBride.)

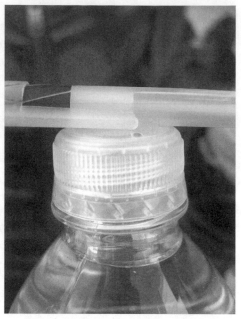

Carefully balance the pen, letting it teeter-totter on top of the bottle cap.

(Photo by Paul Draper. Photo courtesy of Jeff McBride.)

With the pen balanced on top of the bottle cap, extend your right index finger and place it near the bottom (the nonwriting) end of the pen. If you've done everything correctly to this point, the pen will slowly start to move toward your finger! You can get the pen to spin from 180 degrees to 360 degrees by slowly moving your hand in a circle around the bottle. Again, be very careful when you do this. If you touch the pen or it falls off the bottle and hits the table or ground, its static charge will be released and the trick will be over.

Now, this second part is freakin' unbelievable: you say that you can give your telekinetic power to someone else! Ask your spectator to make a fist and extend a forefinger. Take the person's wrist with your right hand and guide her hand so that her forefinger is inches from the bottom of the pen. As you move her hand in a semicircle around the bottle, the pen will follow her hand, just like it did yours. (You should guide the spectator's hand rather than just letting her try it on her own, because, not having practiced it, she might get too close to the pen, causing it to jump to her finger and lose the charge.)

Place your finger near the bottom of the pen. As you move your finger, the pen will follow it.

(Photo by Paul Draper. Photo courtesy of Jeff McBride.)

Hold your spectator's wrist and guide her hand to make the pen spin.

(Photo by Paul Draper. Photo courtesy of Jeff McBride.)

To finish up the trick, tell your helper that you, unfortunately, have to remove their psychokinetic abilities. Pick up the pen (which releases the static charge) and hand it to the spectator. She can try to her heart's content, but the pen won't spin for her now.

If you don't have a bottle handy, this trick works almost equally well on the edge of a table. You have to balance the pen so that its bottom end overhangs the table as precariously as possible without the pen falling off. The effect won't be quite as strong, however: the pen will swing back and forth, but you can't get the spinning motion that's so mystifying when it's balanced on the top of a bottle.

The trick does take some practice. It's a bit touchy because of a few variables, some of them out of your control. As I've mentioned, you have to be careful that you don't accidentally discharge the pen by inadvertently dropping it or touching it against something. And some pens hold the static charge better than others. Also, its success largely depends on the humidity in the air. As you've probably noticed, you pick up more shocks from static electricity on especially dry days. Likewise, this trick works best when there's not a lot of moisture in the air. All that being said, this effect is more than worth overcoming any of these concerns. It genuinely convinces people that you have actual PK powers.

That wraps up our studies in the field of kinky kinetics. Besides, by now you've probably already bent every spoon and fork in the house, so it's time to move on. Let's finish up this part on mental street magic with a series of tricks that border on the bizarre.

The Least You Need to Know

- Psychokinesis is a purported paranormal ability to "influence" objects or energy by using the power of your mind alone. Most often this refers to being able to move an inanimate object without touching it.

- The word *telekinesis* originally referred to objects being moved by ghostly Spirits. Today, the word's synonymous with (and is actually more often used than) *psychokinesis*.

- The modern interest in psychokinesis was ushered in by Israeli psychic Uri Geller, whose demonstrations included being able to bend spoons with his mind.

- Although the most common demonstration of pscyhokinesis is spoon-bending, moving any ordinary object with your mind, such as a cigarette or dollar bill, is equally effective.

Chapter 13

The Powers That Be

In This Chapter

- ◆ The creation of life
- ◆ Unnatural magic in a natural world
- ◆ Stopping your pulse rate and blood flow—mind control or magic?
- ◆ Hypnosis, Mesmer, and mind over matter
- ◆ Magician's Choice, or equivoque

Gurus, visionaries, and prophets throughout history have often coupled their natural charisma with claims of the supernatural, be it the power to commune with the dead or their ability to undergo and endure incredible, superhuman tasks. Blend in a bit of mysticism, and voilà, a cult leader was born.

Many of today's street magicians, though not making divine claims, frequently share many of the same qualities. They commonly profess to use hidden forces from the Unseen World to provoke unusual and startling events with objects from the ordinary to the fantastic. Here's a collection of tricks that could help catapult you into that league.

The Seed of Life

Like spoon-bending, this "trick" was also a favorite of psychic Uri Geller (see Chapter 12), but it's not one of your standard run-of-the-mill mind-reading pieces. This one carries a strong preternatural undercurrent, because it suggests that, as a street magician, you can actually create a living entity.

This miracle doesn't even have to happen in your own hand. You can empower your spectators to have the marvel happen to them! If you've ever wanted to start your own cult group, this may be the trick to do it.

Effect

A seed cupped in your hand begins to sprout.

Preparation

Okay, I admit it up front: this trick takes a lot longer to prepare than most of the other magic tricks in this book, and I'm breaking my rule that you don't have to buy anything extra in order to perform the tricks found here. But I've made an exception here, because it's not every day that you get to create Life. Plus, you don't have to locate a magic shop for any special props. You can find the stuff you need anywhere they sell gardening supplies.

To perform the trick, you must have a few seeds that are just starting to sprout, ones that have little green shoots starting to break through the surface of the seeds. Don't worry: I'm not going to try to turn you into gardeners. But you do have to grow the germinated seeds in advance. Ready for a crash course?

First, go to a nursery, hardware, or home-supply center that sells packets of seeds. For the purpose of this routine, stick with one of the fruits or vegetables that are found in salads or in dinners served at restaurants, because those are the seeds you'll be able to find when you're out performing. I find that corn, peas, and watermelon are good, reliable choices and they have large, visible seeds. Tomato and cantaloupe are easy to find in salads and grow well, but the seeds are tiny. Radish seeds start to sprout almost overnight, but the vegetable isn't as commonly found in dinner salads as some of the other vegetables, and the seeds are also on the small side. (That being said, red radish are Uri Geller's seeds of choice according to his website.) Garden beans are terrific: they grow thick, very visible sprouts, but the packaged seeds don't match the seeds that you'd find if you break open a string bean on your plate at dinner. In the end, the seed you settle on may depend on which one you have the best success growing.

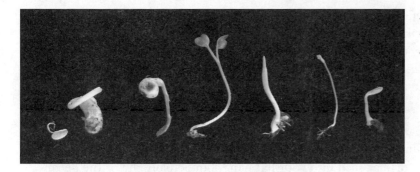

A sampling of germinated seeds after seven days' growth, from left to right: cantaloupe, garden bean, pea, radish, sweet corn, tomato, watermelon.

(Photo courtesy of Titus Photography.)

Take your seeds home along with some of those small, prepackaged soil cubes, peat pots, or pre-filled segmented trays specially designed for germinating seeds. (Yes, you could use gardening soil and Dixie cups, flower pots, or ice cube trays, but compared to the relatively inexpensive peat cubes, that's just too much to bother with.)

Follow the directions on the back of the seed packets to plant the seeds, water them, and keep them warm. You're not growing them into full plants, so just setting the seeded tray on a windowsill should be fine.

About five days later, you'll see little green stems just starting to peek out of the top of the soil. Give them 7 to 10 days, and the sprouts will be very visible. It's harvest time. (If nothing has started to grow by this time, maybe you have a "black thumb," and this trick just isn't for you.) Carefully remove two or three of these newly sprouted seeds, and place them in a pocket where they won't be disturbed until they're needed. (The new sprouts are fragile and could be accidentally snapped off very easily. I carry them in a "snack"-size zipper-lock bag.) Also stick in a few nongerminated seeds. Armed (or more correctly, pocketed) with these seedlings, you're ready to go.

Performance

Here are two versions of the same trick. The first seems a bit more spontaneous, but the second version eliminates a sleight that, depending upon the size of your sprout, might be tricky to pull off. The choice is yours.

Version One

I'd wait to perform this trick until you're with someone who's eating a vegetable or a piece of fruit or a salad that contains the same type of seedling you're carrying. Or, if you're eating out with friends, you may want to order the appropriate dish for yourself so you can do the trick.

For the sake of explanation, let's say you're going to be using a watermelon seedling. Reach into your pocket and secretly finger palm one of the germinated watermelon seeds in your slightly closed right hand. Look through your own fruit salad or ask a spectator to dig out a piece of watermelon from his or her salad for you to use. Squeeze a single watermelon seed out of the slice. Pick up the seed between your right thumb and forefinger and display it.

Hold out your left hand, show both sides to prove that it's empty (without saying so) and hold it open, palm up. Use a Bobo Switch (as described in Chapter 9) to, apparently, toss the single, regular seed into your left hand, but actually throw the germinated seed. Immediately close your left fingers into a loose fist around the seedling, enough to conceal it but not enough to break off its stalk. As soon as is conveniently possible, discard the other seed that's in your right hand by secretly dropping it on the floor.

In the beginning, God created the Heaven and the Earth. Two days later, he got around to creating plants. "And God said, 'Let the earth put forth vegetation yielding seed, each according to its kind.' And God saw that it was good." It was good, but let me show you something great! In order to grow, a seed needs water, and light, and then comes the miracle of Life.

Dip your right forefinger into a glass of water, pick up a drop or two, and let the water drip into your closed left fist. Stare down at your left hand. Squeeze your fist, but don't crush the seedling. Let your hand and forearm tremble a bit. In other words, make the moment mysterious, as if something very significant is happening inside your fist. Slowly, open your hand to display the germinated seed on your open palm. You've just created Life. Hand the seed to your spectator to be inspected. Then, relax. Remember, on the seventh day, even God rested.

If you prefer, you can have the seed begin to sprout in a spectator's hand. Ask your volunteer to hold out one of his hands, palm up. After you've performed the switch and the seedling is in your left hand, open your left fist, flat onto the person's open palm, and dump the seed onto the spectator's hand. Be careful that the spectator doesn't see the sprout. Tell your spectator to close that hand into a loose fist, and then, only after the person's fingers are closed, move your hand away from his. This will transfer the germinated seed from your hand into the spectator's without the seedling being seen too soon. Continue through the patter and routine. Wrap one of your hands around the spectator's and gently squeeze. You might even add a comment such as, "You can do it. Believe!" The spectator will discover the sprouting seed in his own hand.

Charms

If you want to perform this trick but all of the fruit on the table is seedless, you can use one of the seeds you brought. Reach into your pocket and pinch one of the ungerminated seeds between your right thumb and forefinger, hiding it from view. Pretend to see a seed in one of the pieces of fruit on the table, and use your right thumb and forefinger to pluck it out. (Of course, you're really bringing your own seed into view.) Set it on the table or onto a napkin. Perhaps you can ask your spectator to dry it off. Put your right hand back in your pocket and finger palm the sprouting seed. Then pick up the single seed at your right fingertips, and proceed through the remainder of the trick.

Version Two

This is actually my preferred handling, but I explained the other version first, because in this version you have to carry a packet of seeds with you; and most street magicians want their magic to seem completely impromptu. They're afraid that some people might wonder why a street magician (who can supposedly do magic off-the-cuff with anything) has to carry his or her props along. But this particular handling has four benefits:

◆ You don't need to have food being served, so it can be performed many more places.

◆ The seeds can be much larger and, therefore, much more visible.

◆ You don't have to use a Bobo Switch to switch out the seeds; you use a different feint that's less likely to accidentally snap off the sprout.

◆ Because there's no switch, you don't have to get rid of the extra seed at the end of the trick.

Whichever type of seed you decide to use, place a few germinated sprouts in your right pocket along with an unopened packet of seeds. Hand the spectator the packet of seeds. Ask the person to rip the envelope open and pour a bunch of the bean seeds onto her open palm. Take the packet with your right hand, and place it back into your pocket that contains the seedlings. Finger palm one of the germinated seeds. Remove your hand, leaving the envelope behind. While your hand is still at your side, use your thumb to press the shell section of the seed up to the pads of your fingertips, with the sprout lying along your fingers. The back of your fingers should keep both the seed and the sprout hidden from the spectator's sight.

Using your right hand, reach into the spectator's hand and pretend to pick up one of the seeds on her palm. As you do, slide your thumb to your fingertips, which will bring the seed portion of your sprout into view. Pull your right hand away from the spectator's hand. If this is done casually and without hesitation, it will look like you've simply picked up a seed from the spectator's palm. Tell your helper to scatter the rest of the seeds on the ground. As they fall, cry, "Be fruitful and multiply!"

After you've pretended to pick up the seed from the person's palm, let him or her see only the seed portion of the sprout at your fingertips. Keep the sprout hidden, your view.

(Photo courtesy of Titus Photography.)

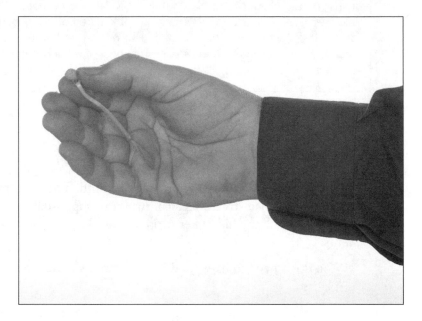

Open your left hand, casually showing it to be empty without saying so. Place your seedling into your left hand, being careful to close your left fingers around the seed before anyone catches a glimpse of the green sprout. Add a few drops of water or say a short spell, and then open your hand. The seed has started to grow.

And yes, this, too, can be done in the spectator's hand. After the other seeds are discarded, carefully place the seedling into the person's hand, making sure that the spectator's fingers are wrapped completely around the plant before you remove your own hand. (And, before you ask, no, they will not feel the little sprout sticking out of the seed.) After you've chanted a few magic charms, exhorting the seed to grow, your spectator opens her hand to discover Life. Warn your spectators to be very careful that night: they're very fertile!

Leaf Shredder

When I first learned this basic magician's trick, I performed it with a tissue. Years later, if I wanted my audience to think I was a Big Spender or thought the investment was worth the payoff, I'd perform it with a dollar bill. (Mind you, because I had to tear up a dollar every time I did the trick, I'd always try to tape the torn pieces back together as soon as I got home.)

But then, one day, when I was challenged to "do something," I simply bent down, picked up a small leaf from the ground, and performed the trick with it. I've never gone back. Because this routine uses something out of your natural surroundings as a prop, it's perfect for a street magician.

Effect

After crumpling a leaf into pieces, the street-smart sorcerer restores it.

Preparation

None.

Performance

What I'm going to attempt is an illustration of a tale as old as civilization itself. It's the legend of the phoenix rising from the ashes or the central story of Christianity itself: Life, Death, and Resurrection.

With your right hand, reach out to a small plant, flower, bush, or low-hanging tree and pluck a small leaf off its stem or branch. As you do, you must secretly pull off a second leaf and finger palm it in the same hand.

That's not as hard to accomplish as it sounds. As you walk over to the plant, turn your back on the spectators. Pull off two leaves that are very close together. You can even use your left hand to help. If the leaves are fresh and green, they'll be very flexible, and you'll be able to easily curl one into a right finger palm very quickly. Remember, at this point the audience doesn't know what you're going to do, so you can pretend to be foraging through the bush or plant to find exactly the right leaf for your demonstration. Besides, what you're doing is hidden from the spectators by your back or shoulder.

With the one leaf secretly palmed, hold out the other leaf so that it can be seen between your right thumb and forefinger. (A nice "magicians' subtlety" is that holding the leaf to display it gives you a reason to keep your hand partially closed, which automatically conceals the other leaf.) Wave the leaf at your fingertips.

What is more fragile than a leaf blowing in the wind? From its arrival in the spring, through the heat of summer, to the turning and falling of the leaves in the autumn. Life, death ... and resurrection!

Using your left hand to help, tear the leaf at your right fingertips into little pieces. Be careful not to accidentally rip up the other leaf that's rolled up and finger palmed as well. Squash the shredded pieces into a tight ball, and hold it at your left fingertips.

Tear up the leaf at your fingertips while finger palming another in your right hand, your view.

(Photo courtesy of Titus Photography.)

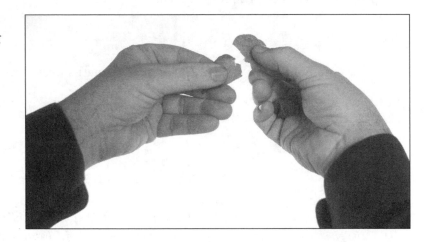

Squeeze the ball more tightly using the fingers of both hands. Under cover of this action, secretly switch the torn pieces at your fingertips with the whole rolled-up leaf that's finger palmed. To get away with this, keep the backs of both hands toward the spectators as you simply roll the two "balls" over one another. Be careful to keep them separated as you exchange them. After the switch, the folded leaf is between your right thumb and forefinger, and the compacted pieces are finger palmed. To the audience, this whole procedure should just look as if you're compressing the pieces of the torn leaf into a smaller bundle.

After a magical gesture to signal the "magic moment" (such as a wave of your hand or a snap of your fingers), use your left fingers to help unfold the "resurrected" leaf. Keep the finger palmed pieces hidden in your right hand. It appears to the audience as if the leaf you destroyed has been restored.

The easiest way to "clean up" after performing this trick is simply to drop both the whole leaf and the pieces together into a trashcan or onto the ground. Trust me, people will not drop down on their hands and knees to inspect the leaf and look for an extra one. If the spectator insists on inspecting the leaf before you discard it, hand it over. You then have plenty of time and misdirection to pocket the pieces.

Several years ago, I was performing on a very small cruise ship with about 100 passengers when we visited an Indonesian island far off the regular tourist map at the special invitation of our cultural liaison onboard. We expected the local mayor to show up, but we were also met on the dock by the island shaman who made a ritual sacrifice of a live chicken (no kidding!) to see if the auspices were good for our visit. (They were.) There were no tourist buses, so using just about any transportation we could find, we traveled up into the hills to visit a village of about a dozen straw huts. Its inhabitants greeted us with native dances and songs. The passengers then dispersed to watch the local women weave on hand looms, so, on the spur of the moment, I decided to do some tricks for the kids standing around. I didn't have any special props with me—I wasn't even carrying any coins or a deck of playing cards—so I started doing tricks with things I could pick up off the ground. I did the ripped and restored leaf, as well as a trick using small pebbles I found around the perimeter of the ceremonial fire circle. Before long, we were all heading back to the ship. As we bounced down the hill in our various jeeps, pickup trucks, and minibuses, our Indonesian guide told me, in complete seriousness, that it was lucky we were leaving when we were. The shaman had heard about my "little show" and was traveling as fast as he could from the other side of the island to challenge me to a magic duel to the death.

The Circle of Life

There are many, many variations of this old favorite in magical literature. Most magicians refer to it simply as "Two in the Hand, One in the Pocket." It's one of the best impromptu close-up tricks I know, because it can be performed with just about any small hand-held object, as long as you can fit three of them inside of a closed fist at one time. You also have to be able to finger palm one of them, but by now that shouldn't be a problem for you.

Effect

You show two pebbles in your left hand. A third placed in your pocket joins them. You repeat this twice. At the end of the trick, all three pebbles disappear.

Preparation

None. When you perform, you're going to need four small, nearly identical objects. For example, in this routine I use common pebbles about a ½-inch in diameter that I pick up off the ground.

> **Tricky Tidbits** _____
>
> I find something that's handy when I'm ready to perform this trick. In restaurants, I've used sugar packets, coffee creamers, and jelly containers. At a bar, I've used bottle caps. (In fact, it's a great trick to perform in conjunction with "The Conjuring Caps" from Chapter 10.) But if you want to go all "Kabbalah" on your crowd, you could carry small crystals or polished colored gemstones with you to perform the trick.

Performance

I was watching a video on the Internet last week that showed a bunch of natives in Africa dancing around a fire surrounded by a large circle of rocks. I didn't know things like that existed anymore. It was called something like a ceremonial fire circle, and it was supposed to have magical powers. The witch doctor—sorry, my bad: shaman—used the fire to call up Spirits of the tribal ancestors, and the enchanted circle was supposed to be a barrier to keep the evil spirits out. Most of the stones were pretty big; some were no larger than these pebbles here.

Reach down with your right hand and pick up four small pebbles that look similar enough that they could pass for each other unless they're closely inspected. There's no rush, so you don't have to grab the first pebbles you see. The audience can only be aware of three of them, so at some point you're going to have to pick up at least two together. If they suspect that you have a fourth pebble, there won't be much of a trick. Once you have all four in your hand, position one of them in a finger palm position.

Sequence One

Throw three pebbles on the table, holding back the fourth one in your right hand. Open your left hand and hold it out, palm up. Pick up one pebble between your right thumb and forefinger. Toss it onto your left palm as you count "One."

Pick up a second pebble between your right thumb and forefinger. Toss it onto your left hand, but, as you do, uncurl your right fingers enough to let the palmed pebble fly into your left hand along with it. The instant the pebbles hit the left palm, close your left hand into a fist. Don't worry about the loud "clink." The audience will assume it's just the second pebble hitting the first one. (I know: this last move looks and feels very similar to the Bobo Switch that you've been using throughout this book. The difference, however, is that here you don't switch the objects when you make the toss. You throw both of them together into your left hand.)

Pick up the last pebble from the table between your right thumb and forefinger. Show it to the audience, casually letting them see that your right hand is otherwise empty. Place your right hand in your pocket, but once your hand is out of sight, finger palm the pebble. Take your hand out of your pocket, and let it hang by your side. Your spectator will assume that you left the pebble in your pocket.

Ask how many pebbles are in your left hand. Regardless of what the audience says, open your left hand to show that all three are there. The one from your pocket has seemingly returned to your hand. Dump the pebbles onto the table.

Sequence Two

Repeat the above series of moves. This time, however, when you place the last pebble in your pocket, actually leave it there. Take out your empty right hand, casually allowing the audience to see that it's empty (without saying so), and drop it to your side. As you did before, ask the audience how many pebbles they think you have in your left hand. Open your hand to reveal three pebbles. Dump them on the table.

Sequence Three

You offer to repeat the trick one last time, but with a small difference. Pick up a pebble with your right hand. Pretend to place it in your left hand, but actually perform a pass to keep the pebble in your right hand. (At the end of the pass, your left hand will be closed in a fist, and a pebble is finger palmed in your right hand.)

With your right hand, pick up the two pebbles on the table together, and add them to the one hidden in your hand. Place your right hand into your pocket, and drop all three pebbles inside. (Again, it doesn't matter if they *talk* as they hit each other.) Bring

The Magic Word

In magical jargon, when two objects that are out of sight can be heard hitting against each other, they are said to **talk**. In some tricks, like "The Circle of Life," it's okay, because it reinforces that the objects are really where they're supposed to be. In other tricks, letting the items "talk" gives away the secret.

your right hand out of your pocket, and casually let the audience see that there's nothing in it.

Ask the audience how many pebbles are in your left hand. Regardless of what the audience guesses, say, "None!" Open both hands, palm up. For emphasis, you might even want to clap them once together. The pebbles have disappeared.

Variation One

One of the great things about a trick that has several possible endings is that you can repeat it later for the same audience but still surprise them at the finish. Here's a twist for the end for the trick you just learned: you don't have to make the pebbles disappear. Instead, you can make them merge into one big stone about three times the size of the others! To do it, we'll use our old friend, the Bobo Switch.

Obviously you have to prepare for this in advance by having the stone that you're going to produce at the end in your right-side pants pocket. The stone has to be visibly bigger than the other pebbles but it still has to be small enough to easily slip out of your pocket and remain hidden when palmed in a loose fist. It also shouldn't make a noticeable bulge in your pants pocket before you remove it.

Perform the first sequence of the original routine. At the end of that section, you'll have just dumped three small pebbles on the table, and you have one more finger palmed in your right hand.

Perform Sequence Two. At the end of that step, instead of merely dropping the fourth pebble into your pocket, switch it for the larger stone. When you remove your hand from your pocket, you're palming the bigger stone. Its size won't allow you to conceal it in a finger palm, so simply close your hand into a loose fist around it. Say that you'll do the trick once more, but this time, you'll do something a little different.

Pick up one of the pebbles on the table with your right thumb and forefinger. Pretend to toss it into your left hand, but perform a Bobo Switch instead. As soon as the big stone hits your left palm, close your fingers around it. To ensure that the spectator doesn't get a peek at it, immediately turn over your left hand, palm down. Pick up the two pebbles remaining on the table, adding them to the one you have hidden in your right hand. Drop all three into your right pants pocket.

The rock circle supposedly provided magical protection. But what if they needed some sort of shield or defense from really evil Spirits? They'd need some big magic—like this!

(If you're performing this as a straight demonstration of sleight-of-hand, you might end instead by saying, "How many do you really think I have in my left hand? One! But it's bigger than the rest!")

Turn your left hand palm up, and open it to reveal the oversized stone.

Variation Two

If you want to produce something for the Big Ending that's too large to palm in your hand (meaning you can't perform a Bobo Switch), here's an alternate handling. Let's say that, instead of a round stone, you're going to produce a long, flat rock about the size of your entire hand.

Just before you're ready to perform, put this larger rock into your right back pants pocket. Most of the rock should be tucked down in the pocket, but enough has to peek out so that you can slip it out quickly when it's needed. (Of course, if you're performing this while seated at a table, you can simply lay the rock in your lap.) Perform the routine up to the point that your left hand is empty, you've discarded all of the pebbles in your right pocket, and your right hand is hanging at your side.

Lean forward and extend your left hand toward your audience as you pull the rock out of your pocket with your right hand, exposed view.

Lean forward and extend your closed left fist, palm up, toward your spectators. Ask them how many pebbles they really think are in your left hand. As you and everyone else are looking at your left hand, reach back with your right hand and pull the rock out of your back pocket. Hold the rock so that your right fingers curl around one end of it and press the rest flat against your palm. (It's okay if the rock extends a bit farther along your wrist, as long as it remains hidden under your forearm.)

Curl your right forefingers around the end of the large, flat rock, and press it against your palm, exposed view. Even though the rock extends past the wrist, it remains hidden under your forearm.

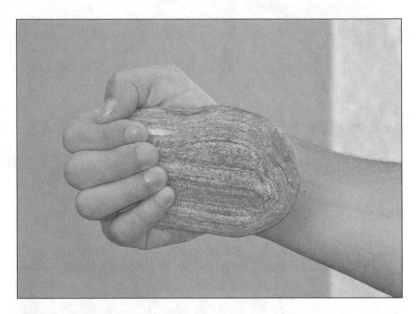

Hold your closed left hand, palm upward, next to your closed right hand, which is held palm down.

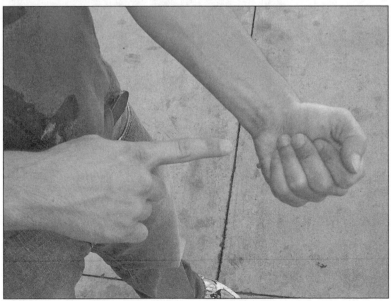

The following actions should be performed in one continuous flow: as you stand upright, bring your right hand out in front of you, palm down, next to but slightly lower than your left hand (which is still closed, palm up.) Turn over both of your hands at the same time as you open them, so that the left hand is palm down and the right hand is palm up. This will reveal the rock on your right hand. If you wish, you can emphasize the appearance of the rock by extending and spreading your fingers wide as you open your hands. Timed correctly, this whole action should look as if you dropped the stone from your left hand into your right hand.

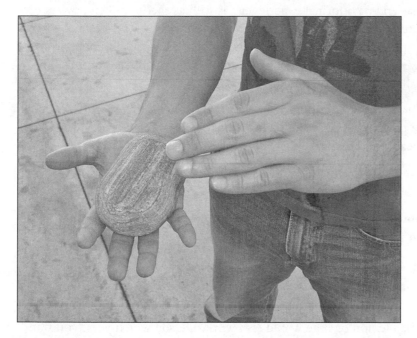

After pretending to toss the stone from your left hand into your right, the left hand is open, palm down, and the right hand is palm up, holding the rock.

Tricky Tidbits

As a final note to this routine, regardless of whether you use the Bobo Switch or the rear-pocket steal, you don't have to change the pebble into a large rock. You could change it into something else entirely. Here are a few ideas:

- A jumbo ball of paper, because in the old children's game "Rock, Scissors, Paper," paper always beats rock

- A tiny hammer or mallet, because it apparently crushed the stone

- A small charm or amulet to ward off wicked spirits

- A comic toy that's a complete nonsequitor or some prop to help you segue to your next trick

If these last two tricks with tales of magic among the witch doctors of Africa didn't rattle your bones, maybe these next two will get your blood pumping—or, in the case of the first one, not moving at all.

Tourniquet Trickery

In this section of the book, we're passing through some of the themes that provide some of the best story ideas for street magicians. In the last two chapters, for example, we investigated ghosts and paranormal experiences as well as the unknown powers of the mind. This chapter, however, has dealt with the metaphysical—the study of time, space, and the true nature of the universe. (Even if you don't know what metaphysics is, it's a great buzzword to drop into a conversation to get people talking about whether magic is real and what it can and cannot do.)

In this trick, you're going to demonstrate your mastery of one of the goals of spiritual meditation—to have power over your bodily functions. (Stop snickering!) In this case, it's controlling the beat of your heart and the flow of your blood.

Effect

Using the psychic power of your mind, you're able to temporarily slow and then stop the beat of your own pulse.

Preparation

You'll need a tennis ball or other hard, small ball. In a pinch (or if you're at a bar where they're handy), a lemon or lime would also work. Decide which wrist you want the spectator to use to check your pulse. Just before you're ready to perform this stunt, slip the ball into the armpit of that arm, under your shirt so the ball can't be seen.

Performance

Have you ever seen one of those magicians on TV have himself buried alive or get frozen in a giant block of ice or placed underwater for days at a time? Why don't they panic? Why don't they use up all of their energy—and their air—in about three seconds? Maybe they practice transcendental meditation, which teaches how to calm yourself, even when you're confronted with your greatest fears. I can't say that I've mastered the art of TM, but I have learned enough to be able to control the rate of my heartbeat.

Hold out the arm under which you're secretly hiding the ball. Turn that hand palm up and offer your forearm to a spectator. Ask the person to find your pulse with one hand and to hold out the forefinger of his other hand. Each time your pulse beats, the person is to give a single light tap on your palm.

Close your eyes. Take several long, deep breaths as if you're trying to ready yourself mentally for the challenge. After your spectator has tapped out a half-dozen beats or so onto your palm, gently squeeze your upper arm against your side. The ball in your armpit will slow the flow of blood through the brachial artery that runs right under your biceps. This, in turn, will limit the flow to the radial artery that branches off from it. It's the throbbing of this radial artery that gives us the pulse on our wrists, so as you press on the ball, your pulse will weaken.

Your spectator will start to tap slower. Soon, your pulse will become undetectable and seem to stop. Most volunteers are visibly shaken when they stop feeling a pulse. The demonstration is over.

You have a perfect reason to excuse yourself for a few minutes while you recover from this difficult physical ordeal. Once you're out of your spectator's sight, remove the ball from under your arm, and stash it somewhere to pick up later.

Curses

You shouldn't restrict your blood for more than a few seconds after the spectator stops tapping your hand, because, in effect, the rubber ball is creating a tourniquet and restricting fresh blood flowing into your arm. (This trick really earns its name.) But don't worry: this short constriction won't cause any permanent damage.

In a Heartbeat

It's often been said that if you could still your mind and body, you would actually feel the almost undetectable but ever-present rhythm of life—its heartbeat, if you will—pulsating beneath all of existence.

Whether you perform it before or after, this trick is perfect to do in conjunction with "Tourniquet Trickery," because it also involves a person's pulse—not yours, but the spectator's. You announce that you've trained yourself in a magical way to detect the heart beating, and you'd like to reciprocate for the last trick by showing the spectator an unusual, even unique, way to check her pulse.

Effect

You balance one toothpick across another in your right hand. You feel for the spectator's pulse with your left hand, and, slowly, one of the toothpicks begins to come to life. It moves, and then beats against the other, matching the tempo of the person's pulse. Suddenly, the toothpick twitches and flies out of your hand. The manifestation is complete.

Preparation

None. You'll need two round toothpicks. (The flat type will work, but not as well.)

Performance

Tell your spectator that you've learned a weird way to take someone's pulse, and you'd be happy to demonstrate.

Pinch one toothpick between your right thumb and forefinger. Slightly curl your right fingers, and lay the toothpick horizontally across the nail of your middle finger. Hold the other toothpick in a vertical position. Place one end of the toothpick into one of the lines that crosses your right palm, and let it rest against the horizontal toothpick being held by your thumb and forefinger. This vertical toothpick should lie to the left little-finger side of your middle finger. Extend your ring and little fingers as flat as possible so that the spectator can get a clear view of the two toothpicks as they balance in a sort of T-formation in your right hand.

Two toothpicks are balanced and ready to take your spectator's pulse.

(Photo courtesy of Titus Photography.)

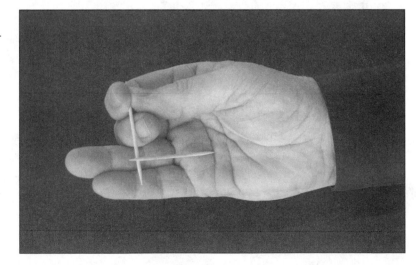

With your left hand, take hold of one of your spectator's wrists, and feel for a pulse. Keep the horizontal toothpick pressed up against the nail of your middle finger, but slowly, imperceptibly, slide the toothpick upward toward the end of your middle finger. Needless to say, the audience can't be aware that you're moving the toothpick.

As the toothpick crosses each small ridge of your fingernail, it sends a tiny vibration down the length of the horizontal toothpick. This results in the vertical toothpick making a series of pronounced individual jumps. (With practice, you can time these hops to match the rhythm of the person's heartbeat.)

Allow the toothpick to bounce in tempo five or six times. Then, secretly scrape the horizontal toothpick upward against the middle fingernail with a short, abrupt movement. This causes the vertical toothpick to jump off and away from the other toothpick. (It often flies completely out of your hand.) This strong "unseen force" signals the end of your demonstration.

And speaking of unseen forces, let's see just how powerful the force of your mind really is. We've seen how you can use it to unlock the secrets of the Dead. We've learned how to use it to control inanimate objeccts in the world around you. But can you also use it to control another person's mind?

Look into My Eyes ...

Are you a magician or a mesmerist? This pseudo-demonstration in which you're able to control the actions of others is pretty darn convincing that you can hypnotize people. No, you can't make a person strip down and hook up for a game of Naked Twister. But after people see you doing this stuff, they may not want to look you directly in the eye. They might be afraid they'll be getting more than they bargained for. Here are some quick demonstrations that look like you really can make people do exactly what you want them to.

Effect

You explain the process of hypnosis and offer to put your spectators into a light trance. You make it impossible for them to keep their fingers apart, to open their eyes, or to stand up from their chairs until you allow it.

Preparation

None.

Performance

All of the preparation in this case is psychological. You have to persuade the spectators that you actually have the power to quickly induce a light hypnotic trance. As a street magician, you already use "power," "authority," and "command" (perhaps even "domination") as themes in some or all of the routines. But if this is your audience's first exposure to you, you must quickly instill a belief in them that you are in control at all times.

At the beginning of the nineteenth century, an Austrian-born doctor named Friedrich (or Franz) Anton Mesmer would put his patients into a light trance state before treating them. (And yes, he is the person we get the word "mesmerize" from.) Most of Mesmer's medical practices were pure quackery, or at least suspect, but at least one, trying to heal people by placing magnets on the affected parts of their bodies, actually made a resurgence in New Age alternative medicine in the late twentieth century.

In the 1840s, a British surgeon named James Braid made up a new word to describe Mesmer's induction and trance state: hypnotism, from the Greek word *hypnos*, meaning "sleep." Braid discovered that while people were mesmerized, they were very open to suggestion and were able to perform seemingly impossible physical and mental tasks. These included being able to endure pain—this at a time when anesthesiology was in its infancy—and to remember long-forgotten people and events.

Today, licensed, clinical hypnotherapists use the techniques of mesmerism to help people …

- Stop bad habits such as smoking
- Control weight and overeating
- Overcome phobias and panic attacks
- Motivate, focus, and energize themselves
- Ease childbirth
- Tolerate chronic pain

Hypnotism is an intriguing subject, and almost anyone can learn the basic induction techniques. If you want to learn more about how to hypnotize and mesmerize, check out *The Complete Idiot's Guide to Hypnosis, Second Edition,* by Roberta Temes (see Appendix B).

Have you ever been hypnotized? Would you like to be? It's not like what you see in the movies. I can't make you go out and kill somebody or drive over a cliff. I couldn't even make you wash my car, which I would sort of like.

And no, I can't make you take off all your clothes—at least not with hypnosis. It won't change a person's basic inhibitions. It can't make you do something you wouldn't do while you're completely awake. Only you know what—and how much—that would be.

But I can show you what it feels like. Now, I'm not going to hypnotize you. Promise. But everybody, close your eyes. Close your eyes. (Pause 2 or 3 seconds.) Open them up. That's what it feels like to be hypnotized. You don't feel any different. You're completely aware of everything that's going on around you. And you don't come out of it in a fog.

Now we're not in exactly the best conditions, but we could try a couple of experiments in light hypnosis and muscle relaxation. You'd be completely conscious the whole time. Does anyone want to try?

You'll find some people very anxious to be hypnotized, some who'll be leery but will play along, and others who will adamantly refuse to try it. That's good, because even though what you're about to do is completely harmless, it's nice to have an aura of danger about it. As few or as many people who want to participate can have a go at it.

The Fake Induction

Before you do any of the following six tests, you have to pretend to hypnotize the subjects. Everybody's seen at least one movie or TV show in which someone's been hypnotized, so they expect you to say certain things when you try to put them under. Here's a simple script for you to use. If you say it word for word, or anything close to do it, in a serious, monotone voice—and you play it straight and not for laughs—people will think you're the real deal. But don't worry; in the short duration that you drone these words, this will not actually hypnotize people.

I want all of you to sit up straight and look out at some point in front of you, maybe a spot on the wall or the ceiling. I want you to look at it, focus on it, concentrate on it, as you listen to my words. I want you to relax. Take a deep breath in. Hold it. Let it out. Again. Breathe in. Hold it. Let it go. Now close you eyes. Relax. I'm going to count backward, slowly, from five to one. When I finish, you'll be asleep. You won't feel any different; it won't seem any different, but you'll be in a light hypnotic sleep. Five. Four. Continuing to relax. Three. You're starting to sleep. Two. And One. Open your eyes. And relax.

Test Number One

This first muscle test is done to convince people that they're actually hypnotized. In truth, the people can't help but follow your command, because it's the way their bodies will naturally respond to your words. All you have to do is have the people act along as you say the following script, and you'll have success. Well, you'll have success with at least 90 percent of the people; the other people will be cheating.

It doesn't matter whether your eyes are open or shut. You're under what's called "waking hypnosis," and I'm going to prove it. Everybody hold out your two hands in front of you, and clasp them together. Interlace the fingers, like you're praying. Clasp them tighter. Tighter still. Clasp your hands as tightly as you can. Now, keep your palms pressed together, but stick out your two forefingers, and hold them about an inch or an inch and a half apart. Are you doing that? Now look down at your fingers, and listen to my words. I'm going to make it impossible for you to hold your forefingers apart. They're getting closer. And closer. Keep your hands tight together. It's like a steel vise is pressing your forefingers closer and closer together. You can't keep them apart. All right. Separate your hands, and relax.

If a person keeps her hands tightly pressed together, it's physically impossible to hold the forefingers separated for any length of time. But as her muscles naturally draw her fingers back together, she's hearing your words and thinks that you're controlling her.

If the spectator keeps his fingers interlaced and palms pressed together, it's impossible to keep the forefingers separated.

(Photo by Paul Draper. Photo courtesy of Jeff McBride.)

Test Number Two

Ask if everyone is ready for Test Number Two. Again, have everyone sit up straight.

All right, this time I want you simply to listen to my voice, and do exactly what I say. Let's try to put you under a little deeper. Once again, I want you to relax. Take a slow, deep breath.

In. And out. In. And out. Now, this time I want to look forward. Keep your head pointing straight out, but I want you to look up with just your eyes, and find an imaginary spot on the ceiling right above you. If you see a real spot, that's okay. Use just your eyes. Look up and focus on that spot. Now your eyes are getting tired, so close your eyelids. Close your eyelids. But keep looking up.

Now say the following words in rapid succession:

But I'm going to make it impossible for you to open your eyes. You can't open your eyes. Your eyelids are now sealed tight, like they're welded together. Go ahead and try. They won't open. You're still looking up at the spot, stare at that spot, but you can't open your eyes. Okay, relax. Everyone look out in front of you. You can open your eyes now. And relax.

Like before, this works because it's a normal muscular phenomenon. It's impossible to open your eyelids while your eyeballs are rolled upward in their sockets. But to gullible—I mean willing—subjects, it's perceived as *you* exerting power over *them*.

Test Number Three

Tell the spectators that you have another experiment to try, but you can only do it with one spectator at a time. Either ask for, or select, someone who was a good subject for both of the previous experiments—in other words, he really couldn't keep his fingers apart or open his eyelids until you told him he could.

All right, let's try another test. Sit up straight, with your back against the chair. Now fold your arms in front of you. That's right, cross them in front of you, and hold them up against your chest. Good. Now close your eyes. And relax. Relax. I want you to imagine that all of your energy, all of your strength, is slipping down, down, down, out of your body. From the top of your head, down your face, across your chest, down your legs, all the way down to the floor. Now open your eyes.

Stand directly in front of your subject, with the toes of your shoes up against his. Stick out your right forefinger, and press it firmly up against the middle of the spectator's forehead.

Keep your arms crossed. Keep your feet flat on the floor. Tilt your head slightly backward as I press my finger against your forehead. I'm going to make it impossible for you to stand up. Go ahead. Try to stand up. Try. But you can't. Keep your arms folded, your feet flat. But try! You can't stand up! You can't get off the chair! (Let him try to stand, unsuccessfully, for about 5 to 10 seconds.) *All right. Relax.* (Remove your finger from the spectator's forehead.) *Unfold your arms, and let them drop. And now, you can stand. Go ahead. Stand up. Sit back down, and relax.*

Why was it impossible for the person to stand up? Sorry, as much as your audience would like to believe that the subject was actually hypnotized, it wasn't your command that did it. In order to stand up, you have to be able to lean your body forward, push upward with your feet, or use your hands to push yourself off the chair. Your instructions removed all those possibilities from the spectator, so he couldn't stand up.

Test Number Four

Here's another Jedi mind trick. Tell your spectator that you're going to make him as weak as a child. Form your hands into fists, extend your forefingers, and touch the tips of your index fingers. Ask your volunteer to face you and wrap one hand around each of your wrists. Ask him to try to pull your hands apart. No matter how hard he tries, he can't separate them.

If the spectator grasps your wrists while you touch the tips of your index fingers as shown, he cannot pull your hands apart.

(Photo by Paul Draper. Photo courtesy of Jeff McBride.)

Test Number Five

Once again you claim that by your great hypnotic powers you're able to rob your spectator of her strength. Openly place your right hand on top of your head. Ask a volunteer to grab hold of your forearm with one or both hands, and try to lift your hand off your head. Try as she might, she's unable to do it.

Simply by holding your hand on top of your head, you're able to prevent the spectator from getting the leverage needed to lift your hand off your head.

(Photo by Paul Draper. Photo courtesy of Jeff McBride.)

Test Number Six

Here's a final test in which you tell all of your spectators that you're going to borrow their energy to use it against them. Have three people line up single-file, one behind the other like a conga line. Stand face to face with the first person in line. Have that person place his hands on your upper chest at the shoulders. Have the other two people place their hands on the back of the person in front of them.

Reach out, place your open palms on the elbows of the person in front of you, and press upward. Tell the people to push with all of their might, but they'll be unable to push you over. The secret is a simple law of physics: by pushing upward on the first person's arms, you deflect all of the combined force of the other people.

Removing the Trance

You can't walk away without pretending to bring the people out of the trance, or later someone might claim that he was still hypnotized when he did something he shouldn't have. And he'll blame you. (Don't laugh: it's happened!) Here's a simple, straightforward script to prevent you from getting into any hot water.

Everybody close your eyes. When I count to three and snap my fingers, you will no longer be hypnotized. You'll be completely awake and refreshed. One. You're starting to wake up. Two. Completely awake and refreshed. Three.

If you press upward on the elbows of the first person in a line of people trying to push you over, they'll be unable to topple you.

(Photo by Paul Draper. Photo courtesy of Jeff McBride.)

Charms

At any point during this routine, of course, anyone can force their bodies to physically overcome your suggestions. But if they do, you can simply dismiss it by saying that they're not naturally good subjects, they're having trouble concentrating, or they just don't want to be hypnotized. It's really a polite form of blaming them. Probably the real reason they're being recalcitrant is they want to show you up, but why bother to point that out?

Pro "Choice"

It would be a simple matter to predict what people were going to do in the future if you had a foolproof, undetectable method to make them do what you wanted them to, wouldn't it? Well, guess what? In magic, there is just such a method, and it's one of magic's most valuable and basic secret weapons. Colloquially, it's known as "Magician's Choice."

Technically, it's a form of *equivoque*—that is to say, you're deliberately being ambiguous or misleading with your words and phrases. In the case of "Magician's Choice," you make your spectators think that they have a free choice (or series of choices) when, in fact, they don't. Remember when you learned how to force a card? Well, this is the same kind of thing, except that you're forcing your spectator to follow your lead with a set of verbal instructions.

The Magic Word

Equivoque, also known as Magician's Choice, is a secret technique to force a person's actions or choices through verbal, psychological, or physical means.

In the simplest form of Magician's Choice, you offer the spectator a choice of three objects. For the sake of explanation, let's say that you have three books in a row on the table, and you want the spectator to choose the one in the middle. In performance, you would start out by saying, "I have three books to choose from. Please pick up two of them."

There are now three possible situations. In the most straightforward scenario, your volunteer picks up the two end books. (For some psychological reason, it's been my experience that this happens more than 50 percent of the time.) Take the books and set them aside without commenting on them. Pick up the remaining book and say, "You have chosen to use …" and read the title of the book you're holding. You've implied, without actually saying so, that the spectator has freely chosen a book by eliminating the other two.

If you are not so lucky, and the volunteer picks the middle book and one of the end books, don't panic. Casually add, "… and hand one of them to me," as if you were completing the thought "Pick up two books, and hand one to me."

Once again, there are now two possibilities. If your volunteer keeps the "force" book and hands you the one that was at the end of the row, nonchalantly set it aside and say, "You have chosen to hold onto …" and read the title.

If, on the other hand, your volunteer hands you the middle book, then look at its title and casually say, "You have handed me …" and read the title. You might ask, "Is there any reason you've chosen this one?" Casually take the other book from the spectator and set it aside with the one that's already been eliminated. Either way, the suggestion is that the volunteer's arrived at a selection by making a free choice through a two-step process of elimination.

Tricky Tidbits _____

Many magicians have taken up the challenge of explaining the theory and practice of the Magician's Choice, as well as other means of forcing. The classic is Ted Annemann's 1933 manuscript *202 Methods of Forcing*. A more recent addition to magical literature is Phil Goldstein's 1977 self-published essay, *A Treatise on the Under-Explored Art of Equivoque: Technique and Applications.*

There are multiple versions of this forcing method, many involving more than three objects, but this is the cleanest handling. The key is the casual way in which you handle the "selected" and "eliminated" books. If you do it properly, your spectators will never suspect that you're manipulating them. In fact, they'll think you're giving them a completely free choice.

So how can you use this tool in your street magic? Well, here's a no-frills trick that cuts right to the chase. Ask your spectators to set down three random objects—anything they want—in front of themselves. (When I've performed this, I've gotten everything from a napkin, to an ice cube, to pieces of clothing.) Tell the people that you think that you're a pretty good judge of character and that many times you have an idea of what the person you're with will do, given a choice. Say that you're getting strong vibrations from that particular person and that you think you'll be able to make a mind-to-mind connection.

Take out a piece of paper or pick up a napkin, and write down the object you plan to force. Either lay it writing-side down on the table, or fold it and hand it to someone. Point out that you have made your prediction, and it's out of your hands: you can't switch or change it later. Using "Magician's Choice," have the person wind up with what you've already written on the paper. Before you reveal your prediction, you can say something like, "Before we started, you saw me write something on a piece of paper. You could have chosen any of these objects, but you picked …. And I wrote …." All you have to do is have your prediction checked and bask in your audience's awe.

Ironically, this trick could also be played as a "force," in which you claim that you used the power of your mind to somehow make the person do your bidding. You could finish the trick by saying, "Now, let's review. You picked three objects to put on the table. They could have been as ordinary or as unusual as you wanted. You could have changed your mind and substituted something else. Then you had to narrow down your choice to pick just one of them. Yet, with all those possibilities, you wound up with …. Tell me, do you think you had a completely fair and free choice? Or do you think I somehow influenced you to make those choices? You decide."

If you like dramatic revelations and you know in advance an object that will definitely be found where you'll be performing, you can write the name of the item on your body in the form of a temporary tattoo. (Note I said "temporary." Use marker ink or hemp tattoos. And I know that "cutting" is popular in some circles, but don't even be tempted to scratch or carve the letters into your flesh for the sake of a simple magic trick, no matter how cool you think it would be.)

And so we wrap up the section on creepy crawlies, mind over matter, and things that go bump in the night. It's time to arm ourselves for the here and now with techno street magic. Got your iPod? Check. Got your cell phone? Check. Got magic?

The Least You Need to Know

◆ Some tricks that seem to be spontaneous require preparation well in advance.

◆ Even the oldest tricks can seem brand new with the use of unusual props or a different patter line. "Everything old is new again."

◆ One trick can have many different, equally satisfying and magical endings.

◆ Tricks and physical demonstrations in which you seem to control your body, such as its heart rate and blood flow, border on the metaphysical.

◆ Pseudo-demonstrations of hypnosis can convince a person that you have incredible control and power over her.

◆ Magician's Choice, or equivoque, enables you to force subjects to make the choices you want them to make.

Part 5

Technotrickery

In this age of information overload, is it possible to fool people with street magic when there's a cell phone or digital camera ready to capture your every move? How can you keep people in the dark when the Internet makes many of magic's most guarded secrets instantly available through a simple Google search? And who's to tell what's real and not real when video software makes trick photography so simple and editing so seamless that impossibilities turn up on YouTube every day?

Not only is it possible to entertain, but it's easier and makes a greater impact than ever because you bring the human element, the emotion, the mystery, and the imagination that's missing in the world of technology. Today's instant-gratification generation gets a rush that's impossible to duplicate through any other medium.

Let's jump into this last part that uses people's own techno toys to fool them. Are you ready to connect?

14

Can You Hear Me Now?

In This Chapter

- ◆ A distant Wizard reads minds over the phone
- ◆ Digital camera magic
- ◆ Magic tricks performed with cell phones

Don't set your cell phone on mute: set it on stunning! As a street magician, you can use your phone or someone else's to perform tricks with text messaging and experiments in ESP. And the spectators might get a call from your mystic mentor, Mr. Wizard himself!

Meet Mr. Wizard

If such a thing as mind-to-mind communication exists, can it exist between people over long distances? There are hundreds of documented cases in which someone knows that something catastrophic has happened to a loved one, even though the person is halfway around the world. Just like we can have physical bonds, we must be able to forge mental bonds as well, and in this trick you prove it!

Effect

A freely selected (or named) playing card is identified by a mysterious voice on a cell phone.

Preparation

This is one of the few tricks in this book in which a stooge is necessary. It has to be someone who's worked on a secret code with you in advance. (I'll explain the code as part of the "Performance.") Because you never know when you'll be performing this trick, it's also best to have someone who's almost always willing and available at a cell phone, day or night, to take your call. Preprogram your secret assistant's number into your speed dial, but *do* memorize the number, just in case someone insists you make the call from his or her phone.

Performance

Did you ever see that old Disney movie where Mickey Mouse was a sorcerer's apprentice? He put on the wizard's hat and made a bunch of brooms come to life. Eventually he had to be saved by the wizard.

When I was growing up I was, sort of, a sorcerer's apprentice. My parents introduced me to one of their friends, this old guy, who offered to show me a few card tricks. At first I thought he was kind of creepy, but before long I was hooked. About once a month he'd come visit my folks, and I'd show him all the new tricks I'd been working on since I'd seen him last. I realize now how bad I must have been, but he always found something good to say, and then, gently, would show me where I was messing up. He was always suggesting some new tricks to practice and, well, he's probably the reason I'm still in magic today. To me, he was always that Wizard from the Mickey Mouse cartoon. My personal Mr. Wizard.

Over the years we discovered we had a kind of mental shorthand, where we could finish each other's sentences. I'd see a magician on TV and go to phone him, but the phone would ring before I could make the call. It was him. A kind of telepathy developed between us, a connection of sorts between our minds no matter how far away from each other we traveled. He must be close to 100 years old now, but, for my money, he's still the Wizard.

Sure, you could have just jumped right into the trick. But then, it becomes just a card trick. This opening creates a strong emotional bond with the audience on many levels. When people think back to seeing "The Sorcerer's Apprentice" segment of *Fantasia* in their childhood, their minds go all warm and fuzzy. You remind them of how awkward they felt when their parents told them to "be nice" to their friends, even if, at first, you were kind of frightened of them. Then how, if they turned out okay, you learned to trust them.

Ask if anyone would like to talk to the Wizard (or, if you prefer, "Mr. Wizard.") Tell your spectator that you're going to have her select a playing card and that you're going to call the Wizard and have him reveal the name of the card.

Charms _____

Almost everyone has had a mentor in some field, someone who's encouraged them along the way, and your admission that you still hold this person so close makes the spectators care about you.

Spread out a deck of playing cards face up on the table. Ask the person to select one and take it out of the deck. Or, if she prefers, she can simply name any card without touching it. Let's say the card that your spectator has chosen is the Three of Spades.

First of all, I want you to be satisfied with your choice. Do you want to change your mind? Also I want you to be sure that there's no way anyone other than us right here could know which card you've picked. There are no secret microphones or cameras hidden anywhere. There's nobody nearby eavesdropping on our conversation. Okay, then. I'm going to call the Wizard.

Take out your cell phone and touch your friend's number on your speed dial. When he answers, say, "Is the Wizard there?" Your friend will immediately recognize your voice, and, if even if he doesn't, who else would start a phone call with that question?

Now comes that secret code I promised. Your friend should slowly start counting in order from Ace to King, leaving a few seconds between each number. As soon as the Wizard says the number of the selected card, you jump in with another question.

In this example, the Wizard would say, "Ace," pause for a second or two, then say, "Two," then pause a second or two, then say, "Three," and before he can say "Four," you say, "Is this the Wizard?" This lets our friend know that the selected card is a Three. Don't worry if it takes a while to get to the value if it's a high card. That's why your first question was "Is the Wizard there?" The audience thinks that whoever answered is going off somewhere to get the Wizard to come to the phone.

As soon as the Wizard knows the number value of the card, he should immediately start naming the four suits in an order that you've prearranged, leaving a gap of a few seconds between them. Again, let's say the order you've decided on is Clubs, Hearts, Spades, Diamonds. You'll start speaking again as soon as the Wizard says the suit of the chosen card.

For example, with the Three of Spades, the Wizard will say, "Clubs," pause for a second or two, then say, "Hearts," pause for a second or two, then say, "Spades," and before he can say Diamonds, you immediately start to speak. The audience chalks up any hesitation here to the Wizard saying hello to you or making small talk. When you abruptly start talking, it'll sound like you're interrupting the old coot to let him know you're actually in the middle of a performance and need his help. But by stopping him after he said, "Spades," your confederate now knows that the chosen card is the Three of Spades.

Wizard, I'm here with [name the person—people love to hear their own name] *and some of her friends at* [name the venue, if you wish], *and she's merely thinking of a card. Can I put her on the line?*

It's that simple. Don't wait too long to hand the phone to your spectator, because you don't want the audience to suspect that you're giving any clues to the person at the other end of the phone. Up until now, your comments ("Is the Wizard there?" and "Is this the Wizard?" have seemed completely innocuous.)

Hand your cell phone to the person who is "thinking" of the card. (Or, if your phone has a speakerphone feature and you're performing for a group, turn it on.) The voice at the other end says in a creaky, weathered voice that you've previously rehearsed with your friend, "You're thinking of the Three of Spades." Then the line goes dead.

You can either play the moment for its mystery and end the trick in silence with a beatific glow of pride on your face, or you can finish with a flippant comic remark such as, "Sorry he cut you off like that. Sometimes he's a little cranky if I get him out of bed."

Curses

Once your spectator has picked a card, never call it the "chosen card" or the "selection." Instead, always refer to it as the card "you're thinking of." Long after the performance is over, when the spectator describes this trick to friends, she will probably forget that other people saw or heard the name of the card and will be much more likely to claim, "And I only thought of the card."

Variation One

Let's take the trick out of the realm of playing cards. If you have a reliable friend who enjoys playing the Wizard, you can create a similar code in which your secret assistant identifies some object that's in the room where you're performing.

Simply make out a list of items that are commonly found in the type of place that you'll be performing. You don't have to be restricted to objects found on the table.

You could use people's personal objects such as a comb, wallet, or lip-gloss. Whatever you decide on, keep them very simple and limited to around a half-dozen objects, because both you and your Wizard will have to memorize them.

When you offer to do the demonstration, collect as many of the items on the list as you can, and set them out on the table in front of you. If people start handing you items that aren't on your list, accept them all at first. Then pretend that the table's getting too crowded to easily display everything, and hand a few things back—making sure that you eliminate anything that's not on your list. With everything in place, ask your spectator to pick one of the articles on the table. When you make your call and say, "Hello. Is the Wizard there?" he will start calling out the stuff on the list. When he hits the selection, ask, "Is this the Wizard?" Your friend will then know what was selected, so you can immediately hand the phone to the spectator.

If your friend is really good at this, you two could memorize other lists with objects that are specific to different types of venues, such as restaurants or bars. The restaurant list might include ketchup and a salt shaker, while the bar list could include a beer, a swizzle stick, or a slice of lime. When the Wizard first picks up, let him know the type of venue you're at, thereby letting him know which list to start calling objects from. For example, you'd say, "Hello. Is the Wizard there? Let him know that it's [your name] calling from [name the venue.] (Make sure your friend recognizes what type of place you're at by it's name: "Joe's" might not be enough information. "We're at "Joe's Pub" is much more specific.)

Variation Two

If you have a friend who's willing to play Mr. Wizard but doesn't want to go to all the trouble of dealing with a code—or is someone you think might not always be in the best condition when you call—you can always resort to forcing the playing card. That way, "Mr. Wizard" only has to memorize one card, and whenever he's called he knows to say the card you've agreed on. This method isn't nearly as strong as giving the spectator a completely free choice, but it still enables you to perform the trick and have a live person playing the Wizard at the other end of the line.

You can even do this with objects in your surroundings. After you've assembled some "random" items, simply use Magician's Choice (see Chapter 13) to force the spectator to choose the one object that the Wizard and you have previously agreed on.

Tricky Tidbits _____

You could also perform this trick by couching it in terms of Haitian voodoo. Tell the spectator that, just like with a voodoo doll, if you touch any part of the spectator's body, say an arm, the hand, the face—and you promise to mind your manners!—the Wizard will feel a sympathetic sensation in his own body and know where your volunteer is being touched. Of course, you've decided the body part in advance and worked it out with your friend who plays the Wizard.

Variation Three

Finally, let's say you want to perform this trick but don't have anyone to play Mr. Wizard. Set up one of your voice mailboxes to have a prerecorded outgoing message that names the playing card that you will later secretly force. Again, this is less effective than having a live person announcing the card, but your patter of having started out as a "sorcerer's apprentice" to a wizard has such strong appeal that the audience will still love the trick.

Fantastic Foto

Once upon a time you actually had to put film in a camera, shoot your picture, take the film to a photo lab, wait a few days, and then finally you got your photos back—only to discover that you had accidentally cut off everyone's head when you took the shots.

Then came Polaroid photos. You only had to wait a minute or two for them to develop, but they often came in odd sizes and had those weird ridges at the bottom.

Finally! With digital, there are true instant photos. And you can shoot them with a camera or your cell phone. You can take the pics, look at 'em, share them with whoever's with you, send them to everyone else, and then post them later on MySpace. You may still cut off everyone's head in the photos. But they're instant! Let's use some of today's up-to-the-moment technology to create an immediate miracle.

Effect

You show several small cards with a different geometric shape on each one, and you ask the spectator to think of one of the symbols. You use your cell-phone camera (or other digital camera) to take a photo of a blank sheet of paper held by a spectator. When you check the photograph, a drawing of the symbol the person is thinking of is on the paper.

Preparation

You'll need to prepare a stack of six cards with one geometric symbol on each. I use blank 3"×5" index cards, and the symbols I use are a circle, a plus sign, a triangle, a square, a five-pointed star, and the six-pointed star sometimes referred to as the "Star of David." (By counting their "sides," these symbols are roughly equivalent to the numbers one through six.) If you want to make this trick seem more impromptu, you can create the "cards" on the spot by ripping a piece of paper into six pieces and drawing a symbol on each or by writing them on the back of people's business cards.

You'll also require two identical pieces of paper about 8½"×11" (the standard size used for photocopies). Stack the papers. Fold them in half and in half again until they're of a convenient size to carry in your pocket. Take the papers out, and unfold and separate them. You'll carry one of these with you when you perform the trick, so for now, refold it and set it aside.

Charms

Much of magic depends upon subtlety to lead people in certain directions or make them believe certain things. You fold both papers before you take the "fake" photograph so that the creases in the paper in the photograph will match the ones in the paper you use when you perform the trick. It's a small detail that will probably not register to anyone consciously, but if you don't do it, people may realize that there's a visual discrepancy. They may not be able to put their finger on what it is, but they'll know that the paper in the photograph and the one that you use when you perform aren't one and the same.

Take the other piece of paper and, with a dark marker, draw one of the six symbols (the one that you want to force) very large and visible on the paper. For the sake of explanation, let's say it's the triangle. Have a friend with nondescript hands (meaning no rings, no tattoos, and no unusual nail-polish colors) hold up the piece of paper in front of a neutral background or one that will be similar to the place in which you'll be performing.

Take a photograph of your friend's hand holding the piece of paper. Because this is supposed to be a close-up shot of the person who's holding the paper when you perform the trick, not even the cuffs of the sleeves can show. On some digital cameras, you have a setting that can put the foreground in sharp focus and blur the background. If you can, focus in on the piece of paper when you take the shot. Store this photo in your phone or camera's memory so that it will be the first photo for you to call back.

(You may wish to take two or three photographs: one of a male's hands holding the paper, another with a female's hands, and perhaps a third of a female with the currently most-popular shade of polish on her nails. This will give you much more flexibility in selecting the spectator when you do the trick.)

The six ESP cards.

Perhaps the most famous tests for ESP, or extrasensory perception, were conducted by J. B. Rhine at Duke University in Durham, North Carolina, from the 1930s to the 1960s. In his most famous set of experiments, he utilized a "deck" of 25 cards comprised of 5 cards each bearing the symbols circle, plus 3 wavy lines, a square, and a star. The deck would be randomly mixed. The "sender" would turn over a card and concentrate on the symbol. A "receiver," who was out of sight of the cards, would then try to identify the symbol. Because the probability of guessing any single card is 1 out of 5, or 20 percent, it was considered noteworthy (though not necessarily proof of extrasensory perception) if anyone showed a significantly higher guess rate over a large number of tests.

Performance

Do you believe in ESP—extrasensory perception? Have you ever been humming a song, and then you turn on the radio and it's playing? Or the phone rings and someone comes to mind who you haven't thought about for years, and they're on the other end? Is it ESP or just coincidence? Or could it be magic? Or maybe a combination of all three? Let's try an experiment. This depends completely on our ability to hook up, mentally—or maybe just a little bit of magic. This usually works best if we're trying to send exact images, so I've made a set of cards with some simple geometric shapes on them to give us something to concentrate on.

Either show or construct the six cards with the ESP symbols on them. Have the spectator mix them so that they're in a random order and then put them, face up, onto the table. The cards shouldn't be dealt in a stack or in a straight line. Instead, they should be scattered haphazardly in a small cluster on the table. Ask the spectator to cover the cards with both hands and shuffle them around even more. When she is finished, note where the force card (in this case, the triangle) is located.

We're going to narrow down the playing field a bit to make it easier to concentrate on just one item. Would you stick out your forefinger and draw a line on the table separating the cards in half?

You're going to be using the Magician's Choice, so you want to have the person split the cards into two equal groups of three cards each, but if you say that, it'll sound suspicious. Most people will automatically split them three and three, but if they don't, add, almost as an afterthought, "Oh, let's make it exactly half and half."

Remove or brush aside the group of cards that doesn't contain the triangle without further comment. You've already said you were going to remove some of the symbols, but you don't want to give the spectator a chance to say, "Wait! Why can't I decide which pile we eliminate?"

Rearrange the other three cards so that they're in a straight line in front of the spectator, with the triangle in the center. Now use the Magician's Choice, as described in Chapter 13, so that the spectator winds up with the triangle.

Many people believe our thoughts are like snapshots, like mental images that our eyes receive and imprint on our brains. I'd like to test that theory with this piece of paper.

(There's no need to call it a "blank piece of paper." Remember our rule from Chapter 4: "Don't run when no one's chasing you!")

Have the spectator hold the paper in her hand, configured the same way that your friend held the paper in the "fake" photo you prepared in advance and have stored in your camera. Tell the person to concentrate—really concentrate—on the selected

ESP symbol and to try to project it onto the piece of paper. Hold up your camera and take a photograph of your spectator, aimed toward the piece of paper. (If you want to involve more than one spectator, have the person who made the selection concentrate on the symbol while a second person holds up the paper.)

Curses

At no time during this trick should you say or even suggest that you're going to take a photograph of the spectator. If you mention where you're going to be aiming at all, emphasize that you're going to be shooting the piece of paper to see if you can capture any kind of mental image on it. That way, you don't have to explain later why you chose to zoom in on the paper rather than including the spectator in the shot.

Take a photo of a spectator holding a blank sheet of paper.

Look down at the screen to check the photo. As you do, secretly switch the photograph you just took for the one that you have stored. Turn you camera so that the spectator(s) can see the photo. The triangle is clearly visible on the piece of paper! The thought transmission has been successful.

Of course, you don't have to use ESP symbols when you do this trick. You could create cards with any type of design on them to project onto the paper, such as numbers, written words, or—if you want to reduce this to just another card trick—the name or a drawing of a playing card.

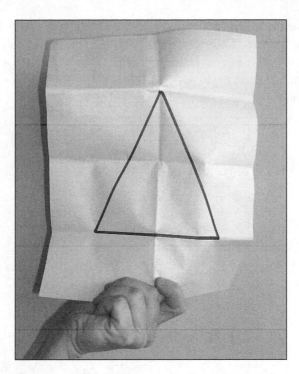

A close-up photo of a hand holding a piece of paper with an ESP symbol on it. (This photo would appear on the screen of your phone or camera.)

Flowers Direct

This trick is a double winner. First of all, you seem to be able to manipulate beams of light at your fingertips. But second, you produce a small bouquet of flowers (or practically any other small object) that you can give away as a present to your spectator. This routine, contributed by Jeff McBride, could turn out to be one of your most popular street tricks.

Effect

You ask a spectator to open her cell phone. With your right fingertips, you "capture" a beam of light from its screen. You transfer it to your left hand, where it solidifies into a mini-bouquet of flowers.

Preparation

First, let's deal with the flowers. Get a bunch of tiny, lightweight paper or fabric flowers that you can find in most arts and crafts stores. (If you're in a major city, there may be a Michael's, a nationwide chain of craft stores, near you that stocks lots of varieties.) Don't use plastic flowers. They look cheap and are very bulky to carry. Take two or three of the small flowers, and twist their individual wire stems together to make a little bouquet. If you're planning to do this several times throughout the evening, you'll find that you can easily carry several bouquets in your pocket at one time.

Paper or fabric flowers such as these are found in most arts and crafts stores.

(Photo by Paul Draper. Photo courtesy of Jeff McBride.)

To produce the beam of light, you'll need a keychain squeeze-light that you can find in most hardware stores or drugstores. These flashlights come in various shapes and sizes. Find one that is small enough to palm in your right hand and can easily fit up your coat sleeve.

Attach the keychain loop of the squeeze-light to the end of a pull, similar to the one you created for "The Vanishing Dagger" in Chapter 10. Because the flashlight isn't as heavy as the knife, you don't need as strong of an elastic cord on this pull. Even two strong rubber bands will work fine.

Attach the safety pin of the pull to your shirt or blouse above your right elbow. When you drop your arm, the light should hang about 2"×3" above your right cuff. Cover your shirt with a jacket that has sleeves loose enough to let the flashlight freely shoot up it when you release the pull.

The elastic pull attached to a squeeze-light.

(Photo by Paul Draper. Photo courtesy of Jeff McBride.)

The elastic cord that attaches the flashlight to the safety pin runs up your right sleeve.

(Photo by Paul Draper. Photo courtesy of Jeff McBride.)

Just before you're ready to perform, reach up your right sleeve and pull the flashlight down into your right hand. The elastic will run along the outside of your shirtsleeve, down your forearm, and across your wrist. Pinch the squeeze-light between your right thumb and index finger, and curl the rest of your fingers loosely around it. You're set to go.

Performance

Tell your spectator that you have something really neat to show her with your cell phone. With your left hand, reach into your left pocket to get it. Instead, grab a bouquet of flowers. Curl your fingers around them so that you're holding the flowers in a loose fist. Say that you forgot your phone. Can you use hers? As she reaches for her phone, remove your left hand from your pocket, and let it hang naturally at your side.

Ask the spectator to open her cell phone. When the screen lights up, point at it with your right index finger. Move your right hand to the phone, and pretend to pluck a beam of light off the screen with your right thumb and forefinger. As your fingers touch the screen, simply squeeze the flashlight palmed in your hand. There'll be a visible glow at your fingertips.

A beam of light is plucked off the screen of an open cell phone.

(Photo by Paul Draper. Photo courtesy of Jeff McBride.)

Raise your right hand and point the light directly into the spectator's eyes. It's a stunning moment for her because she sees a radiant light seemingly detached from any source. But, for your nefarious purposes, it also blinds her—just enough so that she can't see the elastic riding up your sleeve.

Curses _____

Regular squeeze-flashlights will not hurt people's vision if you briefly point it toward their eyes. But be sure that you do *not* use a miniature laser light or pointer, which can cause injury to the eyes.

Bring up your left hand and pretend to pick up the light from your right fingertips. As soon as your left fingers cover the light, release the flashlight and, in the same motion, open your right hand fully. The squeeze-light will shoot up the sleeve of your jacket, undetected. With your right hand, make a magical gesture toward your left hand, or blow on it to create the "magic moment." Open your left hand, reveal the flowers, and present them to your spectator.

The beam of light seems to transform itself into flowers.

(Photo by Paul Draper. Photo courtesy of Jeff McBride.)

These tiny flowers are a great giveaway item, but you could, of course, produce anything that's small enough to carry easily in your pocket and be hidden in your left hand before you reveal it.

"Flowers Direct" from a cell phone.

(Photo by Paul Draper. Photo courtesy of Jeff McBride.)

And you don't have to "transform" the light into a cute giveaway. You could go for pure mystery: If you were actually removing a beam of light and "solidifying" or "freezing" it, what do *you* think it might turn into? A tiny light bulb? A cat's-eye marble? Open your mind to the possibilities.

Well, that's it for the miracles of cell-phone technology. Let's move from oral to aural magic as we check out street tricks performed with your CDs, earbuds, and iPods.

The Least You Need to Know

◆ Street magic is most effective when it's on an emotional level, such as having people recall childhood memories or shared experiences.

◆ Many people will agree to become "secret assistants" at a moment's notice in order to help fool their friends.

◆ Details and subtleties often make the difference between a so-so trick and a mind-blowing miracle!

◆ Even tricks with a "cuteness" factor can be played for their mystery value. The degree to which you present the magic is up to you.

Chapter 15

Music to My Ears

In This Chapter

◆ Tricks with iPods

◆ iPod accessory magic

◆ CD sorcery

◆ Stepping out onto the streets, armed and ready to amaze

It doesn't matter whether they buy them, download them, or share them, kids gotta have their tunes. And to play them, is there anything more ubiquitous—I love big words, don't you?—than the iPod? Here are a bunch of tricks that'll be easy to perform because, no matter where you go, *someone* is going to have an iPod on them. If not, you can use your own. And if worse comes to worst, you can resort to doing magic with the original CDs that the music came from. So listen up!

Buds from Nowhere

"If you're such a good magician, why don't you just produce whatever you want out of thin air?" Once you become known for your street magic, you'll be hearing stuff like this all the time. Well, enough with the insults and taunting: if you want to produce money, your concert ticket, whatever, just reach out into space and—grab it! And to prove that you can, you do—with a set of iPod earbuds.

Effect

You show that both of your hands are empty. You pull up your sleeves, and then produce a set of earbuds at your fingertips.

Preparation

Roll a set of earbuds from your iPod into a ball. Place the rolled-up earbuds on your left sleeve, at the inside bend of your elbow. Bend your arm slightly to hold the buds in place. Make sure they're completely hidden within the folds of your shirt, blouse, or jacket.

The rolled-up earbuds are hidden at the bend in your arm, at the inside of your elbow, exposed view.

(Photo by Claude Piscitelli. Photo courtesy of David Goldrake.)

Performance

Walk up to your friends with your left arm slightly bent, just enough to hold the earbuds in place. (You don't want to look like your arm is paralyzed.) Slowly and openly show both sides of your hands to prove that they're empty.

In one continuous motion, place your right hand directly on top of the balled-up earbuds hidden at the bend of your left arm, and close your right hand into a loose fist around them (thus concealing Mr. Earbuds). With your right hand still at the bend in your arm, use your right thumb and first finger to tug back your left sleeve. Using your left hand, grab your right sleeve at the elbow, and pull that sleeve upward as well. This should look like you're simply pulling up your sleeves to prove there's nothing hidden up them. If this is done casually, no one will pay any particular attention to your closed right hand.

Nothing up my sleeves.

Hide the earbuds in your right hand as you pull up your left sleeve.

(Photo by Claude Piscitelli. Photo courtesy of David Goldrake.)

Cup both hands together, and then separate them quickly to reveal the earbuds. Although it'll take a bit of practice, the best display would be to pinch one bud between the thumb and forefinger of each hand as you separate your hands. This will cause the cords to unfurl as they tumble downward.

Hold one earbud in each hand as you separate them.

(Photo by Claude Piscitelli. Photo courtesy of David Goldrake.)

If you prefer, you can produce the earbuds at the fingertips of your right hand. After you pull up your sleeves, turn so that your right side is toward the people watching you. (This will also help hide the earbuds hidden in your fist.) Look into the empty air to a spot about a foot in front of your eyes. Pretend to see something suspended in the air.

Reach out your right hand, with your thumb and forefinger extended as if you were going to pluck a leaf off a branch. Thrust your arm forward; then stop abruptly as you open up your other fingers. This releases the earbuds from your hand, and the motion propels them forward into sight. Catch them at your fingertips.

The audience won't see the earbuds spring from your hand. Instead, it'll look to them as if you spotted something invisible floating in front of you. You reached for it, and the instant you touched it, it appeared! Something from nothing!

This sleeve method can be used to produce objects besides earbuds, of course. Anything that's small enough to be hidden at the inner bend of your elbow and will fit in your closed right fist can be produced. Once you've got the handling down, you might try doing it with some of your other small electronic devices. The iPod Shuffle, for example, would have no trouble fitting into the crick in your elbow. Although the weight might be a problem, you might even be able to use some of the smaller cell phones out there.

Cut and Restored Buds

Here's a trick that, up-to-date as it is, has a real history to it, dating back at least 500 years! I know: history. Aaargh! But in this particular instance, you might want to use some its storied past as part of your patter when you perform it with earbuds because it involves the Spanish Inquisition and people being burned at the stake for witchcraft.

Among the many tricks that Reginald Scot explained in his book *The Discoverie of Witchcraft (1584)* was the old cut-and-restored rope trick or, as he called it, how "to cut a lace asunder in the middle, and to make it whole again." Believe it or not, what you're about to learn is more or less the same trick but using a method that requires absolutely no sleight-of-hand. I won't claim that the trick is "automatic"—every trick requires at least *some* practice—but it's probably the closest thing to a self-working trick that you're ever going to get. Which is great, because you can concentrate 100 percent of your energy onto mystifying and entertaining your audience instead of worrying whether the trick's gonna work.

Effect

You borrow a set of earbuds, cut one of the cords in half, and then magically put it back together.

Preparation

You have to prepare a secret gimmick. Buy a set of earbuds in a commonly used color. (White is probably your best bet, because it'll match the greatest number of earbuds that you're likely to run across.) Cut off a 2" to 3" section of cord. Bend in it half, and tape the two ends together to create a loop of cord. When you perform the trick, you'll also need a set of earbuds (which can be borrowed) that matches the color of your prepared loop, so you might want to carry an extra set with you. You'll also have to have easy access to a pair of scissors or a sharp knife. When you're ready to perform, finger palm the loop gimmick in your left hand.

Prepare a loop from a small piece of cord.

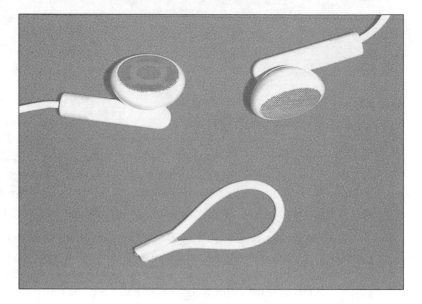

Performance

Borrow a set of earbuds that matches the color of the loop you have finger palmed. You can allow the audience to examine them if you wish, but the fact that a spectator was wearing them should be enough to prove that they're real and that the cord is unbroken. You might want to give the cords a small tug to prove that they're solid.

Fold one of the cords in half, and place the bend in your left hand, allowing the rest of the headset to dangle freely. As you do, make sure that the audience doesn't catch a glimpse of the loop you already have palmed there. Close your left hand into a fist. The bend in the cord should be resting against your left palm, hidden from view, with the ends of that cord and the rest of the headset extending out of the little-finger side of your fist.

Poke your right thumb and forefinger into the forefinger side of your left fist, and grab the bend in the small loop that you have finger palmed there. Pull the bend of the loop into view, being careful that you don't pull it completely free of your fist and that the tape holding the ends of the loop together doesn't show. To the audience, this will look like the center of the cord from the borrowed set of earbuds.

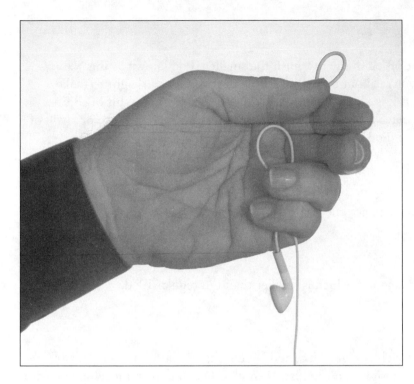

The small loop appears to be part of the earbud cord, exposed view.

(Photo courtesy of Titus Photography.)

Using the scissors or a very sharp knife, cut the loop in half. If you're very brave, let an audience member do the cutting. It's important that you cut the loop with a single snip. If you have to tug or gnaw away, you increase the risk of pulling the whole loop out of your fist and exposing it.

Say that you want to "trim" the ends of the cord. Neatness counts! In actuality, you need to get rid of the evidence. With two or three snips of the scissors, cut away the remaining bits of the loop—including the ends joined by tape. Let the pieces fall to the floor. Don't worry: after the trick is over, no one will bend down, pick up the clipped pieces, and discover that two of them are taped together.

Curses

It shouldn't have to be said, but be careful not snip your fingers rather than the cord! It smarts! Plus, the blood discolors the cord.

To indicate the "magic moment," make a magical gesture, such as snapping your fingers over your hand, waving the scissors like a magic wand, or shouting the magic words "Steve Jobs." Then, with a flourish, open your left hand and immediately tug on the cord of the earbuds to show that it has been completely restored.

Nano to No Pod

Here's a quick sleight-of-hand way to vanish the smaller iPod known as the Nano or Nanopod. What you're about to learn was first developed as a sleight to make a cigarette vanish. But this is a versatile move because, with just a little bit of adjustment, it can be used to make all sorts of things disappear, from a cigarette or a roll of Lifesavers to a full-size iPod or cell phone.

Effect

You vanish a Nanopod held at your left fingertips.

Preparation

None. You'll need a Nanopod, which is smaller than the regular iPod.

Performance

Borrow a Nanopod, which is shaped like and is only slightly larger than a pack of chewing gum. Hold it upright, pinched between your left thumb and forefingers, with your left fingers perpendicular to the floor and the back of your left hand toward the spectators. You'll recognize this grip as the way you first held the cigarette in "Snuff Happens" (see Chapter 8).

Extend your right hand flat, fingers pressed together and with the right palm downward. Hold your right hand about a ½ foot above your left hand. Rest your right fingertips on the top edge of the Nanopod. Slowly press straight downward on the Nanopod, letting it slide between your left thumb and fingers. As it moves down, the Nanopod will be hidden from view behind your left fingers. (If you prefer, instead of using one steady motion, you can push down the Nanopod with a series of light taps.)

When the ends of your right fingers touch your left fingertips, move your right hand slightly forward. The Nanopod will pivot between your left thumb and fingers and tilt upward away from your left palm.

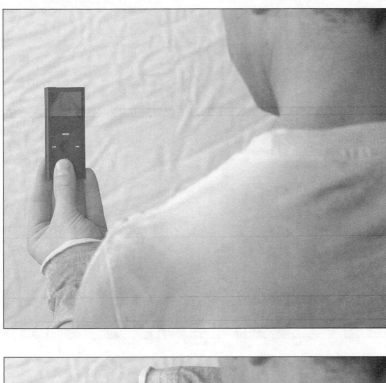

Hold the Nanopod between your left thumb and finger-tips to display it, your view.

(Photo by Claude Piscitelli. Photo courtesy of David Goldrake.)

Push down on the Nanopod with your right fingers, concealing it behind your left fingers, your view.

(Photo by Claude Piscitelli. Photo courtesy of David Goldrake.)

Pivot the Nanopod at your left thumb and fingertips to tilt it up into your hand, exposed view.

(Photo by Claude Piscitelli. Photo courtesy of David Goldrake.)

Slightly curl your right hand, so that one end of the Nanopod rests against the ends of your right fingers and the other end presses (depending upon the size of your hand) against the center of your right palm or the mound at the base of your right thumb. Move your right hand away from your left hand, palming the Nanopod, and casually drop your right hand to your side.

Throughout this action, continue to look at your left hand to focus the spectator's attention there. When your right hand is safely at your side, it's time to make the Nanopod "vanish" from your left hand. Close your hand into a loose fist, and then pretend to crumble the Nanopod into nothingness. Another way would be to pretend to toss the Nanopod upward into the air. Some people will swear they saw the Nanopod leave your hand and disappear in mid-air.

The most effective ending to this trick would be to simply walk away. (And if you're performing with your own Nanopod, you can.) But most likely the spectator will start screaming, "Hey! Where's my iPod?!" Don't expose the trick as a gag by showing everyone how you're simply hiding it in your hand. All this does is say, "Look. I'm smart. You're stupid." Instead, thrust your right hand into your pocket, "find" the Nanopod, take it out, and return it. Or, if you prefer a more magical ending, pluck it out of the air the way you did with the earbuds at the end of "Buds from Nowhere" at the beginning of this chapter. Just be careful not to drop it as it "reappears" at your fingertips.

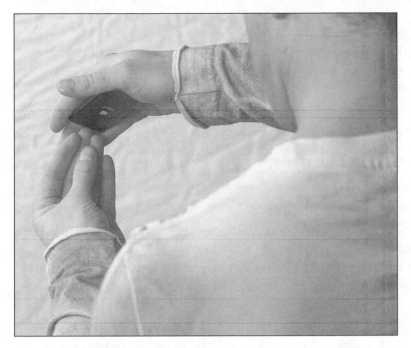

Palming the Nanopod, exposed view.

(Photo by Claude Piscitelli. Photo courtesy of David Goldrake.)

The Vanishing iPod

Who would want to make an iPod vanish, unless it was, perhaps, the maker of a competing MP3 player? What starts out as a joke turns out to be a real fooler when you make your iPod disappear from sight.

Effect

You try to make your iPod disappear using a pen as your "magic wand." Instead, the pen vanishes. You show the spectators that you were just joking: you slipped the pen behind your ear. Then you discover that the iPod really has vanished.

Preparation

None, but you'll need an iPod and a pen, pencil, swizzle stick, soda straw, or similarly shaped object to use as your "magic wand." You also have to be wearing a jacket, pants with a left-side pocket, or an open shoulder bag. You can borrow the iPod, but you'll either have to expose the secret at the end or else go into the next room to remove it from your pocket in order to give it back.

Performance

Position yourself so that your spectator is standing or sitting to your left-hand side. Hold out your iPod in your left hand at about the height of your mid-torso. Show the pen in your right hand.

I can't live without my tunes. Can you? Mine are all right here on my iPod. But guess what? I think I'm getting that disease where you can't remember things—what's it called? Oh, yeah, right: Old Timer's Disease. I keep leaving my iPod at a friend's house or leaving it in my locker at school. One of these days it's just gonna disappear. Wouldn't that suck? Let me show you what that would be like. On the count of three, I'm going to make my iPod disappear using only this magic wand, cleverly disguised as a Bic Pen.

Look down at the iPod. (Remember our lesson, class: everyone's eyes will follow yours, so they'll look at the iPod, too. Besides, they don't want to miss it when the iPod disappears.) Raise your right hand so that the pen is beside the right side of your head. Bring your right arm down quickly, and tap the pen on the iPod as you count, "One."

Lift your arm up to the side of your head a second time so that the pen is close to your right ear, and then immediately bring the pen down to tap the iPod as you say, "Two."

Raise your arm up beside your head again, but this time—and without hesitating in the slightest—slide the pen above your right ear. (If, even after much practice, you find that the pen keeps falling down from your ear, you might try shoving it between your neck and the collar of your shirt, blouse, or jacket instead.) The spectator doesn't see this, of course, because of the angle of your body.

Without pausing, lower your right hand down as if you were still holding the pen. Call out "Three" as you pretend to tap the iPod. Act surprised. Stare at your right hand and say, "Wait! The iPod didn't disappear. The pen vanished!"

Ask the spectators if they'd like to know how the trick was done. Turn even farther to your left, so that they're looking at your right profile. With your right forefinger, point to the pen behind your ear.

It was only a joke. I put the pen behind my ear. See, that's the way magicians fool you. We tell you one thing, but we do something else entirely. We get you looking the wrong way.

With all eyes focused on the iPod in your left hand, slip the pen behind your right ear.

Show your spectator that the pen didn't really disappear. It's actually behind your ear.

While you're saying this and all eyes are looking at the pen behind your ear, casually slip the iPod into your left-side coat pocket, pants pocket, or shoulder bag. Trust me: no one will see you do this! Of course, you have to do it without fumbling so there's no telltale motion of your left arm or elbow. (To help ensure this, if you're going to ditch the iPod in a jacket pocket and the pocket has a flap, make sure it's tucked in before you start the trick.)

Standing with your right side to the audience, slip the iPod into your left pocket.

With your right hand, take the pen out from behind your ear, and then turn to face the spectators. Hold out your empty left hand in front of you as if it were still holding the iPod, but with your hand slightly tilted upward so the back of your hand is toward the spectator. Don't look down at your left hand; instead, keep eye contact with your audience.

Raise your right hand one last time, and say, "Three," as you tap the pen against your open left palm. Pause to let the audience realize that the iPod is gone. Act really surprised! Turn over your left hand, and look at both sides. The iPod has disappeared!

If you really feel you must reproduce the iPod, or if you borrowed it and have to give it back, feel the outside of your pockets as if you were frisking yourself until you "find" the iPod. Reach into your pocket and pull it out, saying, "Fortunately, I always carry a spare. And it already has my (or your) tunes on it!"

This trick doesn't have to performed with an iPod, of course. In fact, it was first described using a small piece of paper and a pencil as "Ear It Is" by playing card and memory expert Harry Lorayne in Volume 7 of the *Tarbell Course in Magic* (see Appendix B). Although the trick's actual invention is uncertain, Lorayne first saw it performed by New York City magic-shop owner Lou Tannen, who in turn was shown it by Pennsylvania illusionist Harry Crawford.

Most magicians who perform this stunt use either a small notepad or a business card instead of the piece of paper. If you decide to do it this way, you could say that every time you try to write down a message, your pen disappears. Then, when you finally find the pen, the notepad is gone!

> **Tricky Tidbits**
>
> The trick is perfect for a Palm Pilot or one of those phones or handheld computers that use a stylus to tap in text. Instead of the pen, you use the stylus. As you pretend to punch in a message, the stylus vanishes from your hand. You find it behind your ear. But then your Palm Pilot disappears. Time to quit work and get a drink!

The Mindreading iPod

At least as far back as the computer HAL in *2001: A Space Odyssey*, science fiction writers have pondered the possibility of machines that become so smart that they're eventually able to take over the human beings who created them. Has this already happened with that iPod you're carrying in your pocket?

This trick depends on an old mathematical principle (often referred to as the "Casting Out of Nines") that reduces a series of numbers subtracted or added to each other to the numeral 9.

Effect

You tell people that you have a mindreading iPod, and it has programmed itself to play 1 of 10 songs that appear on a list taped to the play of the player. The spectator "freely" selects a number and turns on the iPod. It plays the song at that number on the list.

Preparation

Decide what song you want to play as the climax of your trick, and program your iPod to play it first as soon as it's turned on. You must then create a list of songs, number them 1 through 10, and write or print them out on a small rectangular piece of paper that's just slightly smaller than your iPod. The song that you've set your iPod to play should appear as the ninth song on the list. Attach the paper to the back of your iPod using rubber cement or double-sided tape (which will allow the list to be easily removed when you're not performing).

During the trick, you're going to be asking your spectator to do some very simple arithmetic, so you might also want to have a pen and piece of paper in case he can't do the simple subtraction in his head. Or you could hand the person a small pocket calculator, which could be funny because part of the premise of the trick is that machines are so much smarter than we are.

A list of songs, numbered 1 to 10, is attached to the back of your iPod.

(Photo courtesy of Titus Photography.)

Performance

How many tunes are on your iPod? Hundreds? Well, I change mine all the time to play just my Top Ten favorites. But I keep them on "Shuffle" so I never know which is gonna come up next. But somehow or the other, my iPod seems to know what song I want to hear most. Really. I have a mind-reading iPod that knows me better than I know myself.

Charms _____

Here's another possible approach to the trick. Ask the spectators, "Have you ever heard the expression 'AI,' meaning 'Artificial Intelligence?' Do you think that it's possible for machines to have artificial intelligence, to learn from their mistakes to the point that they can make their own judgments and think? If that were possible, it would already be beyond the five senses of human beings. They'd have a kind of extrasensory perception. Maybe it would only be one small step until machines could also read our minds."

The presentation is pretty straightforward on this one. All you have to do is repeat the following patter as the spectator goes through the steps. If his subtraction is correct, the trick works automatically.

Think of any number over 10, which is the number of tunes I'm carrying, up through, say, 99. Any number, just so it has two different digits, like 69. Now reverse the two digits, which gives you a brand new number that even you weren't planning to use. So now you have two two-digit numbers. Tell you what: subtract the smaller number from the bigger number. For example, if you picked 69, now you would subtract 69 from 96. Got it? Take your time. I have no life. I know you weren't expecting a quiz when I walked up, but make sure the answer's right: this thing has a computer brain, and you don't want to be shown up by an iPod.

Now you have yet another new number that no one—not me, not you, not even the iPod—knew you would have. But I only have 10 tunes. Is your answer higher than 10? If it is, add the two numbers together so we have a single digit.

If necessary, hand the person a pocket calculator to do the math, commenting how we all let machines do our thinking for us these days. Of course, if you're performing for a group, let everyone watch the calculations. Or, if you like, at this point you can even help the person or check the math, because he's already made the original free selection. You have to make all of this supervision look very casual, but if the math is wrong, the trick won't work.

The number that the spectator comes up with will always be 9. Show your iPod, and turn it over so that the person can see the list of your Top Ten favorite tunes on the back. Ask him to note what song is at the final number that he is thinking of. (It might be funny to ask the spectator, or everyone, to sing a little bit of the tune.)

Have the spectator put on a set of earbuds, attach them to your iPod, and turn it on. The tune at the number the person is thinking of will play.

In the Loop

Whenever I tell people that I'm a magician, 1 out of 10 ask me, "Oh, what instrument do you play?" I then have to explain that I'm a *magi*cian, not a *musi*cian. Well, this trick combines a little of both: Is it music or magic? Or perhaps a combination of the two—mugic?

Effect

You thread a CD or DVD onto a shoestring, and then pull it free without cutting the cord.

Preparation

None, but you'll need a CD or DVD. Also you'll need a shoelace, thin cord, or a piece of string approximately 2 to 3 feet in length. Both can be borrowed.

Performance

Tie the cord into a small knot at its ends, forming a loop that's about 2 feet in circumference. Ask someone to hold out a CD, vertical, so that its edge is facing you. Thread the loop through the hole on the CD so that about half of the cord's length is on each side. Place your left thumb in the loop that extends out of the left side of the CD as you face it; place your right forefinger in the loop that extends to the right of the CD.

Ask the spectator to hold the CD tightly because you're going to tug slightly on the cord. Open your hands out flat. Move your hands slightly toward your body, but don't pull the string completely taut. Bring your palms together, counting, "One." Spread your hands as you extend your arms a few inches back toward the spectator.

Again, bring your hands slightly toward yourself, tugging the cord against the hole in the CD. Press your palms together and count, "Two." Spread your hands a bit as you extend your arms.

Pull your hands in toward your body a third time, and press the palms together. But this time as they touch, slip your right thumb into the loop on the left-hand side of the CD, directly beside your left thumb.

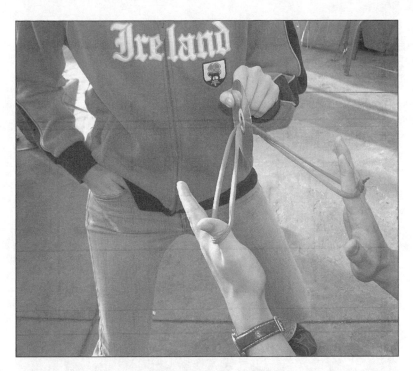

Thread the string through the CD, and have a spectator hold the CD vertical so that its edge is facing you, your view.

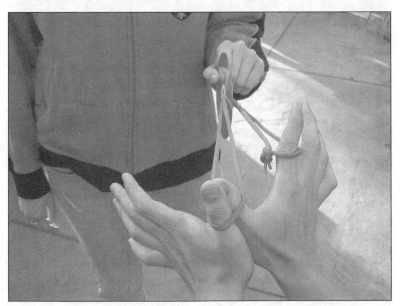

Slip your right thumb next to your left thumb inside the left-hand side of the loop, your view.

Separate your hands; but as they part, allow the right-side portion of the loop to slip off your right forefinger. Without any hesitation, continue to spread your hands wide. Say, "Three!" or maybe, "Free," because the cord will slip free of the CD, looped over your two thumbs.

As the cord pulls free of the CD, widely separate your hands.

You can have the cord penetrate through a post or a person's arm or leg by using the same method but starting with the string behind the object you want to go through.

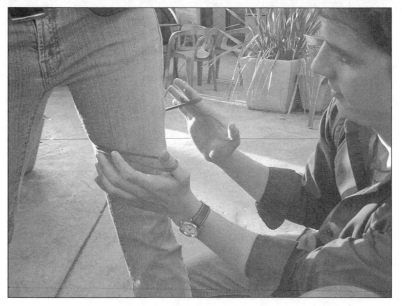

There are many possible variations for the way in which you hold the loop at the beginning of the trick, but this method is the most basic and also has the advantage of leaving your hands in the cleanest-looking position at the end of the trick. No one will notice or mention the slight discrepancy in the way your hands are holding the loop before and after the trick.

You don't have to perform this trick with a CD or DVD, of course. It's possible to use the same moves to pull the cord through a person's arm or leg, or even through a signpost. Simply start with the loop behind the object you want to penetrate.

Well, that's about it. You're now armed, locked, and loaded with an arsenal of street magic to surprise, bewilder, and entertain strangers and friends alike. If you take even a handful of the tricks in this book, perfect them, and perform them in an offbeat, unique style, you'll be well on your way to making your mark as a street magician. But remember: the real magic takes place not in your hands but in the spectators' minds. What they see is only the first step. The mood, character, and memories that you create will linger long after you've disappeared back out onto the streets.

The Least You Need to Know

- With slightly different handling, you can adapt standard sleights to use in tricks other than the ones for which they were invented.

- Sometimes simply using a different object in a trick makes it look completely new. For example, you can use the same method to produce earbuds or a Shuffle, but they look like two different tricks.

- Performing with everyday objects is always effective, because people know what the objects can and cannot do. If it's the spectator's own property, all the better.

- References to movies, songs, people, and events in popular culture make your tricks much more interesting and involving to audiences because it helps set a mood and provides a backdrop against which the magic is performed.

What's That, You Say?

As in any specialized field, there are hundreds of unusual words, phrases, and usages that you'll come across if you continue in your studies of street magic. Here are just some of the "magic words" used as special jargon among magicians and discussed in the pages of this book.

assembly   Any magic routine in which separated objects come together in one place.

billet   An archaic word for a small letter or note. Magicians still use billet as jargon to refer to any small piece of paper, usually one on which secret information is written for use in mind-reading demonstrations.

bizarre magick, bizarre magic   A genre of magic with tricks that have dark, supernatural, or paranormal themes, often performed with unusual-looking props associated with the occult.

burning your hand   Gambler and magician jargon for when the spectator is intently watching your hands, the deck, or any other place or object in order to catch any false moves or sleight-of-hand.

busker, busking   A street entertainer who performs in a public place in return for donations by passersby. When busking, many performers try to gather a small crowd before performing the short show and "passing the hat."

cartomancy   Fortune-telling or divination using a deck of playing cards. The person who predicts the future by dealing and interpreting the cards' meaning is known as a card reader, or simply a reader.

center tear   A method to obtain and read a message on the center portion of a folded paper as you rip it up.

closer   Pronounced *cloz-er*. The last trick you perform at a particular sitting. It should have high impact both magically and emotionally, with a satisfactory feel of "conclusion" about it.

close-up magic   Intimate sleight-of-hand performed one-on-one or for a very small group using hand-held objects such as playing cards and coins. Sometimes also referred to as micro magic (especially in Europe), tabletop magic, pocket magic, and vest pocket magic.

confederate   *See* stooge.

control   Any method that moves a specific playing card or cards to a known position in the deck. When you secretly move a chosen card to where you want it, you're controlling the card.

convincer move   Any action that seems to prove an implied condition or state. In other words, the subtlety convinces the audience that everything is exactly the way you claim it is.

crimp   Slightly bending (but not creasing) all or part of a playing card—often just a single corner—to hold or mark a position in a deck. The bend itself is also referred to as a crimp.

dealer's position   Holding the playing cards in your hand in the position used to deal cards from the top of the deck.

effect   In magic jargon, what the audience thinks they see happen during the trick, or the basic law of nature that's magically broken. Although lists vary, most magicians agree on at least seven basic effects: Productions, Vanishes, Transposition, Transformation, Penetration, Restoration, and Levitation.

equivoque   A secret technique to guide a spectator's actions or choices through verbal, psychological, or physical means, often through the use of suggestion or ambiguous words. Also known as "Magician's Choice."

fakir   A Hindu mystic who lives only by begging and whose religious practices sometimes include the performance of feats of physical endurance. The word is commonly used to refer to any Indian street performer whose "act" consists of odd or torturous stunts.

flourish   A deliberate show of skill.

force   To secretly cause a member of the audience to perform an action or make a particular selection without him or her realizing it. Also the action itself.

gimmick   Also sometimes called a gaff, something that has been specially prepared in order to accomplish a trick. An object that has been altered or secretly prepared in order to later perform a trick is said to be gimmicked or gaffed.

glimpse   *See* peek.

ideomotor activity   Body motions caused by thoughts, even subconscious ones, rather than any external stimuli.

jog   A playing card is said to be *jogged* when one of its edges is deliberately extended out of the deck. An *out-jog* protrudes from the outer or front side of the deck (the edge toward the audience); an *in-jog* sticks out of the inner or back side (the edge toward you); a *side-jog* protrudes from one side of the deck or the other.

key card   Any card whose identity and position you know in a deck of playing cards. You can locate a selected card by knowing its position in relation to your key card. Also known as a locater card.

lapping, lap   Lapping is the technique of secretly dropping an object into your lap in order to vanish or ditch it, or, less frequently, the use of the lap to hold an object until it's ready or use or to obtain an object from your lap.

layperson   A nonmagician.

levitation   The act of floating or rising into the air without any visible means of support.

living or dead test   A genre of mind-reading trick in which you discern whether an individual is living or dead just by reading or hearing the name.

locater card   *See* key card.

Magician's Choice   *See* equivoque.

mesmerist, mesmerized   A hypnotist, hypnotized. Coined from the name of Austrian-born physician Friedrich (or Franz) Anton Mesmer (1734–1815), who put his patients into a trance state before treating them. The term "hypnosis" (from the Greek *hypnos*, meaning "sleep") wasn't coined until the 1840s by British surgeon James Braid (1795–1860).

micro magic   *See* close-up magic.

misdirection   Any method that directs the audience's attention away from any secret action that you want to conceal.

mountebank   A traveling performer or itinerant street peddler, generally having the connotation of someone who deceives the public.

move   *See* sleight, sleight-of-hand.

opener   The first trick in your performance. It must be carefully chosen to grab the attention of your audience and fully engage them with your personality and persona.

packet   A small bunch or group of playing cards, usually numbering from four to a dozen.

palm, palming   Concealing any object in the hand is known as palming. The types of palms are named according to where or how the item is held, such as the classic palm (concealed in the center of the palm), the finger palm (held in a loose fist at the base of the middle and ring fingers), and the thumb palm.

pass   A sleight-of-hand move in which you pretend to place (i.e., pass) an object from one hand into the other while secretly retaining it in the original hand. There are many types of passes of varying difficulty depending upon the position in which the hands are held, the size and type of object being concealed, and the angle from which the audience is watching.

patter   The words or script that you say while performing a trick.

peek   A brief glance unseen by the spectator to give you some sort of secret information, often the identity of a playing card in a card trick. Magicians will say they peek, or glimpse, the card.

plant   *See* stooge.

pocket magic   *See* close-up magic.

prestidigitation, prestidigitator   A formal word for sleight-of-hand, coined around 1855–1860 from French and Italian root words for rapid hand motions. The performer is known as a prestidigitator.

psychokinesis (PK)   A paranormal ability to manipulate matter and energy using mental, not physical, power. An example is using the mind to bend spoons. *See also* telekinesis.

pull   A pull is a secret gimmick used to vanish objects up your sleeve or into your jacket. Pulls usually involve an elastic or rubber cord fastened up a sleeve or inside a jacket and stretched to the object that's to be vanished. The end of the pull could also be a receptacle or holder of some sort in which the object that you want to make disappear is placed.

reader, card reader   *See* cartomancy.

real work   A closely guarded tip or information not found in the general instructions provided with a trick that will make it more effective or easier to perform.

revelation   The way in which you announce or display (i.e., reveal) the identity of a selected card at the end of a card trick.

ribbon spread   When the cards are spread in an even, straight line on the table, the cards are said to be in a ribbon spread. The magician is also said to ribbon spread the cards.

routine, routining   The process of placing the tricks that you perform at a single sitting into a particular order so that they seem to naturally follow one another and achieve maximum impact. Also, the individual steps of an individual trick or the manner in which you perform them.

secret assistant   *See* stooge.

shill   *See* stooge.

sleeving   Using the sleeve of a shirt, blouse, or jacket for magical purposes, usually making an object disappear by secretly shooting it up your sleeve. Conversely, by having something hidden up your sleeve and lowering your hand to your side, the object will drop into your hand to be produced later.

sleight, sleight-of-hand   From an Old Norse word meaning slyness, sleight-of-hand is any secret motion performed with the hands in order to accomplish a magic trick. The action itself (the "move") is called a sleight.

stooge   Someone you've let "in" on the secret and usually rehearsed the trick with in advance, and then placed among the regular spectators in the audience. Also known as a secret assistant, confederate, plant, or shill.

street magic   Until the late 1990s, the term "street magic" most often meant busking, in which a magician would gather a small audience and then perform in return for tips. Since the late 1990s (generally marked by the 1997 TV special *David Blaine: Street Magic*), street magic has referred to the genre in which the magician shows up unannounced, performs one or two seemingly impromptu tricks (frequently with bizarre or edgy storylines), and then leaves without expectation of payment.

sucker trick   Any routine in which you perform a trick, show how it is done, and then repeat the trick using a different method to fool the audience again.

suspension   An illusion in which something or someone floats or hovers in a single place but doesn't rise or fall.

tabletop magic   *See* close-up magic.

talk   Magical jargon. When two objects that are out of sight can be heard hitting against each other, they are said to talk.

target   Street magic slang for the person who the magician zeroes in on and decides to approach.

telekinesis (TK)   A synonym for psychokinesis, but often specifically meaning the ability to make an object move without touching it.

tell   Gambler and magician jargon, an unconscious mannerism, tick, twitch, or change in body language that reveals a person's thoughts and moods.

thumb palm   A sleight in which an object is hidden in the hand, clipped between the base of the thumb and the forefinger. *See* palm, palming.

vest pocket magic   *See* close-up magic.

The Source

It's almost impossible to believe in this Age of Information Overload, where everything is available 24/7, that at the beginning of the twentieth century, it was difficult to find anything at all written about the art of magic. In many places, the knowledge was still being passed down from master to student. Often, magic was a "trade" that stayed in the same family for generations.

By the 1950s, however, magical literature was growing by leaps and bounds. There were several important (but some short-lived) magazines and, as the years went along, more and more books were being written to explain the great secrets of magic. Some were very specialized and dealt only with certain expertise, such as with playing cards.

Rather than offer a laundry list of books that might be considered "recommended reading" for students of general magic, let me share with you some of the books and DVDs that I consulted while writing this book on the specific field of street magic. Some of these books were written for the public and can be found through regular booksellers. Others can only be found in magic shops or through magic dealers online.

In some cases it's been impossible to provide complete bibliographic information, especially in the cases of books that were self-published or have long been out of print. But don't worry: if a book's not readily available at your local magic shop or bookstore, you'll only need the name of the book and its author to locate it through Internet sources such as Amazon.com and eBay.

Although many magic dealers carry some hard-to-locate titles, one of the best, searchable Internet sources is H&R Magic Books (magicbookshop.com), started by Richard Hatch and Charlie Randall in 1990. Located in Humble, Texas, the bookseller usually has around 5,000 new, used, and out-of-print titles in stock.

Books

Ahlquist, Diane. *The Complete Idiot's Guide to Fortune Telling*. Indianapolis: Alpha Books, 2006. A beginner's guide to the history and techniques of predicting the future, using a variety of methods.

Angel, Criss, with Laura Morton. *Mindfreak: Secret Revelations*. New York: HarperCollins, 2007. In the first half of his premiere book, Criss Angel tells about his start as a performer, his growth as an artist, and his philosophy of magic. The second half of the book explains 40 simple tricks. Some of them are classics and can be found in this book as well.

Annemann, Ted. *202 Methods of Forcing*. New York: Max Holden, 1933. The classic study of how to force spectators to make the seemingly "free choices" you want them to. Although the original hardback edition is a collector's item, more recent paperback editions are still readily available.

Blaine, David. *Mysterious Stranger: A Book of Magic*. New York: Villard, 2002. In his first book, David Blaine discusses his inspirations for his work, his early career, his thoughts on street magic, and his public endurance stunts. The book is also sprinkled with the instructions to a handful of easy-to-do street magic tricks that can be performed by readers.

Bobo, J. B. *Modern Coin Magic*. Chicago: Magic, Inc., 1966. This is the "Bible" of coin magic. First published in 1952, it's had several revised editions, most notably those by Magic, Inc. (Chicago, 1966) and Dover Publication (Brooklyn, NY, 1982). There have been other popular books on coin work through the years, such as T. Nelson Downs' *Modern Coin Manipulations* (edited but also largely written by William J. Hilliar, first published in 1900) and *David Roth's Expert Coin Magic*, written by Richard Kaufman (New York: Kaufman and Greenberg, 1985); but "Bobo," as magicians refer to *Modern Coin Magic*, is still considered the preeminent work on the subject.

Burger, Eugene. *Spirit Theater*. New York: Richard Kaufman and Alan Greenberg, 1986.

———. *The Experience of Magic*. New York: Richard Kaufman and Alan Greenberg, 1989.

———. *Strange Ceremonies.* New York: Richard Kaufman and Alan Greenberg, 1991.

———. *Mastering the Art of Magic.* Washington, D.C.: Kaufman and Company, 2000.

Burger, Eugene, and Robert E. Neale. *Magic and Meaning.* Seattle: Hermetic Press, 1995. Eugene Burger is one of the great theorists in modern magic, especially when the subject matter turns dark and bizarre. Any books by him are on my "must-read" list. All of these books, though now difficult to obtain, are well worth the search, because Burger's magical thinking can be applied to every aspect of a street magician's performance, style, character, and patter.

Christopher, Milbourne. *The Illustrated History of Magic.* New York: Thomas Y. Crowell Company, 1973.

———. *Panorama of Magic.* New York: Dover Publications, 1962. These two books by Milbourne Christopher on the history of magic, liberally illustrated with engravings and photographs, were written for the general public, but they also became very popular with magicians. Detailed enough to satisfy most magic historians, they are full of enough colorful anecdotes to interest even the casual reader. Although some minor facts have since been challenged, Christopher's basic scholarship has not, and the books remain highly collectible and valuable resources among magicians.

Claflin, Edward. *Street Magic: An Illustrated History of Wandering Magicians and Their Conjuring Arts.* Garden City, NY: Dolphin Books, 1977. Claflin provides a history of the busking style of street magic from its early itinerant street entertainers up through modern times. Besides providing a good overview of the art itself, the book also profiles Jeff Sheridan, perhaps the premier American street magician of the 1970s.

Gardner, Martin. *The Encyclopedia of Impromptu Magic.* Chicago: Magic, Inc., 1978. This fascinating book teaches stunts, puzzles, bits of business, and bar bets ("betchas") with everyday objects in addition to simple magic tricks. Gardner originally published much of the material in his long-running column in Hugard's *Magic Monthly* magazine.

Goldstein, Phil. *A Treatise on the Under-Explored Art of Equivoque: Technique and Applications.* Boston: Phil Goldstein, 1977. A major essay on the use of "Magician's Choice" to influence a spectator's actions.

Groves, David. *Be a Street Magician!* Los Angeles: Aha Press, 1998. This book was one of the first how-to guides to performing magic on the street. It gives practical information on all aspects of the "busking" style of street performing. The book tells how to pick tricks that work on the streets, create a show, and attract a crowd. It also deals with the legal aspects of street performing, dealing with topics such as "Do I need a permit?" and "What about the cops?" See the author's website, david-groves.com.

Jillette, Penn. *Cruel Tricks for Dear Friends*. New York: Villard, 1989.

———. *Penn & Teller's How to Play with Your Food*. New York: Random House, 1992.

———. *Penn & Teller's How to Play in Traffic*. New York: Boulevard Books (Penguin Putnam), 1997. Part of the appeal of Penn & Teller, the self-styled "Bad Boys of Magic," is their willingness to reveal the secret to how some of their tricks are done. They perform in an outrageous, in-your-face style that carries through into their first three books of magic tricks written for the general public. Close to 200,000 copies were sold of the hilariously nasty *Cruel Tricks* alone.

King, Mac, and Mark Levy. *Tricks with Your Head: Hilarious Magic Tricks and Stunts to Disgust and Delight*. New York: Three Rivers Press, 2002. If you liked Mac King's "Eyescream" in Chapter 9, then this is the book for you! It's filled with comical tricks just like that which, as the title suggests, you can do with all or parts of your head.

Lorayne, Harry. *The Tarbell Course in Magic, Volume 7*. New York: Lou Tannen, 1972. This is the seventh volume of a gargantuan course in magic started as individual mail order lessons by Dr. Harlan Tarbell in the 1920s. The home-study magic course was eventually collected into book form beginning in 1941. Tarbell completed six volumes and proposed a seventh volume and even prepared a few tricks for it before his death in 1960. Harry Lorayne included these few tricks along with other material in Volume 7, along with an index to the material in all seven books. Steven Burton and Richard Kaufman later prepared Volume 8, which included material from the original course that wasn't included in the previous bound volumes, as well as Tarbell writings that had appeared in magic magazines and Tarbell tricks that were contributed by his peers.

Maven, Max. *Max Maven's Book of Fortunetelling*. New York: Prentice Hall, 1992. Internationally acclaimed mentalist Max Maven traces the history and techniques of every conceivable type of fortune-telling, from gazing into crystal balls to reading palms and tea leaves. Whether you ever intend to try your hand at prophecy, this book will provide ideas for themes and patter lines for your mind-reading tricks.

Page, Patrick, and Albert Goshman. *Magic By Gosh: The Life and Times of Albert Goshman*. Los Angeles: Albert Goshman, 1985. This collection of routines by one of twentieth-century American magic's most idiosyncratic performers includes the handling that formed the basis for "The Conjuring Caps," which you'll find in Chapter 10 of this book. Goshman, who died in 1991, is credited with being the first magician to perform the trick with bottle caps. The routines in Goshman's book are just waiting for some modern street magician to update and make them his or her own.

Ogden, Tom. *The Complete Idiot's Guide to Magic Tricks*. Indianapolis: Alpha Books, 1999. If you can get hold of this book, you'll find dozens of tricks written in the simple-to-follow *Idiot's Guide* style. Although originally written for a more generalized audience, many of the routines can be sharpened with an edgy slant for your street magic.

Scot, Reginald. *The Discoverie of Witchcraft*. First published in 1584. Although King James I of England ordered that all copies of this book be burned, a few escaped the flames and new editions were available almost immediately. In modern times, Dover Publications has kept an unabridged reprint of the 1930 John Rodker (London) edition available.

Sumpter, Gary. *Ultimate Street Magic: Amazing Tricks for the Urban Magician*. London: New Holland, 2006. British magician Gary Sumpter reveals some of the classics of street magic, from impossible card revelations to seemingly spontaneous levitations on the street.

Tognetti, Arlene, and Lisa Lenard. *The Complete Idiot's Guide to Tarot, Second Edition*. Indianapolis: Alpha Books, 2000. Everything you've ever needed to know about reading tarot cards, from their ancient beginnings and selecting the right deck to identifying and interpreting the meanings of the cards.

Tarbell, Harlan. *The Tarbell Course in Magic, Volume 1*. New York: N.L. Magic Company, 1941. This first volume of the famous series, described earlier, includes Tarbell's own version of "The Jumping Rubber Band" found in Chapter 10 of this book.

Temes, Roberta. *The Complete Idiot's Guide to Hypnosis, Second Edition*. Indianapolis: Alpha Books, 2004. Pscyhologist and hypnotherapist Roberta Temes shows how to use hypnosis, including self-hypnosis, to improve one's quality of life. The first edition was the bestselling book on hypnosis on the market.

Zenon, Paul. *Street Magic: Great Tricks and Close-Up Secrets Revealed*. London: Carlton Books, 2005. Paul Zenon teaches the brand of street magic that's brought him success and notoriety in his native England, with an emphasis on cards and cons.

DVDs

David Blaine and Criss Angel, the two foremost American street magicians in recent years, have released much of their work on DVD.

Rather than release individual DVDs, David Blaine put out an edited compilation disk of his first three specials (*Street Magic*, *Magic Man*, and *Frozen in Time*) with extras as *David Blaine—Fearless*. Buena Vista Home Entertainment, 2002.

Much of Criss Angel's television performance work is also now available on DVD. Titles include:

Criss Angel's Made in Japan. His first television special, originally aired in Japan.

Criss Angel Mindfreak. Originally aired as an A&E Halloween special in 2002.

Criss Angel Supernatural. Originally aired as a TV special in 2003.

Mindfreak: Complete Season One. Originally aired on A&E, beginning in 2005.

Mindfreak: Complete Season Two. Originally aired on A&E, beginning in 2006.

Criss Angel has also released a five-volume instructional DVD series of street magic entitled *Master Mindfreaks*, superseding the earlier release of two volumes under the title *Masterminds*.

Other instructional videotapes of interest to street magicians include the following:

Christian, Brad. *How to Do Street Magic.* Ellusionist.com, 2006.

King, Corey. *Levitation: King Rising.* Ellusionist.com, 2006.

Magic Makers. *Underground Magic.* Sioux Falls, SD: Magic Makers, 2004.

Tracz, Arthur. *The Art of Levitation.* Fun, Inc., 2005.

Also of special note is *Penn & Teller's Magic & Mystery Tour* (Acorn Media, 2005). This compilation DVD of three Canadian television specials by Penn & Teller follow their footsteps as they trace the origins and modern manifestations of street magic in Egypt, China, and India.

Tell Me More!

The pursuit of street magic is a never-ending process. There are always more tricks to learn, new and better ways to perform them, and endless variations. Then there's the practical experience that can only be gained by getting out there in the trenches and performing for real people. Here are just a few of the many ways to learn more about the art of street magic.

Be a Bookworm

Oh, no! Not the library! Books are an invaluable source for magic material. Even David Blaine and Criss Angel have released their own books—yes, books—on street magic (see Appendix B for these and other books). Almost every trick that has ever been created eventually winds up in a book. Most of this secret information is already there now.

What you're practicing is a relatively new, focused field, so you might not find too many books on the shelves that actually have the words "street magic" in their titles. But fear not. With the lessons you've learned from this book, you can take thousands of the tricks in those books and adapt them for street magic. So it's time to visit the 793 stacks in the old Dewey Decimal System.

Of course, in addition to the books in the library, most of which were written for the general public, there are books written specifically for magicians that can only be purchased through magic dealers. We'll look at magic shops in a few minutes. You'll also find these stores to be a great source for videos and DVDs if you prefer learning that way.

Instructional books and DVDs have different pros and cons. Books are hard to hold flat and turn pages while you're trying to hold a deck of cards in your hands. But as you work through the moves described in a written text, you'll find that you naturally find the best ways to fit the moves to your own hands. DVDs have the advantage of showing you exactly what the moves should look like, expertly done. The downside is the real danger of mimicking the moves so closely that you unconsciously become a clone of whoever made the tape; and once you've picked up their mannerisms, it's sometimes hard to develop your own unique style.

On the Rack

The twentieth century saw a number of notable American magic magazines and journals come and go. Some of the early ones, such as *The Jinx* and *The Phoenix*, were so revolutionary for their time that their original issues are now collector items; in recent years, bound reprints have been published.

Among the bound volumes of magazines that would be of most interest to street magicians is *The Complete (New) Invocation* because it offered occult-themed routines for practitioners of so-called bizarre magick. Many of the Indian fakir routines that were too dangerous or extreme to include in this book, such as swallowing needles or slicing off your tongue, are outlined in the pages of *Swami* and *Mantra*, two magazines that were published in the 1970s by Sam Dalal of Calcutta, India. *Swami* ran for just 36 issues, from January 1972 to December 1974, and *Mantra* ran for even fewer issues—a mere 28—from April 1975 to July 1977.

The two current magic magazines that offer the most general up-to-date information on the magic scene are *MAGIC* and *GENII*. Both include feature articles on magicians and events, as well as new products, reviews, and advertising. They can be reached at:

MAGIC, An Independent Magazine for Magicians
Stan Allen, Editor
6220 Stevenson Way
Las Vegas, NV 89120
(702) 798-0099
magicmagazine.com

Genii, The Conjurors' Magazine
Richard Kaufman, Editor
The Genii Corporation
4200 Wisconsin Avenue, Suite 106–384
Washington, DC 20016
(301) 652-5800
www.geniimagazine.com

The first issue of *Street Magic Magazine*, a new high-gloss magazine edited by James L. Clark and dedicated specifically to the growing field of street sorcery, hit magic stores in March/April 2007. Japanese street magician Cyril Takayama is featured on the cover of the premiere issue. Subscription and other information can be found at:

Street Magic Magazine
(877) 877-7878
www.streetmagicmagazine.com

Two other major magic magazines, *The Linking Ring* and *M.U.M.*, are only available through their fraternal organizations, the International Brotherhood of Magicians and the Society of American Magicians, respectively. (You'll be reading about these clubs a bit later on in this appendix.)

Do You See What I See?

One of the best ways to increase the breadth of your magical wisdom is to see other magicians perform. Not to steal their tricks. Never! That's one of magic's "Thou Shalt Not" commandments. But by seeing other magicians, either live or on TV, you'll get to see what's hot and what kind of tricks are getting the strongest reactions from the crowds you want to attract.

Besides the tricks, you should also be watching other performers—not just magicians—to study their stagecraft and showmanship. Why did they get the response they got? *How* did they get it? Watch with a critical eye to see what performance tips you can pick up to use in your own work.

Enroll at Hogwarts

Unfortunately, there are few real schools of magic out there that have regular classes. Sometimes a local hobbyist or a full- or part-time professional offers lessons in their area. The classes are often held evenings at a YMCA, YWCA, community college, or some similar institution. Check out continuing education calendars in your area. Also, many magic shops offer their own classes. Or, if you see a magician in your area whose work you admire, you might consider the possibility of arranging private lessons.

McBride's Magic & Mystery School (magicalwisdom.com or mcbridemagic.com), begun by Jeff McBride and located in Las Vegas, offers intensive master classes to very small groups (usually limited to an enrollment of 15 people) that teach much more than just tricks. Aided by the school's dean, Eugene Burger, a veritable guru of magic, the instructors, guest artists, and staff give personal attention to your development as a performer, an artist, and a person. I'm not being hokey when I say that: there are few opportunities to be as inspired, challenged, and rewarded as you will be by attending any of McBride's classes. For a very different experience, McBride also offers four-day retreats in which students meet for concentrated study and reflection in magic, mythology, performance, and creative play.

The Chavez Studio of Magic was the first bona fide school of magic and was founded by Ben and Marian Chavez in 1941. (In fact, it was the only school for magicians in America where veterans of World War II could study under the G.I. Bill of Rights.) It's a one-of-a-kind "school" that offers instruction in specific areas of sleight-of-hand with such objects as playing cards, coins, cigarettes, and billiard balls. It also teaches the "real work" on the Zombie (see "The Floating Ball" in Chapter 5). The course covers showmanship, stagecraft, and routining as well. Today, the school is operated by Dale Salwak, who lives in greater Los Angeles. For more information on the Chavez course, contact Dale Salwak at www.dalesalwak.com.

Shop 'Til You Drop

If you're looking for new tricks, you may want to find a magic shop or magic dealer in your area. If there's a storefront location (instead of being simply an online magic supplier), a magic shop's a great place to find out what kind of tricks and props are available. And you have the opportunity to see them firsthand before you buy them. If you become a "regular," the shop's staff will get to know the type of street magic you like and make suggestions. Magic shops are also a good place to meet other local magicians.

A word of warning, however. Always remember that magic shops are in the magic *business*. Some dealers, both online and in storefront locations, sell anything to anybody. There's almost never a problem with the workmanship of the stuff you buy.

It doesn't fall apart. But it might not work the way you expect it to just from reading about it or hearing it described.

I'll give you a personal example. When I was around twelve, I was going to order my first trick through a mail order catalog: you stack several cardboard boxes, and they come to life as a walking robot! Of course, the catalog didn't explain that you couldn't do this trick alone. You needed to have a hidden assistant who *somehow* has to crawl onto the stage unseen and get into the boxes to make the robot move. Fortunately, I was a "sorcerer's apprentice" to a magic mentor who wisely steered me in another direction. If I had been left to my own devices, I would have ordered a trick that would have been totally useless to me.

Even when the description of a trick is totally accurate, without any humbug, there are all sorts of things that could make it impractical for a street magician. Some tricks can only be performed as "openers," your first trick, because you have to be rigged up in some fashion. Other tricks may require you to wear gimmicks, such as a hidden magnet under your shirt, that make the tricks too bulky or uncomfortable for you. Some have severe angles, require special lighting, or have other restrictions that make the trick impossible to do in the venues or the way in which you want to perform. So just be careful with your purchases: once you know the secret, the trick can't be returned.

Your best bet is to be up front with the magic dealer, whether you're meeting the person face-to-face or chatting through the CONTACT US link of a website. Let him know the level of experience you have, what other kinds of tricks you already do, and how you want to use the trick in question. Any reputable dealer will steer you in the right direction; he knows that, in the long run, it's in his own best interest to keep you as a satisfied customer.

Here are a few of the most well-established, long-running storefront magic shops around the United States:

Abbott's Magic Company
124 St. Joseph Street
Colon, MI 49040
(269) 432-3235

Daytona Magic Shop
136 South Beach Street
Daytona Beach, FL 32114-4402
(386) 252-6767
daytonamagic.com

Denny & Lee Magic Studio
Baltimore location:
325 South Marlyn Avenue
Baltimore, MD 21221
(410) 686-3914

Las Vegas location:
5115 Dean Martin Drive, Suite #907
Las Vegas, NV 89118
(702) 740-3500 and (702) 740-3501
dennymagic.com

Eagle Magic & Joke Store
708 Portland Avenue
Minneapolis, MN 55415
(612) 333-4702
eaglemagicstore.com
Eagle Magic is the oldest continuing operating magic shop in the United States.

Fantasma Magic
421 Seventh Avenue, 2nd Floor
(Entrance on 33rd St. between 6th and 7th avenues)
New York, NY 10001
(212) 244-3633
fantasmamagic.com

Hank Lee's Magic Factory
Showroom:
127 South Street
Boston, MA 02111
(617) 482-8749
hanklee.org and magicfact.com

Hollywood Magic
6614 Hollywood Blvd.
Hollywood, CA 90028
(323) 464-5610
hollywoodmagic.net

Ken-Zo's Yogi Magic Mart
1025-29 South Charles Street
Baltimore, MD 21230
(410) 727-5811

Magic, Inc.
5082 North Lincoln Avenue
Chicago, IL 60625
(773) 334-2855
magicinc.net

Magicland
304 Park Forest Center
Dallas, TX 75234-4137
(972) 241-9898

Misdirections Magic Shop
1236 Ninth Avenue
San Francisco, CA 94122
(415) 566-2180
misdirections.com

Stevens Magic Emporium
2520 E. Douglas
Wichita, KS 67214
(316) 683-9582
stevensmagic.com

Tannen's Magic
45 W. 34th Street, Suite 608
New York, NY 10001
(212) 929-4500
tannens.com

Twin Cities Magic & Costume Co.
241 W. 7th Street
Saint Paul, MN 55102
(651) 227-7888
twincitiesmagic.com

I won't even attempt a complete survey of the dozens of magic dealers that are found exclusively or primarily online, because the list changes almost as frequently as your most recent software upgrade.

Ellusionist.com, founded by Brad Christian, must be mentioned first in any book on this subject, however, because it has positioned itself as the Internet magical supply center for all things having to do with street magic, be it apparatus, accessories, gear, or DVDs. In addition to selling products, the site has its own forum and newsletter. Besides their home site, they can also be found at www.myspace.com/ellusionist.

A few other online shops deserve special mention because they've established themselves as reliable, with a good track record for magicians' satisfaction and service:

Elmagicshop.com
"Earth's Largest Magic Shop," operated by David Malek.

Mymagic.com
Operated by Meir Yedid.

Hocus-pocus.com
Began as a storefront location, opened by Paul Gross in 1977 in Fresno, California. Internet-based shop started in 1997.

Elmwoodmagic.com
Operated by Paul Richards. A walk-in shop since 1993, Elmwood Magic moved exclusively online in 2006.

Llpub.com
Although primarily known as a manufacturer and distributor of their own line of instructional magic videos, L&L Publishing, located in Lake Tahoe, also offers a complete line of magic products.

Join the Club

The International Brotherhood of Magicians, known as the I.B.M., is the world's largest magicians' fraternal organization. It has more than 14,000 members and more than 300 local chapters, known as *Rings*, in more than 70 countries. Among its member benefits are a monthly magazine, *The Linking Ring*. The I.B.M. also sponsors an annual convention, usually held over the July 4th weekend, somewhere in the United States.

The I.B.M. was founded in 1922 by Len Vintus, Gene Gordon, and Don Rogers. Active and Affiliate members (who don't belong to a local Ring) must be sponsored into the organization and must be at least 18 years old; there are junior memberships as well.

The I.B.M. can be contacted at:

The International Brotherhood of Magicians
11155-C South Towne Square
St. Louis, MO 63123-7819
(314) 845-9200
www.magician.org

The Society of American Magicians, or S.A.M., started with just 21 members and was founded on May 10, 1902, in Martinka's, a magic shop in New York City. One of the club's early luminaries was Harry Houdini, who became a member in 1903 and was elected National President in 1917. He held the post until his death in 1926.

The S.A.M. meets in approximately 250 chapters known as *Assemblies*, located throughout the world. The clubs' official journal is *M-U-M*, which in an acronym for Magic-Unity-Might. The S.A.M. holds an annual national convention, usually in July somewhere in the United States. The S.A.M. has several categories of membership, determined by the magician's age and local assembly affiliation.

In 1984, five members of the S.A.M. founded the Society of Young Magicians (the S.Y.M.) for magicians between the ages of 7 and 17. In 1988, S.A.M. changed its constitution to extend membership to Young Members (Y.M.) and adopted the S.Y.M. as its official youth program. There are now more than 100 chartered S.Y.M. Assemblies. Their official publication in the *Magic SYMbol*.

The S.A.M. and the S.Y.M. can be both be contacted through:

The Society of American Magicians and the Society of Young Magicians
Richard Blowers, National Administrator
P.O. Box 510260
St. Louis, MO 63151
(314) 846-5659
magicsam.com

The Web

Still not satisfied? That's why we have the Internet. There are literally thousands of websites dedicated to magic on the World Wide Web. If you type the word "magic" into your search engine, though, don't be surprised if most of the sites have nothing to do with magical entertainment, much less street magic. Most of the sites deal with the occult or mysticism, the MAGIC role-playing game, or pages that simply use the word "magic" so often that their URLs turn up.

But don't worry. There are plenty of sites out there for *our* type of magic that should be of interest to anyone who wants to seriously pursue street magic. There are also online magic magazines, bulletin boards, and newsgroups as well as sites for individual magicians. And if you want *see* performances, just type "street magic" into YouTube, and be prepared to see hours and hours of street entertainers (of every level of ability, from the mundane to the incredible) from all over the world.

To help you get started on your cyber-search, I'll list just two sites that offer hundreds of links to other websites of interest to street magicians:

◆ www.linkingpage.com

◆ allmagicguide.com

Index

A

Above the Below stunt, 11
Academy of Magical Arts, 15
Airdrop Turnover method, card revealing, 105-107
Anderson, Harry, 5
Angel, Criss
    attire, 31
    modern magician, 11-13
arm tricks, Stretching a Point, 150
    effect, 150
    performance, 150-152
    preparation, 150
Ashes to Ashes trick, 137
    effect, 137
    performance, 138-141
    preparation, 138
Asrah, 83
attire, creating character, 31-32
attitude, creating character, 32
audiences
    engaging senses, 45
    performing live, 47
        approaching people, 47
        knowing uninterested audience, 47-48

B

Balducci, Ed, 87
Balducci Levitation trick, 87
    effect, 87
    performance, 88-93
    preparation, 88
Barry, Keith, 16
Beginner Bending Spoon trick, 240
    effect, 240
    performance, 240-244

Bending Spoon trick, 244
    effect, 245
    performance, 245-248
    preparation, 245
Benn, J.B., 16
Blackstone, Harry, 5
Blaine, David, 8-9, 31
Blistered trick, 165
    effect, 165
    performance, 166-169
    preparation, 165
body language, trick details, 43
Braun, John, 123
Breaking Point trick, 251
    effect, 251
    performance, 253-255
    preparation, 251-253
Brown, Derren, modern magician, 13-14
Buds from Nowhere trick, 321-322
    effect, 322
    performance, 323-325
    preparation, 322
buskers, street magic history, 5-6
Busted! trick, 255
buzzwords, 34-35

C

Capehart, Chris, 6
card tricks
    forcing cards, 108-109
        Criss Cross force, 109-110
        Hindu Shuffle, 110-113
        revealing, 113-118
    history, 98
    Is This Your Card? tricks, 104-108

Karate Kard trick, 118
  effect, 119
  performance, 119-121
  preparation, 119-120
Pick It and Stick It trick, 99
  effect, 99
  performance, 99-104
  preparation, 99
Singed Card trick, 122-123
Slop Shuffle trick, 123
  effect, 123
  performance, 124-126
  preparation, 124
CDs, In the Loop trick, 338
  effect, 338
  performance, 338, 341
cell phones
  Fantastic Foto trick, 310
    effect, 310
    performance, 313-314
    preparation, 311-312
  Flowers Direct trick, 315
    effect, 315
    performance, 318-320
    preparation, 315-318
  Mr. Wizard trick, 305
    effect, 306
    performance, 306-310
    preparation, 306
Cellini, Jim, 6
center tear, 223
character
  creating persona, 30
    as if tool, 30
    attire, 31-32
    attitude, 32
    grooming, 32
    magic wands, 33
  patter, 33-34
    buzzwords, 34-35
    emotive key words, 37
    myths and legends, 37
    stimulating questions, 36
  routine, 28-30
  selecting magic tricks

appropriate content, 26
basic effects, 27-28
doing what's right, 27
learning numerous tricks, 28
making streetwise, 26
cigarettes
  Snuff trick, 141
    effect, 142
    performance, 142-145
    preparation, 142
  Vanishing trick, 145
    effect, 145
    performance, 146-148
Circle of Life trick, 281
  effect, 282
  performance, 282-288
  preparation, 282
Clapper method, card revealing, 107-108
classic palming, 203
Cole, Danny, 16
Commando Act, The, 6
confederates, 51
Conjuring Caps trick, 202
  effect, 202
  performance, 204-207
  preparation, 203
Copperfield, David, 5, 31
costs, street magic, 20-21
Covered Levitation trick, 83
  effect, 83
  performance, 84-87
  preparation, 83-84
Crawl Space trick, 78
  effect, 78
  performance, 78-80
  preparation, 78
crimping cards, 107
Criss Angel Made in Japan, 12
Criss Angel Mindfreak, 11
Criss Cross force, 109-110
Cut and Restored Buds trick, 325
  effect, 325
  performance, 326-327
  preparation, 325

D

Dante, 5
David, Blaine, modern magician, 9-11
Discovery of Witchcraft, The, 22
Double Whammy trick, 259
    effect, 259
    performance, 261-262
    preparation, 259-260
doubts, street magic, 22-24
Drowned Alive stunt, 11
DVDs, In the Loop trick, 338
    effect, 338
    performance, 338-341

E

ear tricks
    Nose Candy, 169
        effect, 170
        performance, 170-172
        preparation, 170
    Pierced! trick
        effect, 161
        performance, 161-165
effects
    Ashes to Ashes trick, 137
    Balducci Levitation trick, 87
    Beginner Bending Spoon trick, 240
    Bending Spoon trick, 245
    Blistered trick, 165
    Breaking Point trick, 251
    Buds from Nowhere trick, 322
    Busted! trick, 255
    Circle of Life trick, 282
    Conjuring Caps trick, 202
    Covered Levitation trick, 83
    Crawl Space trick, 78
    Cut and Restored Buds trick, 325
    Double Whammy trick, 259
    Eyescream trick, 172
    Fantastic Foto trick, 310
    Floating Ball trick, 56
    Flowers Direct trick, 315

Fly By trick, 76
Folding Coin trick, 263
Ghost Whisperer trick, 220
Go Fly a Kite trick, 187
Great Escape, The, 182
Gypsy Switch trick, 199
Heads or Tails trick, 128
In a Heartbeat trick, 290
In the Loop trick, 338
Jumping Rubber Band trick, 178
Karate Kard trick, 119
Leaf Shredder trick, 279
Levitating Lady trick, 66
Look into My Eyes trick, 291
Mindreading iPod trick, 335
Miracle of Life trick, 230
Mr. Wizard trick, 306
Nano to No Pod trick, 328
Nose Candy trick, 170
Oh, Fork! trick, 256
Pentagram of Doom trick, 223
Pick It and Stick It trick, 99
Pierced! trick, 161
Pin Head trick, 155
Pin-etration trick, 158
PK Pen trick, 268
Rising Ring trick, 70
Rubber Spoon trick, 239
Salt of the Earth trick, 195
Seed of Life trick, 274
selecting magic tricks, 27-28
Slop Shuffle trick, 123
Snuffing Cigarette trick, 142
Spinning in Your Grave trick, 227
Static Electricity trick, 62
Stretching a Point trick, 150
Thumb Tack trick, 153
Tourniquet Trickery, 288
Trapdoor Trickery trick, 192
Under Cover trick, 131
Undercover Ascension trick, 80
Up the Sleeve trick, 210
Up Yours trick, 207
Vanishing Cigarette trick, 145
Vanishing Dagger trick, 212

Vanishing iPod trick, 331
You Bent It! trick, 248
emotive key words, stimulating audience, 37
Encyclopedia of Impromptu Magic, The, 128
equivoque, 299
eye tricks
    Eyescream, 172
        effect, 172
        performance, 172-173, 176
        preparation, 172
    Nose Candy, 169
        effect, 170
        performance, 170-172
        preparation, 170
Eyescream trick, 172
    effect, 172
    performance, 172-173, 176
    preparation, 172

F

F.I.S.M. (International Federation of Magic
    Societies), 15
fairs, street magic history, 4-5
fakirs, 7
Fantastic Foto trick, 310
    effect, 310
    performance, 313-314
    preparation, 311-312
Fawkes, Isaac, 4
finger palming, 132
fire, 22
    Ashes to Ashes trick, 137
        effect, 137
        performance, 138-141
        preparation, 138
    Heads or Tails trick, 127-128
        effect, 128
        performance, 129-131
        preparation, 128
    Snuffing Cigarette trick, 141
        effect, 142
        performance, 142-145
        preparation, 142

Under Cover trick, 131
    effect, 131
    performance, 135-137
    preparation, 131-134
Vanishing Cigarette trick, 145
    effect, 145
    performance, 146-148
Flashpoint method, card revealing, 105
Floating Ball trick, 55-56
    effect, 56
    performance, 57-61
    preparation, 56
flotation. *See also* levitation
    Balducci Levitation trick, 87
        effect, 87
        performance, 88-93
        preparation, 88
    Covered Levitation trick, 83
        effect, 83
        performance, 84-87
        preparation, 83-84
    Crawl Space trick, 78
        effect, 78
        performance, 78-80
        preparation, 78
    Fly By trick, 76
    Undercover Ascension trick, 80
        effect, 80
        performance, 81-83
        preparation, 80
flourishes, 44
Flowers Direct trick, 315
    effect, 315
    performance, 318-320
    preparation, 315-318
Fly By trick, 76
Folding Coin trick, 262
    effect, 263
    performance, 264-265
    preparation, 263
forcing cards, 108-109
    Criss Cross force, 109-110
    Hindu Shuffle, 110-113

revealing, 113-114
    handwritten notes, 114-115
    marking on own body, 117-118
Frozen in Time, 10
Frozen in Time stunt, 10

G

Gardner, Martin, 128
Gazzo, 6
Geller, Uri, 237, 244
ghosts
    Ghost Whisperer trick, 220
        effect, 220
        performance, 220-223
    Miracle of Life trick, 230
        effect, 230
        performance, 232-234
        preparation, 230-231
    Pentagram of Doom trick, 223
        effect, 223
        performance, 224-227
        preparation, 223-224
    Spinning in Your Grave trick, 227
        effect, 227
        performance, 228-230
        preparation, 228
Ghost Whisperer trick, 220
    effect, 220
    performance, 220-223
gimmicks, 70
glimpses, 102
Go Fly a Kite trick, 186-187
    effect, 187
    performance, 187, 190-192
    preparation, 187-189
Golden Rule, 32
Gongora, Chris, 16
Goshman, Albert, 202
Grasso, Michael, 16
Great Escape, The, 181-182
    effect, 182
    performance, 182-186
    preparation, 182

grooming, creating characters, 32
Gypsy Switch trick, 198-199
    effect, 199
    performance, 199-202
    preparation, 199

H

hand tricks
    Blistered, 165
        effect, 165
        performance, 166-169
        preparation, 165
    Pierced!, 161
        effect, 161
        performance, 161-165
    Pin Head, 155
        effect, 155
        performance, 157-158
        preparation, 155-156
    Pin-etration, 158
        effect, 158
        performance, 159-161
        preparation, 158
    Thumb Tack, 152
        effect, 153
        performance, 153-155
        preparation, 153
handwritten notes, forced card revealing, 114-115
Heads or Tails trick, 127-128
    effect, 128
    performance, 129-131
    preparation, 128
Henning, Doug, 5, 31
Hindu Shuffle, 110-113
history
    card tricks, 98
    street magic
        buskers, 5-6
        levitation, 7-9
        levitators, 9
        McBride, Jeff, 6
        regional fairs, 4-5

Hogarth, William, 4
Holt, Henry, 238
Houdini, Harry, 5
How to Play with Your Food, 172

I

In a Heartbeat trick, 289
    effect, 290
    performance, 290-291
In the Loop trick, 338
    effect, 338
    performance, 338-341
in-jogging cards, 106
International Federation of Magic Societies
    (F.I.S.M.), 15
iPods
    Buds from Nowhere trick, 321-322
        effect, 322
        performance, 323-325
        preparation, 322
    Cut and Restored Buds trick, 325
        effect, 325
        performance, 326-327
        preparation, 325
    Mindreading iPod trick, 335
        effect, 335
        performance, 336-337
        preparation, 336
    Nano to No Pod trick, 328
        effect, 328
        performance, 328-330
    Vanishing iPod trick, 331
        effect, 331
        performance, 332-335
        preparation, 331
Is This Your Card? tricks, 104-108

J-K

jogging cards, 106
Judah, Stewart, 123
Jumping Rubber Band trick, 177-178
    effect, 178
    performance, 178-181

Karate Kard trick, 118
    effect, 119
    performance, 119-121
    preparation, 119-120
Karson, Joe, Floating Ball trick, 56
key-card method, card tricks, 104-108
King, Mac, Eyescream trick, 172
KISS principle, 45-46
Korn, Chris, 16
Kredible, Justin, 16

L

lapping, 196
Leaf Shredder trick, 279
    effect, 279
    performance, 279-281
legends, 37
Levitating Lady trick, 66
    effect, 66
    performance, 66-70
    preparation, 66
levitation. *See also* flotation
    Balducci Levitation trick, 87
        effect, 87
        performance, 88-93
        preparation, 88
    Covered Levitation trick, 83
        effect, 83
        performance, 84-87
        preparation, 83-84
    Crawl Space trick, 78
        effect, 78
        performance, 78-80
        preparation, 78
    Floating Ball trick, 55-56
        effect, 56
        performance, 57-61
        preparation, 56
    Fly By trick, 76
    Levitating Lady trick, 66
        effect, 66
        performance, 66-70
        preparation, 66

Rising Ring trick, 70
    effect, 70
    performance, 71-73
    preparation, 71
Static Electricity trick, 61-62
    effect, 62
    performance, 62-66
    preparation, 62
street magic history, 7-9
Undercover Ascension trick, 80
    effect, 80
    performance, 81-83
    preparation, 80
levitators, street magic history, 9
Levy, Mark, 172
Lie Detector method, card revealing, 105
living or dead tests, 220
Look into My Eyes trick, 291
    effect, 291
    performance, 292-298
Lorraine, Sid, Slop Shuffle trick, 123

M

Magic Man, 10
Magic Mirror method, card revealing, 105
magic wands, creating characters, 33
Magic X, 15
Magician's Choice, 298-301
magicians
    history
        buskers, 5-6
        levitation, 7-9
        levitators, 9
        McBride, Jeff, 6
        regional fairs, 4-5
    modern, 9
        Angel, Criss, 11-13
        Blaine, David, 9-11
        Brown, Derren, 13-14
        Takayama, Cyril, 15-16
        Zenon, Paul, 13-14

Mask, Myth & Magic, 6
McBride, Jeff, street magic history, 6
McBride's Magic and Mystery School
  website, 6
Meier, Thomas, 16
mind control
    Beginner Bending Spoon trick, 240
        effect, 240
        performance, 240-244
    Bending Spoon trick, 244
        effect, 245
        performance, 245-248
        preparation, 245
    Breaking Point trick, 251
        effect, 251
        performance, 253-255
        preparation, 251-253
    Busted! trick, 255
    Double Whammy trick, 259
        effect, 259
        performance, 261-262
        preparation, 259-260
    Folding Coin trick, 262
        effect, 263
        performance, 264-265
        preparation, 263
    Oh, Fork! trick, 256
        effect, 256
        performance, 257-259
        preparation, 256
    paper psychokinesis, 265
        Rolling Papers trick, 265-267
        Timber! trick, 267-268
    PK Pen trick, 268
        effect, 268
        performance, 269-272
        preparation, 269
    Rubber Spoon trick, 238-239
    telekinesis, 237-238
    You Bent It! trick, 248
        effect, 248
        performance, 248-251
Mindfreak, *Secret Revelations*, 13

Mindreading iPod trick, 335
    effect, 335
    performance, 336-337
    preparation, 336
Miracle of Life trick, 230
    effect, 230
    performance, 232-234
    preparation, 230-231
misdirection, 198
mountebanks, 4
moves, sleight-of-hand, 131
Mr. Wizard trick, 305
    effect, 306
    performance, 306-310
    preparation, 306
Mysterious Stranger, 11
myths, 37

N

Nano to No Pod trick, 328
    effect, 328
    performance, 328-330
Neistadt, Jason, 16
Nichols, Sutton, 4
Nose Candy trick, 169
    effect, 170
    performance, 170-172
    preparation, 170
nose tricks, Nose Candy, 169
    effect, 170
    performance, 170-172
    preparation, 170
Nu, Alain, 16

O

objects
    Conjuring Caps trick, 202
        effect, 202
        performance, 204-207
        preparation, 203

Go Fly a Kite, 186-187
    effect, 187
    performance, 187, 190-192
    preparation, 187-189
Great Escape, The, 181-182
    effect, 182
    performance, 182-186
    preparation, 182
Gypsy Switch trick, 198-199
    effect, 199
    performance, 199-202
    preparation, 199
Jumping Rubber Band trick, 177-178
    effect, 178
    performance, 178-181
Salt of the Earth trick, 195
    effect, 195
    performance, 195-198
    preparation, 195
Trapdoor Trickery, 192
    effect, 192
    performance, 192-194
    preparation, 192
Up the Sleeve trick, 209
    effect, 210
    performance, 210-211
    preparation, 210
Up Yours trick, 207
    effect, 207
    performance, 207-208
Vanishing Dagger trick, 211
    effect, 212
    performance, 213-215
    preparation, 212
Oh, Fork! trick, 256
    effect, 256
    performance, 257-259
    preparation, 256
On the Cosmic Relations, 238
out-jogging cards, 106

P

palming, 132, 146, 203
paper tricks, 265
    Rolling Papers trick, 265-267
    Timber! trick, 267-268
passes
    deceptive moves, 137
    sleight-of-hand, 131
patter, creating characters, 33-34
    buzzwords, 34-35
    emotive key words, 37
    myths and legends, 37
    stimulating questions, 36
peeks, 102
Penn & Teller, 5
Pentagram of Doom trick, 223
    effect, 223
    performance, 224-227
    preparation, 223-224
Pepys, Samuel, 4
performance
    Ashes to Ashes trick, 138-141
    Balducci Levitation trick, 88-93
    Beginner Bending Spoon trick, 240-244
    Bending Spoon trick, 245-248
    Blistered trick, 166-169
    Breaking Point trick, 253-255
    Buds from Nowhere trick, 323-325
    Busted! trick, 255
    Circle of Life trick, 282-288
    Conjuring Caps trick, 204-207
    Covered Levitation trick, 84-87
    Crawl Space trick, 78-80
    Cut and Restored Buds trick, 326-327
    Double Whammy trick, 261-262
    Eyescream trick, 172-173, 176
    Fantastic Foto trick, 313-314
    Floating Ball trick, 57-61
    Flowers Direct trick, 318-320
    Fly By trick, 76
    Folding Coin trick, 264-265
    Ghost Whisperer trick, 220-223
    Go Fly a Kite trick, 187, 190-192

Great Escape, The, 182-186
Gypsy Switch trick, 199-202
Heads or Tails trick, 129-131
In a Heartbeat trick, 290-291
In the Loop trick, 338, 341
Jumping Rubber Band trick, 178-181
Karate Kard trick, 119-121
Leaf Shredder trick, 279-281
Levitating Lady trick, 66-70
live audiences, 47
    approaching people, 47
    knowing uninterested audience, 47-48
Look into My Eyes trick, 292-298
Mindreading iPod trick, 336-337
Miracle of Life trick, 232-234
Mr. Wizard trick, 306-310
Nano to No Pod trick, 328-330
Nose Candy trick, 170-172
Oh, Fork! trick, 257-259
Pentagram of Doom trick, 224-227
perfecting tricks, 41-42
Pick It and Stick It trick, 99-104
Pierced! trick, 161-165
Pin Head trick, 157-158
Pin-etration trick, 159-161
PK Pen trick, 269-272
Rising Ring trick, 71-73
Rubber Spoon trick, 239
rules
    never announce tricks in advance, 40
    never repeat tricks, 41
    never reveal secrets, 40
Salt of the Earth trick, 195-198
Seed of Life trick, 275-278
Slop Shuffle trick, 124-126
Snuffing Cigarette trick, 142-145
Spinning in Your Grave trick, 228-230
Static Electricity trick, 62-66
stealing other magicians' work, 46
Stretching a Point trick, 150-152
Thumb Tack trick, 153-155
too-perfect theory, 46
Tourniquet Trickery, 288-289
Trapdoor Trickery trick, 192-194
trick details, 42

be natural, 43-44
body language, 43
engaging senses, 45
flourishes, 44
KISS principle, 45-46
meaningful moments, 44
Under Cover trick, 135-137
Undercover Ascension trick, 81-83
Up the Sleeve trick, 210-211
Up Yours trick, 207-208
Vanishing Cigarette trick, 146-148
Vanishing Dagger trick, 213-215
Vanishing iPod trick, 332-335
when something goes wrong, 49-51
You Bent It! trick, 248-251
personas, creating, 30
as if tool, 30
attire, 31-32
attitude, 32
grooming, 32
magic wands, 33
Peterson, Fred, 128
Phoenix, The, 242
phones
Fantastic Foto trick, 310
effect, 310
performance, 313-314
preparation, 311-312
Flowers Direct trick, 315
effect, 315
performance, 318-320
preparation, 315-318
Meet Mr. Wizard trick, 305
effect, 306
performance, 306-310
preparation, 306
Pick It and Stick It trick, 99
effect, 99
performance, 99-104
preparation, 99
Pierced! trick
effect, 161
performance, 161-165

Pin Head trick, 155
effect, 155
performance, 157-158
preparation, 155-156
Pin-etration trick, 158
effect, 158
performance, 159-161
preparation, 158
PK Pen trick, 268
effect, 268
performance, 269-272
preparation, 269
plants, 51
practice
live audiences, 47
approaching people, 47
knowing uninterested audience, 47-48
perfecting tricks, 41-42
rules
never announce tricks in advance , 40
never repeat tricks, 41
never reveal secrets, 40
too-perfect theory, 46
trick details, 42
be natural, 43-44
body language, 43
engaging senses, 45
flourishes, 44
KISS principle, 45-46
meaningful moments, 44
when something goes wrong, 49-51
Premature Burial stunt, 10
preparation
Ashes to Ashes trick, 138
Balducci Levitation trick, 88
Bending Spoon trick, 245
Blistered trick, 165
Breaking Point trick, 251-253
Buds from Nowhere trick, 322
Busted! trick, 255
Circle of Life trick, 282
Conjuring Caps trick, 203
Covered Levitation trick, 83-84
Crawl Space trick, 78

Cut and Restored Buds trick, 325
Double Whammy trick, 259-260
Eyescream trick, 172
Fantastic Foto trick, 311-312
Floating Ball trick, 56
Flowers Direct trick, 315-318
Fly By trick, 76
Folding Coin trick, 263
Go Fly a Kite trick, 187-189
Great Escape, The, 182
Gypsy Switch trick, 199
Heads or Tails trick, 128
Karate Kard trick, 119-120
Levitating Lady trick, 66
Mindreading iPod trick, 336
Miracle of Life trick, 230-231
Mr. Wizard trick, 306
Nose Candy trick, 170
Oh, Fork! trick, 256
Pentagram of Doom trick, 223-224
Pick It and Stick It trick, 99
Pin Head trick, 155-156
Pin-etration trick, 158
PK Pen trick, 269
Rising Ring trick, 71
Salt of the Earth trick, 195
Seed of Life trick, 274-275
Slop Shuffle trick, 124
Snuffing Cigarette trick, 142
Spinning In Your Grave trick, 228
Static Electricity trick, 62
Stretching a Point trick, 150
Thumb Tack trick, 153
Tourniquet Trickery, 288
Trapdoor Trickery trick, 192
Under Cover trick, 131-134
Undercover Ascension trick, 80
Up the Sleeve trick, 210
Vanishing Dagger trick, 212
Vanishing iPod trick, 331
pretend, playing, 30
psychokinesis, 238
paper tricks, 265
Rolling Papers trick, 265-267
Timber! trick, 267-268

PK Pen trick, 268
effect, 268
performance, 269-272
preparation, 269
pulls, 212
Pusey, Joshua, 128

Q-R

questions, stimulating audience, 36

revelations, 104
reverse Balducci, 92
Revolution stunt, 11
Rising Ring trick, 70
effect, 70
performance, 71-73
preparation, 71
Robert-Houdin, Jean Eugene, 8, 31
Rolling Papers trick, 265-267
routines, 28-30
routining, 29
Rubber Spoon trick, 238-239
rules
never announce tricks in advance, 40
never repeat tricks, 41
never reveal secrets, 40

S

safety, street magic, 21-22
Salt of the Earth trick, 195
effect, 195
performance, 195-198
preparation, 195
Scot, Reginald, 22
secret assistants, 51
secrets, never reveal, 40
Seed of Life trick, 274
effect, 274
performance, 275-278
preparation, 274-275
Sheridan, Jeff, 6
Sheshal, 7
shills, 51

side-jogging cards, 106
Singed Card trick, 122-123
sleeving, 209
sleight-of-hand, 131
Slop Shuffle trick, 123
   effect, 123
   performance, 124-126
   preparation, 124
Snuffing Cigarette trick, 141
   effect, 142
   performance, 142-145
   preparation, 142
Spinning in Your Grave trick, 227
   effect, 227
   performance, 228-230
   preparation, 228
spirit world
   Ghost Whisperer trick, 220
      effect, 220
      performance, 220-223
   Miracle of Life trick, 230
      effect, 230
      performance, 232-234
      preparation, 230-231
   Pentagram of Doom trick, 223
      effect, 223
      performance, 224-227
      preparation, 223-224
   Spinning in Your Grave trick, 227
      effect, 227
      performance, 228-230
      preparation, 228
Stars of Magic, 202
Static Electricity trick, 61-62
   effect, 62
   performance, 62-66
   preparation, 62
stooges, 51
street magic
   ability to perform, 18-19
   costs, 20-21
   defined, 17-18
   history
      buskers, 5-6
      levitation, 7-9

      levitators, 9
      McBride, Jeff, 6
      regional fairs, 4-5
   modern-day magicians, 9
      Angel, Criss, 11-13
      Blaine, David, 9-11
      Brown, Derren, 13-14
      Takayama, Cyril, 15-16
      Zenon, Paul, 13-14
   reasons for doing, 19-20
   safe practice, 21-22
   self-doubt, 22-24
Street Magic, 6, 9
Stretching a Point trick, 150
   effect, 150
   performance, 150-152
   preparation, 150
Subtle Problems You Will Do, 123
Successor, The, 244
sucker tricks, 62
supernatural
   Circle of Life trick, 281
      effect, 282
      performance, 282-288
      preparation, 282
   In a Heartbeat trick, 289
      effect, 290
      performance, 290-291
   Leaf Shredder trick, 279
      effect, 279
      performance, 279-281
   Look into My Eyes trick, 291
      effect, 291
      performance, 292-298
   Magician's Choice, 298-301
   Seed of Life trick, 274
      effect, 274
      performance, 275-278
      preparation, 274-275
   Tourniquet Trickery, 288
      effect, 288
      performance, 288-289
      preparation, 288
Supernatural, 12

suspension, 8
suspension of disbelief, 43

T

Takayama, Cyril, modern magician, 15-16
Tannen, Louis, 202
Tarbell Course in Magic, The, 165, 335
telekinesis, 237-238
    Beginner Bending Spoon trick, 240
        effect, 240
        performance, 240-244
    Bending Spoon trick, 244
        effect, 245
        performance, 245-248
        preparation, 245
    Breaking Point trick, 251
        effect, 251
        performance, 253-255
        preparation, 251-253
    Busted! trick, 255
    Double Whammy trick, 259
        effect, 259
        performance, 261-262
        preparation, 259-260
    Folding Coin trick, 262
        effect, 263
        performance, 264-265
        preparation, 263
    Oh, Fork! trick, 256
        effect, 256
        performance, 257-259
        preparation, 256
    Rubber Spoon trick, 238-239
    You Bent It! trick, 248
        effect, 248
        performance, 248-251
Tempest, Marco, 16
T.H.E.M. (Totally Hidden Extreme Magic),
    15
Thompson, J.G. Jr., 104
Thumb Tack trick, 152
    effect, 153
    performance, 153-155
    preparation, 153

thumb palming, 146
Thurston, Howard, 5, 56
Tillar, Jack, Blistered trick, 165
Timber! trick, 267-268
too-perfect theory, 46
Totally Hidden Extreme Magic (T.H.E.M.),
    15
Tourniquet Trickery, 288
    effect, 288
    performance, 288-289
    preparation, 288
Trapdoor Trickery trick, 192
    effect, 192
    performance, 192-194
    preparation, 192
tricks. *See also* individual trick names
    Ashes to Ashes trick, 138-141
    Balducci Levitation trick, 88-93
    Beginner Bending Spoon trick, 240-244
    Bending Spoon trick, 245-248
    Blistered trick, 166-169
    Breaking Point trick, 253-255
    Buds from Nowhere trick, 323-325
    Busted! trick, 255
    Circle of Life trick, 282-288
    Conjuring Caps trick, 204-207
    Covered Levitation trick, 84-87
    Crawl Space trick, 78-80
    Cut and Restored Buds trick, 326-327
    Double Whammy trick, 261-262
    Eyescream trick, 172-173, 176
    Fantastic Foto trick, 313-314
    Floating Ball trick, 57-61
    Flowers Direct trick, 318-320
    Fly By trick, 76
    Folding Coin trick, 264-265
    Ghost Whisperer trick, 220-223
    Go Fly a Kite trick, 187, 190-192
    Great Escape, The, 182-186
    Gypsy Switch trick, 199-202
    Heads or Tails trick, 129-131
    In a Heartbeat trick, 290-291
    In the Loop trick, 338, 341
    Jumping Rubber Band trick, 178-181
    Karate Kard trick, 119-121

Leaf Shredder trick, 279-281
Levitating Lady trick, 66-70
live audiences, 47
     approaching people, 47
     knowing uninterested audience, 47-48
Look into My Eyes trick, 292-298
Mindreading iPod trick, 336-337
Miracle of Life trick, 232-234
Mr. Wizard trick, 306-310
Nano to No Pod trick, 328-330
Nose Candy trick, 170-172
Oh, Fork! trick, 257-259
Pentagram of Doom trick, 224-227
perfecting tricks, 41-42
Pick It and Stick It trick, 99-104
Pierced! trick, 161-165
Pin Head trick, 157-158
Pin-etration trick, 159-161
PK Pen trick, 269-272
Rising Ring trick, 71-73
Rubber Spoon trick, 239
rules
     never announce tricks in advance, 40
     never repeat tricks, 41
     never reveal secrets, 40
Salt of the Earth trick, 195-198
Seed of Life trick, 275-278
Slop Shuffle trick, 124-126
Snuffing Cigarette trick, 142-145
Spinning in Your Grave trick, 228-230
Static Electricity trick, 62-66
stealing other magicians' work, 46
Stretching a Point trick, 150-152
Thumb Tack trick, 153-155
too-perfect theory, 46
Tourniquet Trickery, 288-289
Trapdoor Trickery trick, 192-194
trick details, 42
     be natural, 43-44
     body language, 43
     engaging senses, 45
     flourishes, 44
     KISS principle, 45-46
     meaningful moments, 44

Under Cover trick, 135-137
Undercover Ascension trick, 81-83
Up the Sleeve trick, 210-211
Up Yours trick, 207-208
Vanishing Cigarette trick, 146-148
Vanishing Dagger trick, 213-215
Vanishing iPod trick, 332-335
when something goes wrong, 49-51
You Bent It! trick, 248-251
Tricks with Your Head, 172

U

Under Cover trick, 131
     effect, 131
     performance, 135-137
     preparation, 131-134
Undercover Ascension trick, 80
     effect, 80
     performance, 81-83
     preparation, 80
Up the Sleeve trick, 209
     effect, 210
     performance, 210-211
     preparation, 210
Up Yours trick, 207
     effect, 207
     performance, 207-208

V

Vanishing Cigarette trick, 145
     effect, 145
     performance, 146-148
Vanishing Dagger trick, 211
     effect, 212
     performance, 213-215
     preparation, 212
Vanishing iPod trick, 331
     effect, 331
     performance, 332-335
     preparation, 331
Vega, Enrico de la, 16

Vegas, Lisa de la, 16
Vernon, Dai, 242
Vertigo stunt, 11
Voice Detector method, card revealing, 105
Vulcan Mind Meld method, card revealing, 105

W–X–Y–Z

wands, creating character, 33
websites
    Blaine, David, 9
    McBride's Magic and Mystery School, 6
    Takayama, Cyril, 15

You Bent It! trick, 248
    effect, 248
    performance, 248-251

Zenon, Paul, modern magician, 13-14
Zombie, 56